PEPPER IN OUR EYES

EDITED BY W. WESLEY PUE

PEPPER IN OUR EYES:
THE APEC AFFAIR

UBCPress · Vancouver · Toronto

In memory of Gil Puder
11 July 1959 - 12 November 1999

Printed in Canada on acid-free paper ∞

ISBN 0-7748-0779-2

Canadian Cataloguing in Publication Data

Main title under title:

Pepper in our eyes

Includes bibliographical references and index.
ISBN 0-7748-0779-2

1. Asia Pacific Economic Cooperation (Organization). Ministerial Meeting (1977: Vancouver, BC). 2. Demonstrations – British Columbia – Vancouver. 3. Civil rights – Canada. 4. Police – Complaints against – Canada. 5. Police and mass media – Canada. I. Pue, W. Wesley.

JC599.C3P46 2000   323'.0971   C00-910128-4

UBC Press acknowledges the financial support of the Government of Canada through the Book Publishing Industry Development Program (BPIDP) for our publishing activities.

Canadä

We also gratefully acknowledge the support of the Canada Council for the Arts for our publishing program, as well as the support of the British Columbia Arts Council.

UBC Press
University of British Columbia
2029 West Mall, Vancouver, BC V6T 1Z2
(604) 822-5959
Fax: (604) 822-6083
E-mail: info@ubcpress.ubc.ca
www.ubcpress.ubc.ca

CONTENTS

PREFACE

In November 1997 Canada hosted a meeting of government leaders from countries surrounding the Pacific Ocean. The annual gathering of the heads of the Asia-Pacific Economic Cooperation (APEC) "economies" brought important world leaders to Vancouver at a time of crisis for many Asian economies. The meeting provided them with a unique opportunity to explore some urgent issues.

The major news story coming out of the conference, however, had little to do with trade, cooperation, or the pageantry of summitry. Instead, the summit topped Canadian news broadcasts in a most dramatic and most surprising way when an entirely predictable student protest met with a peculiarly strong police response.

The lasting image of the summit, seared in Canada's collective memory, was that of a Canadian Broadcasting Corporation television cameraman being pepper-sprayed by an irate-looking police officer. Newsworthy and dramatic, video footage of this incident has been broadcast repeatedly since.

Such images jarred Canada's self-understanding. Using noxious chemicals to attack non-violent protesters who appeared to be *obeying* police orders seemed un-Canadian. The apparent "taking out" of a news camera looked more like something that police and soldiers in other, less civil, countries would do.

The pepper spray unleashed that day incapacitated its immediate victims, blurring their vision and leaving them writhing in agony. It has also "peppered" all of our eyes, for the image obscures as much as it reveals about the matters of substance behind the "APEC affair." This powerful single image has kept public attention focused on the issue of aggressive police conduct – always easily condemned or condoned – rather than on the underlying questions concerning the duties of police in democratic countries, their accountability under law, and the command and control structures under which they operate. Our ability to discern and understand such fundamental issues has been hampered in part by the power of a picture.

More importantly, however, great fogs of obfuscation, unclear thinking, and disinformation about some very important fundamentals of public life have rolled out in the aftermath of the 1997 summit. This compounds the difficulties we face in understanding some complex issues relating to policing, the rule of law, and accountability in a liberal democracy. While it clearly serves some interests to deliberately muddy the waters here, the truth is that such complex issues are not easily rendered in newspaper headlines or television broadcasts.

It did not take long for it to become clear that matters of considerable substance were raised by the events of the day. Issues larger than the use of force by police (itself no small matter, of course) began to appear through the haze. Two dozen University of British Columbia law professors wrote to Prime Minister Jean Chrétien, recording a number of serious constitutional violations that had taken place on their campus. Experts in other areas expressed similar concerns. The British Columbia Civil Liberties Association complained about police conduct. Craig Jones, who was arrested and held for fourteen hours for displaying a sign saying "Free Speech," launched legal proceedings, naming the Royal Canadian Mounted Police and the government of Canada as defendants. More lawsuits followed. The groundbreaking journalism of CBC-TV's Terry Milewski kept the issue front and centre, raising important questions relating to the command and control of police by politicians. The Prime Minister's conduct was questioned. Despite initial denials by both the Prime Minister's Office and the RCMP, a document trail that became public clearly showed deep political involvement in policing arrangements.

Then an important but normally obscure tribunal – the RCMP Public Complaints Commission (PCC) – launched an inquiry into the whole matter. Things started slowly but the pace quickened as new documents casting the Prime Minister's Office or the RCMP in a bad light became public. It quickened again when witnesses began to testify in the autumn of 1998. The fall sitting of the House of Commons that year started with intense focus by the opposition parties on allegations that the Prime Minister had improperly ordered the police to supress Canadians' fundamental rights and that many *law-abiding citizens* had been arrested as a result. (No responsible politician or commentator has ever suggested that the arrest of individuals engaged in criminal conduct would be improper.) The attack came from all sides: the Progressive Conservative Party in the centre, the Reform Party on the right, and the New Democratic Party to the left all agreed on the importance of the fundamental principle that the police are not supposed to do the bidding of politicians. News flowed quickly, almost daily, contributing to a growing sense of scandal.

The government wished that the issue would go away. The Prime Minister's Office launched an unprecedented attack on Milewski and an "unrelated" attack on the autonomy of the CBC. The CBC's management caved in, pulling its award-winning journalist from the story. No shred of evidence has ever been introduced to show either that his reports were inaccurate or that the techniques he employed in pursuing investigative journalism violated the norms of journalistic ethics. In fact CBC Ombudsman Marcel Pépin fully exonerated Milewski of any wrongdoing. Silenced he remained, however. Prime ministers are powerful people.

Meanwhile, the Prime Minister responded daily to questions in the House of Commons with advice to opposition parties to "let the RCMP Public Complaints Commission get on with its business." Throughout the autumn of 1998, however, the government appeared to be oddly unsupportive of the commissioners investigating the matter. This first became clear when funding to ensure that complainants obtained adequate legal representation was repeatedly denied. The government persisted in its refusal despite the insistence of both the PCC panel and the Federal Court of Canada that such support was needed to ensure a full and proper inquiry. Of course, in the topsy-turvy world that is Ottawa, the very government whose actions were being investigated controlled the purse strings for those who claimed to be victims of government and police wrongdoing. Limited funding was eventually granted to complainants, but only in 1999 and only after an entirely new RCMP complaints tribunal was constituted.

What happened to the *first* panel? During the autumn of 1998, there were allegations of political interference with the tribunal's work. A cabinet minister had to resign. The panel chair, Gerald Morin, also resigned, in the face of some very peculiar challenges to his impartiality, followed by the rest of the three-person tribunal. At the time of writing, a new RCMP PCC panel, presided over by a sole commissioner, E.N. (Ted) Hughes, QC, is under way. Its findings lie in the future.

For all the sound and fury – and there has been much of that – many Canadians are left wondering "why the fuss?" Most probably share the view of a mid-career lawyer who asked, as the issue crescendoed in the House of Commons, "*So what* if the Prime Minister gave orders to the police?"

The "so what" question is important. If the complainants' allegations are borne out, the conduct of government and police before, during, and after Vancouver's APEC summit amounts to a fundamental violation of the

Canadian constitution. Countries where the police respond to political command are not democracies. They tend to be brutal, inhumane places.

The issues are more subtle and complex than thirty-second news clips can deal with. Central though they are to the meaning of Canada, they are not well understood. Disturbingly, one senses that an entire generation of political leaders may have no understanding of the issues at all.

This book is intended to fill a void by providing a "primer" on Canadian civics. It arises from reflections on the APEC affair but makes no attempt to offer a definitive legal, historical, philosophical, or political assessment of those events. Any such effort would be premature. Rather, this book consists of contributions by distinguished experts in a variety of fields, who draw upon their expertise to explain, in ordinary English, the background issues and the values at stake.

Canada's APEC summit raised questions relating to constitutional principle, the role of police in democratic society, and the effects of "globalization" on rights and politics in Canada. It is those substantive issues that this book addresses.

ACKNOWLEDGMENTS

Thanks are due to Peter Milroy and Emily Andrew (director and acquisitions editor, respectively, of UBC Press), the staff of UBC Press, and three anonymous expert referees who reviewed the manuscript. Their guidance, expertise, and advice are much appreciated.

I am grateful to the contributors, all of whom are recognized experts in their fields. Each enthusiastically agreed to contribute to this project, met impossible deadlines, and showed integrity, knowledge, courage, and wisdom throughout. Their advice has always been good.

The University of Adelaide provided an outstanding research and writing environment during my term as Distinguished Visiting Professor in History, Law, and British Studies from May to September 1999. Colleagues there and colleagues, students, and employees at the University of British Columbia did much to inform this book. Mark McVicar, Russell Jutlah, Karen Pearlston, Carolyn Andersson and James Kim were most helpful at various stages. This project was supported by research assistance made possible by the University of British Columbia's Faculty of Law Endowment Fund.

I am also grateful to innumerable individuals who provided me with information or perspective on the important matters this book addresses. They include James D. Service, QC (a fine Liberal), student activists, corporate lawyers, university faculty, police officers, family members, graduate students, journalists, schoolteachers, law students, and the passengers of Van Pool 40.

Finally, of course, I acknowledge the loving support and encouragement of Joanne Pue and our daughters, Heather and Colleen.

CHRONOLOGY OF EVENTS

8 January 1997

Prime Minister Jean Chrétien announces that the APEC Economic Leaders' Meeting (AELM) will be held in Vancouver on 24 and 25 November 1997: "I am confident it will be the highlight of 1997 – Canada's Year of Asia Pacific – which will celebrate and strengthen our longstanding social, cultural and business ties within the Pacific community." A press release from the Prime Minister's Office (PMO) explains: "The leaders' meeting will be held in the Great Hall of Arthur Erickson's award-winning Museum of Anthropology, located on the campus of the University of British Columbia."

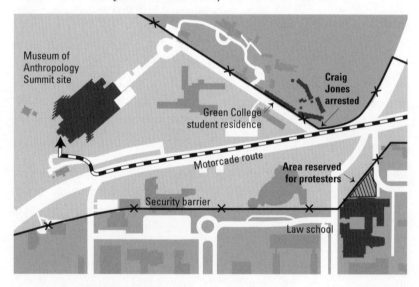

Summer and autumn 1997

Indonesia's President Suharto repeatedly expresses concern about the possibility of encountering "embarrassing" demonstrations while in Canada. He indicates that he will boycott the meetings unless assured that there will be no affront to his dignity.

Suharto or his officials are reassured on numerous occasions by Canadian officials at all levels, including officials from the APEC Canada Coordinating

Office (ACCO), RCMP officers, External Affairs Minister Lloyd Axworthy, and the Prime Minister. Promises are made to protect Suharto's "comfort" or "dignity," or to attend to his "security and other arrangements." Assurances are given that demonstrators "will not be permitted in close proximity to the President."

The RCMP enlarge the perimeter of a fenced area that they had deemed necessary for security purposes at UBC in order to accommodate PM's "specific wish that this is a retreat and leaders should not be distracted by demos, etc." (notes of RCMP Supt. Wayne May, 27 August 1997).

September to November 1997

Disquiet is expressed (*sotto voce*) in certain quarters concerning the propriety and/or legality of restricting demonstrations for reasons unrelated to security: "The PMO had expressed concerns about the security perimeter at UBC, not so much from a security point of view but to avoid embarrassments to APEC leaders. ACCO and the RCMP are looking at that issue. The response (as suggested in fact by Donolo) is that we have to find a balance that meets both concerns (we do not wish student demonstrations and efforts by the govt to suppress the freedom of expression to become a major media story)" (memo from Robert Vanderloo, 12 September 1997).

17 November 1997

Research by the UBC Legal Office reveals that neither the RCMP nor UBC has legal authority to control excessive noise on campus.

22 November 1997

Karen Pearlston, a graduate law student residing at Green College (a graduate student residence and the building closest to the APEC motorcade route at UBC), is told by police that they have orders from the PMO that there should be "no signs and no people" on the Green College side of the motorcade route. She is threatened with arrest when she asserts her constitutional rights. Asked on what charge, the police respond, "We'll make something up."

In the evening, student protesters camped near the Museum of Anthropology are arrested. Police documents had stated that the PMO was "very concerned" about their presence (e-mail from Insp. Dingwall to Supt. May and others, 20 November 1997) even though the campers apparently did not pose a security threat.

"APEC command centre logs show that on one occasion, Jean Carle, the Director of Operations for the Prime Minister's office, phoned Wayne May. May is the RCMP Superintendent who headed up security at the summit. The call came just days before the meeting at UBC, and it centred on the student protesters camped near the summit site" (*Newsworld Online*, 23 August 1999).

22-23 November 1997

Individuals arrested on these dates are required to sign "Conditions for Undertakings Before an Officer in Charge" containing the following clause as a condition of release: "I will not participate or be found in attendance at any public demonstration or rally that has gathered together for the sole purpose of demonstrating against the Asia-Pacific Economic Cooperation or any nation participating in the so named conference." Individuals who either refuse to sign or who breach these terms are held in custody, some-times without charge, until the APEC conference is over. The RCMP would later admit that this was improper and that the conditions were unlawful.

24 November 1997

Anti-APEC organizer Jaggi Singh is arrested on the charge of assaulting a UBC security guard (who also served as a volunteer auxiliary RCMP con-stable) by *speaking* loudly into a megaphone on 7 November, more than two weeks earlier. Released after signing an undertaking, Singh is rearrested later the same day for breaching its conditions. (Two weeks before his trial date, in February 1999, the charges are dropped, prompting him to ask, "Why did I spend four days in jail and why was I nabbed?")

The APEC Threat Assessment Joint Intelligence Group (TAG) Daily Bulletin reports that "two members of the media attending UBC last night as invited observers were noted to be overly sympathetic to the APEC Alert protesters. Both subjects have had their accreditation seized."

Law student Craig Jones places paper signs reading "Free Speech," "Democracy," and "Human Rights" on fences surrounding Green College "in a manner that did not present any security or line-of-sight concerns for the police. Each page of the signs was printed with a notice warning that the signs had been properly and lawfully erected by a Canadian citizen exercising his right of free expression under the Canadian Charter of Rights and Freedoms and that removal of the signs would violate the laws of Canada" (from court documents filed by Jones). At midnight, police remove the signs.

25 November 1997

The APEC Economic Leaders' Meeting takes place at the UBC Museum of Anthropology.

At approximately 7:50 a.m., Craig Jones, aided by a pro-APEC organizer, displays signs reading simply "Free Speech," "Democracy," and "Human Rights" on Green College property. The signs, on 8½ × 11" sheets of paper, are visible from the planned APEC motorcade route but are behind police security fences. The "Human Rights" sign is laid out on the sidewalk near the roadway. The others are displayed from portable coat racks. An RCMP inspector orders the signs removed. Jones would later assert that "at no time was it ever suggested ... that the means by which his sign was mounted posed any security risk." He is arrested, held for fourteen hours, and eventually released without charge.

At approximately 8:30 a.m., Mike Thoms, a doctoral student in history, briefly displays a "textile banner." He is told by RCMP officers that he cannot do this and that he will be arrested for "an obstruction of justice" if he persists. Police seize the banner.

Other individuals wishing to display signs on the Green College side of security fences are told by police that signs are not allowed. RCMP Inspector Dingwall "had ordered student protesters to get off the sidewalk along the APEC leaders' route. At the time Dingwall said they were obstructing pedestrian traffic. And he repeated the claim in a subsequent memo. But when asked about the memo during Public Complaints Commission testimony, Dingwall admitted he lied to the students to get them to move because he was uncomfortable with them being on the sidewalk that the leaders' motorcade would be passing" (CBC *Newsworld*, 11 September 1999).

Police remove a Tibetan flag flying at a considerable distance from the APEC leaders' meeting site.

"PMO aide, Jean Carle ... told the [APEC] inquiry he 'expressed opinions' about the placement of student protesters, so their flag waving and yelling wouldn't embarrass the APEC leaders. But he said he never directly told police to move the protesters" (*Newsworld Online*, 26 August 1999).

Insp. Bill Dingwall "told the [APEC] inquiry the Mounties never tried to hide or restrict demonstrators to limit any political embarrassment ... The positioning of protest banners was not a security issue, yet in one of his many e-mails, Dingwall discussed options for removing them from a university building" (*Newsworld Online*, 7 September 1999). Dingwall and other RCMP officers also denied taking orders from the Prime Minister's staff.

The Prime Minister's staff cancel a scheduled speech to APEC leaders by Chief Gail Sparrow of the Musqueam Nation. She had intended to allude briefly to human rights issues.

Students are pepper-sprayed by police on several occasions. A Canadian Broadcasting Corporation cameraman is also doused with pepper spray. It has been alleged that individuals carrying cellular telephones or amplifying equipment were arrested and that women, but not men, were strip-searched by RCMP officers.

"According to an RCMP source, audio tapes of police radio transmissions at APEC were punctuated with 'Jean Carle wants this' and 'Jean Carle wants that.' The tapes have gone missing, and on Monday Mr. Carle admitted shredding most of his APEC memos, too" (*National Post*, 28 August 1999).

5 December 1997

The *Vancouver Sun* reports that a ten-page RCMP internal memorandum titled "Most Frequency [sic] Asked Questions about APEC Security Measures" told members of the Force that "the Prime Minister's Office was not involved in RCMP security arrangements."

8 December 1997

Craig Jones files suit against the RCMP, the government of Canada, and individual RCMP officers.

Kay Stockholder, President of the BC Civil Liberties Association, files a complaint with the RCMP Public Complaints Commission and becomes the first to call for public hearings into events at APEC 1997.

10 December 1997

At a UBC Senate meeting, senior university officials confirm the direct involvement of senior officials from the PMO in establishing "security perimeters" around the AELM meeting site.

14 December 1997

Officials with Elections Canada (a non-partisan independent agency) interrogate two anti-APEC organizers (Jonathan Oppenheim and Victoria Scott) with a view to charging them for the destruction of *their own* ballots during the 1997 federal election, held almost seven months earlier.

20 February 1998
Shirley Heafey, chair of the RCMP Public Complaints Commission (PCC), appoints a panel to investigate matters arising from the 1997 APEC summit. The panel consisted of Gerald Morin (chair), Vina Starr, and John Wright.

20 July 1998
Justice Barbara Reed of the Federal Court of Canada rules that the PCC panel can properly make "a recommendation to the federal government that the [APEC complainants] be provided with funding. The other side is already fully funded by the federal government ... the issue at stake is of fundamental public importance addressing as it does the boundary between freedom of expression and police security ... The complainant ... acts as a representative of the public interest – the public interest in ensuring that the police do not overstep the bounds of what is proper conduct."

August 1998
Federal Solicitor General Andy Scott refuses to provide funding to pay the legal expenses of the APEC complainants.

Autumn 1998
The fall sitting of the House of Commons is dominated by questions concerning the APEC Inquiry.

25 September 1998
The *Toronto Star* reports that New Democratic Party leader Alexa McDonough, speaking in the House of Commons, asserted: "We learned that former operations director, Jean Carle, has admitted to destroying documents pertaining to spray-PEC." However, PCC counsel Chris Considine is quoted as saying that "we have no evidence to suggest at this time that there has been a deliberate destruction of documents."

5 October 1998
NDP Member of Parliament Dick Proctor reports in Parliament that he overheard Solicitor General Scott say that he was acting as Prime Minister

Chrétien's "cover" in the APEC affair and that "it will all come out in the inquiry that four or five Mounties overreacted for five minutes. No one knows this. I think it was excessive."

6 October 1998

The *Vancouver Sun* reports: "Chrétien has said he will not testify even if the RCMP public complaints commission calls him." Liberal MP and constitutional expert "Ted McWhinney (Vancouver Quadra) was kicked off the House foreign affairs committee after saying last week that students involved in the protest at the Asia-Pacific Economic Cooperation forum should have their legal bills paid. The committee was to vote on the request for funding this week."

16 October 1998

Solicitor General Scott writes to Gerald Morin, chair of the PCC APEC panel, reiterating the government's refusal to provide funding to assist with the complainants' legal fees despite the panel's earlier representations that "public confidence in our findings and recommendations may require separate funded legal representatives for the complainants."

Peter Donolo, the Prime Minister's communications director, writes to the Canadian Broadcasting Corporation alleging that award-winning CBC journalist Terry Milewski is biased against the Prime Minister. No specific inaccuracies or violations of professional journalistic standards are alleged. Milewski is taken off the story.

18 October 1998

The *Province* reports that delegates to the convention of the federal Liberal Party's BC wing passed a resolution calling on the government to provide funding for complainants before the APEC Inquiry.

19 October 1998

Prime Minister Chrétien defends police use of pepper spray at the APEC summit: "Rather than taking a baseball bat or something, they're trying to use civilized measures."

The RCMP PCC panel, chaired by Gerald Morin, resumes hearings but refuses to "read into the record" a statement regarding funding for complainants as instructed by Shirley Heafey, administrative head of the RCMP PCC.

23 October 1998

The *Vancouver Sun* reports that "the federal government raised an allegation of bias against Morin," founded on reports allegedly overheard in Prince Albert, Saskatchewan, some months earlier by RCMP Constable Russell Black.

5 November 1998

The federal government, "which first raised the issue of bias against chairman Gerald Morin, decided it will not make a formal application against the panel." However, lawyers for RCMP officers announce that they will seek a court ruling that the panel is biased *and* an interim order prohibiting "the panel from reconvening before the application for disqualification is heard" (*Vancouver Sun* and *National Post*, 5 November 1998).

6 November 1998

An internal CBC investigation into the Prime Minister's Office's complaints clears Terry Milewski of wrongdoing. He is not reassigned to cover the story.

23 November 1998

Andy Scott resigns as Solicitor General and is replaced by Lawrence MacAulay of Prince Edward Island.

4 December 1998

Gerald Morin resigns from the APEC Inquiry panel. Peter Mansbridge reports on CBC's *The National:* "Gerald Morin blamed interference from his boss, a political appointee, and even raised the possibility of break-ins and bugging of his car and office." According to CBC reporter Ian Hanomansing, "Gerald Morin says the person in charge of the commission, Shirley Heafey, a political appointee, interfered three times."

10 December 1998

Morin's fellow commissioners, Vina Starr and John Wright, resign. PCC chair Shirley Heafey (the administrative head of the commission but not the head of individual panels) "kept the resignations secret for reasons she did not disclose" (*Vancouver Sun*, 18 December 1998).

17 December 1998

The resignations of commissioners Starr and Wright are made public, after Parliament has recessed for the Christmas holidays. Alexa McDonough says: "People are properly shocked that the Public Complaints Commission chose to hide the resignations from the public for a whole week. It hardly inspires confidence" (*Globe and Mail*, 18 December 1998).

21 December 1998
E.N. (Ted) Hughes is appointed as sole commissioner to investigate the matters before the PCC relating to the 1997 APEC summit: "Investigating allegations of political interference in the security measures at the summit is not part of Hughes' mandate, his boss, commission chairwoman Shirley Heafey, confirmed at an Ottawa press conference" (*Vancouver Sun*, 22 December 1998).

5 February 1999
Commissioner Hughes writes to Solicitor General MacAulay urging the federal government to pay for lawyers representing the APEC complainants. He also indicates that he is looking into whether he has "authority to order that it [state-funded counsel] be provided."

Commissioner Hughes rules that, in proper circumstances, the PCC has jurisdiction to investigate and to make recommendations concerning questions relating to the role of the Prime Minister or of his officials in giving improper orders, if any, to the RCMP.

15 February 1999
Solicitor General MacAulay agrees to provide funding for modest legal representation for APEC complainants before the PCC with the following restrictions: (1) it will not cover expenses incurred before 21 December 1998 (when Hughes was appointed); (2) only three lawyers will be paid for; and (3) the lawyers' fees will be restricted to Department of Justice scale. Reform MP Jim Abbott comments: "It makes me think of a rowboat up against a battleship." He estimates that there are "20-odd" lawyers on the other side.

5 March 1999
Commissioner Hughes rules that no person is exempt from being summoned as a witness before the commission if the evidence points in their direction (that is, the Prime Minister could be subject to a summons).

19 March 1999

CBC Ombudsman Marcel Pépin issues a report fully exonerating Terry Milewski: "For six months, the Watergate break-in was regarded as a second-rate break-in, until the two reporters from the *Washington Post* presented the other version we know now ... in the practice of journalism, skepticism and tenacity are not necessarily shortcomings and even less evidence that questioning the official versions confirms an unacceptable bias ... The content of the reports by Mr. Milewski and their presentation by the CBC are consistent with the rules of good journalism and the CBC's Journalistic Standards and Practices."

6 May 1999

Elections Canada drops charges of destroying their own ballots against anti-APEC organizers Jonathan Oppenheim and Victoria Scott.

25 June 1999

Mr. Justice William McKeown of the Federal Court of Canada upholds the federal cabinet's right to withhold documents germane to the APEC Inquiry even though those documents might prove helpful to the complainants' case.

24 August 1999

Jean Carle testifies before the PCC panel: "While Mr. Carle admitted his duties brought him into frequent contact with the RCMP officers organizing summit security, he said the only thing he did was make a few suggestions. He denied that those suggestions were orders or that they were designed to spare Suharto from seeing demonstrations criticizing his regime" (*National Post*, 24 August 1999).

27 September 1999

New evidence is disclosed by the RCMP reporting the following comments by Supt. Wayne May during a conversation between police officers in the days immediately before the APEC summit at UBC: "You know, we know how we normally treat these things, and the normal course of action that we follow, but ah – then the ah – Prime Minister is not directly involved. When we're, you know, in dealing with tree huggers and that sort of thing. But right now, the Prime Minister of our Country is directly involved and he's going to start giving orders, and it might be something that we can't live with, or it's going to create a lot of backlash in final analysis."

8 November 1999
Vancouver lawyer Marvin Storrow resigns as lead counsel to the PCC investigating the APEC affair following suggestions that his attendance at a $400-a-plate fundraising dinner for Prime Minister Jean Chrétien was improper.

20 January 2000
Lawyers for the government of Canada and commission counsel argue that the PCC has no jurisdiction with respect to anyone who is not a member of the RCMP and that accordingly the Prime Minister cannot be called as a witness.

25 February 2000
Commissioner Hughes rules that he has no jurisdiction under the terms of the RCMP Act or under his terms of reference to compel the attendance of the Prime Minister as a witness. Nonetheless, expressing concern that his report might be under a "cloud" if the Prime Minister does not testify, he extended an invitation to the Prime Minister to appear of his own volition.

28 February 2000
Ivan Whitehall, counsel for the government of Canada and the RCMP, indicates formally that the Prime Minister will not testify at the APEC Inquiry, reiterating only that the Prime Minister did not give "improper orders or directions to RCMP members."

29 February 2000
Jonathan Oppenheim, Jaggi Singh, and Rob West, three of the APEC complainants, withdraw their complaints from the the inquiry into RCMP conduct at the November 1997 APEC meetings. "Without the prospect of Mr. Chrétien's testimony, many protesters say the hearing has lost its authority and crucial political context" (Jane Armstrong, "Protesters withdraw complaints from APEC summit inquiry," *Globe and Mail*, 1 March 2000, A7).

PART 1:
CANADA'S APEC SUMMIT, 1997

As I and about 30 other protesters stood chanting 'We are not the enemy,' I think I saw regret in the eyes of some police officers. This wasn't your average protest chant – this was a group of students, overcome with fear, anger, and sadness, pleading in hushed tones with a group of men and women whom they had always thought were there to protect them.

– J. Clark, *Ubyssey,* 28 November 1997

It's such an innocuous name for such a brutally painful thing, really. When asked about it Jean Chrétien said, "For me, I put pepper on my plate." I saw those people writhing, face on fire, eyes shut so tight that the tears could barely roll out, screaming. Screaming so hard I thought they'd break apart. I put pepper on my plate, he said, and the media laughed like Chrétien was Johnny Carson.

– Bruce Arthur, *Ubyssey,*
28 November 1997

1

Policing, the Rule of Law, and Accountability in Canada: Lessons from the APEC Summit

W. WESLEY PUE

This is a book about "civics." It addresses basic questions about what it means to live in a fundamentally decent, humane country of the sort that Canada aspires to be. It is a book about government, human rights, economic power, free speech, police, constitutions, democracy, the accountability of government officials, and state power.

A useful starting point for considering such issues is provided by Lord Acton's well-known adage: "Power tends to corrupt and absolute power corrupts absolutely." Power corrupts good people as well as evil, brilliant intellectuals as well as ordinary mortals. In recognition of this we have created constitutions, parliaments, courts, and the like. All of these exist in the knowledge that it is only by providing explicit limits backed by a series of checks and balances that power's natural tendencies can be constrained.

Ultimately, however, institutional structures alone cannot resist power's corrosive effects. Our main protection lies in our own vigilance. No single institution, person, association, or idea can long defend any democracy, however stable it seems, from power's corrupting effects. A watchful citizenry, well informed about the basic principles of democratic government, is indispensable to liberal democracy. The hallmarks of freedom and constitutional liberty need to be understood, absorbed, internalized, and discussed by all of us.

Because of this, fundamental principles of democratic governance are too important to be entrusted exclusively to members of Parliament, ministers of the Crown, police officers, soldiers, courts, broadcasters, and newspapers. Knowledge and discussion of the foundations of constitutional liberty must not be restricted to the traditional "chattering classes," and should not be the exclusive preserve of lawyers, human rights advocates, philosophers, university professors, and journalists.

In the hurly-burly of daily life, however, *they* too need to pause occasionally to reflect quietly on such matters.

Mr. Chrétien's APEC Summit

This book arises from reflections on a bizarre series of incidents that took place on a university campus and their even stranger aftermath. On 25 November 1997 Canadian Prime Minister Jean Chrétien hosted a summit of nearly twenty political leaders representing the Asia-Pacific Economic Cooperation (APEC) economies (APEC never refers to its members as "states" or "countries"). The Museum of Anthropology at the University of British Columbia was the chosen site.

There were obvious reasons for its selection. Canada's top-ranked university in 1997, UBC provided a prestigious setting for the summit. The museum is a very special place, sitting on a point of land that juts into the Pacific Ocean, with Burrard Inlet and the city of Vancouver sparkling to the east and the picture-perfect scenery of an ocean fjord enveloped by mountain peaks to the north. The magnificent "gulf islands" dot the waters of the Strait of Georgia to the west. Temperate rain forests, beaches, and cliffs surround the museum. Spectacular views of ocean and snow-capped peaks lie in all directions. One of the most beautiful spots on the planet, the museum was a perfect setting for the "photo-ops" beloved by democrats and dictators alike.

The people who attended the APEC summit were no random collection of democrats and dictators, however, just as APEC is no ordinary international organization. Unlike most international bodies, APEC is entirely unidimensional. It focuses exclusively on the promotion of trade, maintaining a studied disregard for "ancillary" matters such as human rights, world peace, labour or environmental standards, the promotion of democratic values, and so on.

In the real world, unlike in the rarefied atmosphere of summitry, it is of course impossible to separate economics from politics quite so neatly. In fact, most long-standing international organizations acknowledge the inseparability of the two spheres. The United Nations, the North Atlantic Treaty Organization, the European Community, the Commonwealth of Nations, the North American Free Trade Agreement, and other organizations concern themselves, to greater or lesser degrees, with matters relating to political values as well as defence, trade, or whatever their principal purpose may be. The APEC club of "economies" was, however, deliberately created without moral, political, or ethical standards. As a result, the government leaders who met in Vancouver in 1997 included some rather nasty individuals. Strong-arm dictators, blatantly corrupt politicians, and an individual whose curriculum vitae included well-documented genocide joined more respectable politicians at the conference table.

Not surprisingly, some people consider the very existence of this odd organization to be something of an affront. Viewing APEC as contemptuous of human rights, damaging to social and political progress, and even detrimental to the long-term economic well-being of the people who live in its member states, critics are often highly suspicious of government policies supportive of APEC and the ideology it represents. The November 1997 summit provided an ideal opportunity for people holding such views to protest both APEC itself and new Canadian policies that they believed ran counter to traditional Canadian values.

The 1997 APEC leaders' summit was greeted by one of the largest campus demonstrations in recent Canadian history. Small, isolated expressions of protest during the lead-up to the leaders' meeting culminated in mass demonstrations on 25 November 1997. Thousands poured onto the UBC campus in protest. The crowds of committed anti-APEC demonstrators were swelled considerably by many who, with little previous knowledge of APEC, showed up to register other concerns. Thousands had heard stories about alleged excesses of the Royal Canadian Mounted Police on the campus in the lead-up to the summit, and many probably showed up on the day primarily to show their disapproval of the RCMP's actions. For such individuals APEC itself began to look bad because of its association with "un-Canadian" police activities in Vancouver.

Policing APEC 1997

What did police do in the autumn of 1997 to so stir the University of British Columbia's notoriously docile students?

Separating rumour and ill-founded allegation from fact can be difficult, even with the benefit of hindsight. This book was written during the course of 1999, at some distance from the events of 1997 but well in advance of the findings of any official inquiry. As the book was being written, the events surrounding Vancouver's APEC summit were under inquiry by the RCMP Public Complaints Commission (PCC) and several lawsuits had been filed against the RCMP, the Prime Minister, and the government of Canada. No final conclusions had been reached in any of these forums.

Whatever may ultimately be found *proved by the evidence,* a number of reasonably well substantiated allegations are deeply disturbing. The restrictions necessarily imposed by the law of evidence means that legally proved "facts" are often considerably more or less than what actually happened (the divergent outcomes of the two O.J. Simpson trials in the United States illustrates this). For this reason, among others, it is hard to predict what the ultimate outcome of legal processes will be. The task is all the more difficult because legal standards of proof operate at a higher threshold than those applied by historians, political scientists, or ordinary Canadians.

The current investigations focus on a wide range of alleged unlawful police conduct, including a bit of "roughing-up," excessive use of pepper spray, arrest on flimsy grounds, and the imposition of unlawful release conditions. There have been allegations that police officers assaulted and detained peaceful individuals for displaying signs, *or* for using cell phones, *or* for possessing megaphones or other amplifying equipment – *none of which is even remotely unlawful.* There have also been complaints that individual police officers used pepper spray to punish (if proved, they would be guilty of criminal assault) rather than to subdue lawbreakers or to effect lawful arrests (which, in proper circumstances, is permissible). Other police officers are said to have told Canadians that UBC, in effect, was a "Charter-free zone" (there is no such thing in Canadian law), while still others are alleged to have engaged in sex-discriminatory strip searches and prophylactic arrest. There have been allegations that law-abiding individuals who wished to display signs, flags, or other symbols of their beliefs were harassed or even arrested. A good deal of evidence has come out suggesting that the RCMP imposed unreasonable restrictions on the freedom of movement, association, and expression of law-abiding Canadian citizens. Complainants have alleged that they did so under instructions from the Prime Minister's staff, an allegation supported by documents released by the UBC administration and by evidence from other sources.

Of course, many people have a good deal of sympathy for police officers, most of whom view their job as an important public service. Many Canadians also have little patience for "student radicals," "professional activists," and their ilk. It is natural to fall back on well-rehearsed scripts in interpreting events such as the APEC summit. For most Canadians, these scripts suggest a rather easy dismissal of concern about the matter: "predictable student protests are predictably contained by police, followed, predictably, by whining about police conduct the protesters themselves had provoked."

Such scripts do not fit this particular event, however. Not everyone pepper-sprayed, handcuffed, roughed-up, or arrested during the APEC summit even remotely fit the mould of "student radical" (not that student radicals should be abused by police either, of course). Consider the following account, written by Roger and Paula Barnsley in an open letter to friends and colleagues shortly after the events it describes:

> The night before the APEC meeting at UBC, a Green College resident (she is about thirty, completing her PhD in Pharmacology and a Swedish-trained physician) reported the following events at dinner (we eat all of our meals as a community). During the day (Monday) she had stopped, with several other Green College residents, to listen to a person telling a group of students about alleged RCMP misconduct earlier in the day. This event did not take place in any secure zone. During the talk another student climbed a nearby flagpole which prompted about five RCMP officers to move through the group of students who were listening to the speaker. Then, without any warning, the RCMP officers assaulted the speaker (his head hit the flagpole twice) and then they "pepper-sprayed" him in the face three times. Immediately after this event they directly and intentionally "pepper-sprayed" about six persons who were listening to the talk. Four of these people were Green College members, including the physician who told the story. The speaker and a number of other students who verbally expressed their dismay with this act were handcuffed and detained.

Although secondhand, this account nonetheless originated with a source close to the authors, who were visitors to UBC residing temporarily in Green College. Paula Barnsley was a senior lawyer from Fredericton, New Brunswick, and Roger was academic vice president of St. Thomas University. Both were pursuing advanced research at the college in the autumn of 1997. The proper interpretation to be put upon the events described by the Barnsleys is, of course, a matter of dispute before the RCMP PCC. At minimum however, their report shows that concern about policing at APEC rapidly expanded well beyond the predictable circle of student protesters.

Consider also the better-known case of Craig Jones, who was arrested the day of the meeting on the lawn of his university residence. His arrest has become an important focus of media coverage. Like the physician in the Barnsleys' account, Jones's background and interests made him an unlikely candidate for trouble with the police. A thirty-something law student intent on a career in corporate law, Jones is a former Canadian soldier, intensely proud of his service in the Seaforth Highlanders. He was a life-long supporter of the Liberal Party of Canada (at least until the time of his arrest). On 25 November 1997, Jones stood *behind* police barricades – just where he was supposed to be – displaying signs saying "Human Rights," "Free Speech," and "Democracy." Ironically, these words reflect the official policies of the Liberal Party and form the foundation of the law that Canadian police officers are duty-bound to uphold. Despite this, Jones alleged that he was arrested simply for displaying these signs on the lawn of his residence: they could have been construed as being critical of one or more of the visiting dictators.

These are strange tales and there are many others like them. This book can neither report on all such stories nor probe the particular allegations in any depth. To do so would be inappropriate at a time when legal proceedings are under way. In all likelihood, the final outcome of the various hearings will be mixed. Some of the many, many allegations of police or political wrongdoing will probably be proved to the satisfaction of the PCC and/or the courts, some will likely be found "unproven," and some may be conclusively found to be unsubstantiated.

The most disturbing allegations currently under investigation, however, relate not to *what* the police did in November 1997 but rather to *what motivated their actions*. Evidence has been introduced both to the PCC and in the House of Commons suggesting that the police not only acted unlawfully but did so with unlawful purpose. Furthermore, it has been suggested that they did so *not* of their own doing but in order to further the wishes of the Prime Minister of Canada or his senior staff. If this interpretation of events is correct, it is possible that other members of the federal cabinet may have been involved.

It is allegations of this sort that raise the APEC affair from the mundane to the level of principle.

Men and Women with Guns
Even law-abiding citizens of democratic states need to always be wary of police power.

This is because police officers have unusual jobs. They are required to work in a highly organized paramilitary fashion, to carry guns, to arrest and detain fellow citizens, and sometimes to use lethal force. The organizations they work for have no close equivalent in democratic societies (apart from the military), and their unique characteristics make them potentially and uniquely dangerous. Combining Lord Acton's adage about the corrupting influence of power with Chairman Mao's thought that "political power grows out of the barrel of a gun," we can immediately appreciate that there is cause for concern whenever the police and politics mix.

"Bad" cops are among the worst enemies of law. Our legal system, policing bureaucracies, and constitution are carefully designed to protect all of us from corrupt, overzealous, or incompetent cops. Good officers know this and are well aware of the importance of acting with the highest integrity. They strive always to work within the law, not against it. When police go wrong, human error or "bad" individuals are often to blame. Corrupt, poorly trained, emotionally strung-out, overtired, or merely stupid police officers are dangerous. The core allegations of the APEC affair suggest, however, that forces may have been at work that were much more serious – and far more frightening – than simple excess by "dumb cops."

The possibility that Canada's most senior political figures deliberately set in motion a chain of events that ended in the violation of the fundamental rights of large numbers of Canadians is disturbing. These are the very individuals to whom, first and foremost, we entrust our constitutional rights and liberties. Less savoury still, the complainants have alleged that Canadian police and politicians alike did improper things in order to appease the sensibilities of one or more of the dictators whom the Prime Minister wished to entertain at his showcase summit.

If such allegations are borne out by the slow grind of evidentiary processes, we will be forced to conclude that the RCMP were deployed by the government of the day for *political*, not law enforcement, purposes. This is a line that ought never to be approached. No functioning democracy – in fact, no reasonably humane autocratic state – tolerates a direct connection between the whims of the executive branch and the strong arm of law enforcement.

More is at stake, however, than the character, lawfulness, or good behaviour of key government and police officials. The APEC affair points to possible deficiencies in the mechanisms and structures that govern the relationship between politicians and police in Canada. Buffering police and military forces (the two are interchangeable when wrongly employed) from political control is the first and primary objective of the rule of law, the crowning achievement of centuries of Canadian-Anglo constitutional development. Despite past failings, the importance of the principle itself has never been lost sight of. Paradoxically, our long history of relatively humane and liberal democratic government makes the profound importance of this key principle easy to overlook. Canadians have been blessed with both long-standing political stability and tolerable government fidelity to the principles of the rule of law. As a result, most of us have never focused our minds on a layer of constitutional principle so fundamental that it is the bedrock on which everything else rests.

Taking the foundations for granted, generations of politicians, lawyers, philosophers, historians, and journalists have turned their attentions elsewhere. Colleges and universities – even faculties of law – no longer teach much about the constitutional fundamentals. We have become preoccupied with other things: arguments about the division of powers between the federal government and the provinces; endless wrangling between Ottawa and the Quebec sovereignists; the creation of the Canadian Charter of Rights and Freedoms; and controversial court rulings on gender discrimination, Aboriginal rights, union picketing, gay and lesbian relationships, the rights of criminals or victims, and so on. Each of these is a weighty matter. They come into play, however, only at the second tier of importance and preoccupy us only because we have long had the luxury of taking the first tier – the principle that police and other armed forces are to be used *only* to enforce the law, not to do the political bidding of government officials – for granted.

It is easier to understand what is ultimately at stake by casting an eye abroad. The experience of countries less fortunate than Canada underlines the importance of keeping politicians and police apart. Indeed, Canada recently went to war with Yugoslavia in large part to protect people who were being subjected to terrible suffering because this boundary was routinely violated. It is clear that the problems of Kosovo and the rest of the former Yugoslavia did not originate primarily in the formal structures of the Yugoslav state. That country has a reasonably decent-looking constitution, with many of the trappings of constitutional rights and accountable government structures. Some institutional structures may be missing, but more important than these structures is the fact that the psychological and political preconditions of freedom have not been internalized by key officials at all levels: the human connection between paper rights and lives lived is not strong. Laws on paper amount to little when politicians, police, and military officers conspire to subvert them. Kosovo's misery provides an extreme example of the consequences when government officials, soldiers, and police have no desire to submit willingly to the constraint of lawful principle. In the 1990s their sense of self-limitation and of restraint under the law gave way to other, baser instincts. Power corrupted.

Similar points can be made regarding Indonesian conduct in East Timor, political repression in Malaysia, and, indeed, the daily conduct of government in most of the world's nastier places.

What Is a Police State?

Now, Canada is not Kosovo, East Timor, or Malaysia, and no one seriously suggests that we have become a "police state." Nonetheless, such comparisons serve to sharpen our focus on some very important principles.

Vancouver talk show host and retired Social Credit cabinet minister Rafe Mair has aptly observed that "a police state is not where the police take over the government but where the government takes over the police."

In fact, however, it can work either way. Consider the victims of official violence in Kosovo or East Timor: it doesn't much matter to them whether the police and soldiers who engaged in atrocities hatched their plans all on their own or did such things in response to orders from government officials. The *results* are the same either way. In either situation the proper buffer between political will and the application of force by police breaks down. Repressive regimes of all stripes in all corners of the earth share this common feature: law gives way to will with disastrous effect. The outcome is equally "lawless" regardless of the direction in which power flows.

Canadians expect their police to act within the constraints of law and to be above political interference. In Canada the most important buffers to secure this end originate in human conscience, in constitutional history, in convention, in public morality, and in the moral culture of government and policing. Because an increasing concentration of power is transforming all "Westminster-style democracies" into one-person prime-ministerial shows, it is cause for concern that these fundamental principles of constitutional propriety exist mostly as matters of convention. They are part of a deeply rooted constitutional order whose paramount principles find only partial expression in statutes or constitutional documents. Such principles are very real and are supremely important, but there is and can be no complete code of Canadian constitutionalism. They need to be learned, thought about, and understood by each succeeding generation of politicians, police, and citizens.

Shielding police from politicians is the foundation of the rule of law, the most important of our constitutional principles. In 1985 the Commissioner of the RCMP told the Solicitor General (the federal cabinet minister responsible for the RCMP) that "a police state emerges when a Government uses its police agencies as instruments of repression against the citizens of the state. It is against that very concern that the police are given a high degree of independence." Dictionary definitions differ little. *Merriam-Webster's Collegiate Dictionary* (10th edition), for example, defines "police state" as "a political unit characterized by repressive governmental control of political, economic, and social life usually by an arbitrary exercise of power by police and especially secret police in place of regular operation of administrative and judicial organs of the government according to publicly known legal procedures."

Canadian cops are human, like the rest of us. This being the case, individual police officers do from time to time transgress their proper role. It is entirely predictable – though not acceptable – that this will happen even in the best-run police agencies staffed by the very best officers. When police misbehave, it is essential that their wrongdoing be remedied, not just as a matter of fairness to aggrieved individuals but also as a matter of public policy.

Police officers are carefully instructed in this fundamental principle of Canadian civics before they are ever allowed in a squad car. According to author John Sawatsky, traditional RCMP training "pounds into them the concept that they are the servants of the law and not the government and that the role of the police in a democratic society is to uphold the law and nobody, regardless who the transgressor is, can interfere. If the Prime Minister makes an illegal U-turn, he must receive a ticket." Every decent police training program in the country drums this into the heads of all would-be police officers.

The commonplace principle is strikingly at variance with what is alleged to have happened at the University of British Columbia in November 1997. Those events are important not so much for what happened – a minor tremor on the Richter scale of world evil – but for the principles at stake.

The Unsavoury Politics of Scandal

The importance of the principles involved was recognized by all political parties in the House of Commons. Even a few members of Parliament on the government benches recognized the importance of the allegations against the Prime Minister and his office. (Admittedly, you had to be watching closely to notice this, as these MPs were muted by party discipline with lightning speed.)

Canada's APEC summit dominated Question Period in the House of Commons during the entire autumn sitting in 1998, ministerial careers were threatened, one cabinet minister was forced to resign on an ancillary matter, and the public image of the Mounties suffered a serious blow. Prime Minister Chrétien's reputation was tarnished as never before. Nonetheless, the noise and fury of political battle did little to illuminate the key public issues that the APEC crisis pointed to. The event seemed to carry the scent of a routine, run-of-the-mill, media-and-opposition-manufactured scandal of little consequence. (In fact, acting on a strong instinct to shoot the messenger, the Prime Minister's first line of defence was to blame the media: award-winning Canadian Broadcasting Corporation journalist Terry Milewski was pulled from the story when the Prime Minister's director of communications complained about him to CBC management. The attack was effective and Milewski permanently sidelined even though the Prime Minister's Office [PMO] was entirely unable to point to either error of fact or failure of journalistic ethics in Milewski's coverage.)

Superficial similarities do make the APEC affair resemble other, lesser scandals. Too often played out for crass political effect, the pattern of manufactured scandal is well known: allegation, leaked evidence, denial, evasion, "technically, legally correct" statements, further leaks, and so on. That script is recurrent and tedious, often generating sound and fury out of all proportion to whatever matters of substance lie behind the fuss.

This resemblance was reinforced too by an odd coincidence of timing. News stories about political interference with policing at APEC 1997 peaked during the autumn of 1998, just as the United States was experiencing considerable turmoil about less constitutionally weighty matters. During this period a highly partisan political feeding frenzy was under way, focusing largely on President Bill Clinton's sexual behaviour in general and his relationship with Monica Lewinsky in particular. Bad behaviour perhaps, but hardly high *constitutional* crime. The Clinton impeachment process was simultaneously better TV, easier to understand, and less consequential than Canada's unfolding political crisis. APEC-related stories were frequently carried in the same newscasts that revealed salacious details about the sexual preferences of the US president. The juxtaposition of these two quite different events made it easy to underestimate the importance of the allegations against our own government.

Canadians, in fact, had little taste for scandal-driven politics even before the nonsense around "Monicagate" exhausted their patience entirely. Knowing this and finding himself in trouble, Mr. Chrétien hid behind Mr. Clinton's problems. The Canadian government played up superficial similarities between the two political crises as much as possible, knowing full well that the suggestion that we shouldn't be as silly as the Americans would have intrinsic appeal north of the 49th parallel. It was a good political strategy, effectively obscuring the gravity of allegations against the Prime Minister. Even opposition politicians who raised the issue repeatedly in the House of Commons often seemed to be acting out a script they had not properly studied, playing roles they did not fully understand. As a result they sometimes *actually looked like* politicians in search of scandal, unaware even as they spoke that proof of the central allegations in the APEC affair – if it comes to light – would be the substance of a first-order constitutional crisis.

An abundance of confusing detail and constitutional subtlety made the events surrounding Vancouver's APEC summit both harder to understand and harder to focus on than the salacious revelations about the sexual trysts that the most powerful man in the world had with a woman half his age in the Oval Office. Other circumstances also helped obscure the central issues. Everyone understands that visiting heads of state need to be protected from foreseeable threats and that this might sometimes quite properly require the deployment of large numbers of police. Common sense suggests that security was important at the APEC meetings, that the Prime Minister would be concerned, and that the mix of crowds of demonstrators and large numbers of police was likely to produce problems. Many parents tell their children to keep away from large demonstrations precisely because they know that in such circumstances a certain amount of jostling, shoving, arrests, even dousing with pepper spray and a bit of roughing-up is predictable, unremarkable. In heated circumstances the occasional excesses of "bad" or merely stressed-out cops also seems mundane. Such abuses of police power need to be remedied, perhaps, but in themselves hardly rise to the stature of a "national scandal."

Moreover, "radicals," students, and demonstrators are, almost by definition, never particularly popular. Some of the complainants in the APEC affair struck many ordinary Canadians as distinctly lacking in "respectability" and hence little deserving of sympathy. Some could be relatively easily dismissed as lawbreakers, others as overexuberant student demonstrators, still others as "professional activists," political extremists, troublemakers, and so on. It served the interests of powerful bureaucracies – in the police and in politics – to play as much as possible to interpretations of events coloured by these lenses. Sometimes the complainants or other demonstrators themselves gave plausibility to such characterizations. Video footage of some individuals pulling down a security fence, apparently deliberately, cast all demonstrators in a bad light. No doubt a thousand Canadians switched off their televisions every time a demonstrator appeared claiming a right to disrupt the meetings or to "arrest" a visiting head of state (an idea that was a lot less plausible before the arrest of former Chilean president Augusto Pinochet in England). It is the nature of protest that such claims are made, and the nature of television news that they are broadcast repeatedly without adequate context and without any serious assessment. Part of the "street theatre" of protest, overreaching claims are by and large unwelcome in middle Canada. Neither did the habits of speech, the dress, and the political views of many demonstrators resonate well with mainstream Canadians.

The Politicians' Indigestion Protection Bill

In order to understand the civics issues behind the APEC affair, it is helpful to step back a bit from the details, to see past the youthful demonstrators of whom we may disapprove, and to look beyond a cause with which we may disagree. It is important not to miss the forest for the trees.

To reach a dispassionate understanding of key issues, we need to focus resolutely on matters of constitutional principle. The most serious *allegations* run something like this:

1   For political reasons, the Prime Minister wished to ensure the attendance of former Indonesian president Suharto at the 1997 Vancouver APEC summit. (It has been suggested that the participation of other dictators may also have been at issue. The Indonesian connection, however, is by far the best documented.)
2   Suharto indicated that he would not attend unless he was protected from being "embarrassed" by protests, demonstrations, banners, placards, signs, and so on.
3   The Prime Minister ordered his aides either:
    (a) to ensure that Suharto would be spared embarrassment (not just protected from assassination, injury, or assault)
        or
    (b) to instruct the RCMP to ensure that Suharto would be spared embarrassment.

In either event,

4   The Prime Minister's senior staff gave orders to the RCMP. These orders resulted in the violation of constitutionally protected freedoms (free assembly, free speech, freedom from arbitrary arrest, among others) for reasons *that had nothing to do with security needs.* As a result dozens were arrested and hundreds of *law-abiding* individuals were interfered with or assaulted by police as they exercised their constitutionally protected rights as citizens of a democratic country.

A fairly complete paper trail supports some such interpretation of events, and the Prime Minister's complete refusal during months of controversy to offer a candid, unambiguous, and comprehensive account of his conduct is certainly troubling. Nonetheless, it must be emphasized that at the time of writing, none of these allegations have been accepted as proved by any competent forum.

Even assuming some such interpretation of events to be entirely accurate, however, many wonder what the fuss is about. It may help to imagine an only slightly modified set of facts. What would happen if a bill were introduced to prohibit the display of posters displeasing to the Prime Minister or, perhaps, to mandate that no one within 100 metres of a Canadian politician should utter words displeasing to him or her – a proposal for a "Politicians' Indigestion Protection Act," if you will.

This of course is absurd because no constitutionally minded Commons, Senate, or Governor General would even contemplate the passage of such legislation. If they did, the resulting statute would be struck down by *any* court without a second thought. Such legislation would violate every principle of free speech and democracy on which the constitution rests.

Nor could such draconian measures be justified on the grounds that certain words might cause offence to foreign despots or trading partners. No such rationale could provide legal justification under the terms of the Canadian Charter of Rights and Freedoms, within the spirit of a free and democratic society (Constitution Act, 1982), or under a constitution similar in principle to that of the United Kingdom (Constitution Act, 1867). Freedom is not made of such material.

Now if the government can't do these things up front (by introducing legislation, debating it, obtaining passage through the Houses of Parliament, and securing royal assent), it clearly shouldn't be able to do so through the back door. If Parliament is prohibited from doing something, so too are prime ministers, their aides, and police. "Reason of state" cannot be casually invoked by democratic leaders, even if the "reason" is that we don't want to offend one of the Prime Minister's dinner guests. The despot's mantra, "reason of state" is the conceptual opposite of Canada's most important single constitutional principle, the rule of law.

The Rule of Law

This principle comes in two parts. First, no one can be interfered with, harassed, or made to suffer except for a distinct breach of law established in the ordinary legal manner before the ordinary courts. Second, *everyone* is bound by the law: police, PMO staff, MPs, the Prime Minister, even the Governor General in Council.

In common with all decent countries, Canada has well-developed mechanisms that are supposed to protect the police from political interference and to protect citizens from political policing. The reason is simple: blurring this boundary renders the rest of the constitution irrelevant.

The rule of law can be represented graphically by reference to two possible lines of authority, portraying quite different ways in which the state's power might come to be exercised against its citizens:

Line A: Rule of Law
Constitution –> Queen in Parliament –> police –> courts –> citizen

Line B: Despotism
Prime Minister –> flunky's decree –> police –> truncheon –> citizen

Line A is a short-form expression of the rule of law. It presumes that before citizens' liberties and freedoms are restricted, the full protection of constitutional rights *and* the political protections provided by our parliamentary system of government will be brought into play. In this model the legislature determines what should be lawful and what should not, the police enforce the law and only the law, the courts adjudicate, and citizens are punished only for violation of law, established in the proper ways. At every point along this chain, power is confined within the channels of lawful authority and constitutional propriety. Law constrains will.

Line B is dictatorship. In it the will of politicians subverts law. This is so even if assault by pepper spray and plastic handcuff is substituted for the truncheon of old. In this model, the police do the bidding of politicians or bureaucrats unmediated by court, Parliament, or constitutional propriety. If the principles of lawful governance (summarized in Line A) can be freely violated, the political use of police forces to harass journalists, political opponents, and other inconvenient individuals is no longer unthinkable. This happens routinely in many countries, and the possibility that something similar occurred in Vancouver in 1997 is the core concern raised by the APEC affair.

Whatever is eventually proved about the particular incidents of alleged police wrongdoing, a mountain of evidence points to an unusually close relationship between the Prime Minister and the RCMP. This alone suggests that all may not be well with Canada's federal police force, an impression confirmed, disturbingly, by eminent Canadian political scientist Donald Savoie's 1999 observation that "the relationship between the commissioner of the RCMP ... and the prime minister ... has become so close over the past twenty years or so that the minister responsible – the Solicitor General – ... is now effectively cut out of some of the most important discussions and decisions."

This is a significant distortion of established constitutional channels in that one of the Solicitor General's most important duties as a "law officer of the Crown" is to serve the *law*, to protect police from improper political pressures even if they come from the head of the cabinet in which the Solicitor General serves. The Solicitor General, like the Attorney General, is much more than just another political minister.

Of course if the Prime Minister's staff gave unlawful orders – for example, that individuals displaying signs displeasing to President Suharto should be stopped or arrested – any professional police force should have refused to act on those orders. They were legally as well as morally bound to do so. And they should have been supported in doing so by both the RCMP Commissioner and the Solicitor General. In a democracy the police are there to enforce the law, a task that should never be confused with simply doing the bidding of politicians. A very slippery slope lies between student protesters and the rest of us. Central principles of public life, once compromised, lose their force.

Prime Ministers, Police, and the Unwritten Constitution

If confirmed, the emerging story line about Canada's APEC summit would be deeply troubling. It would reveal a shocking disrespect for the principle of the political independence of the police on the part of senior police officers, members of cabinet, the Prime Minister, and the Prime Minister's staff. It would represent a fundamental violation of the principle of the rule of law, striking at the very heart of our constitution.

To recap partially, this is because a direct connection of the executive branch to police short-circuits the entire constitutional apparatus: the House of Commons (and the rest of the "Queen in Parliament"), the courts, the juries, the independent bar, and the rest. Other mechanisms that civil societies use to ensure a proper buffer between the police and the politicians include police commissions (or commissioners), the very special cabinet offices of Solicitor General and Attorney General (the senior "law officer of the Crown"), and a variety of understandings, constitutional conventions, or usages limiting the means and types of legitimate communication between government officials and police officers. Such understandings, conventions, and usages constitute an important part of the "unwritten constitution."

Contrary to what most people think, the larger part of the Canadian constitution is not neatly summarized in statute or Charter but is found precisely in this nebulous constitutional realm. Nebulous though they may be, if the mechanisms shielding armed force from political deployment or improper ministerial control fail, the rest – constitutional documents, the Charter of Rights and Freedoms, human rights commissions, and Parliament itself – become a mere chimera that can be ignored.

It is of course important that police be accountable to the public. There is a world of difference, however, between public accountability and political control. We are accustomed to thinking of the Prime Minister as the "chief executive officer" of government, of cabinet as a "board of directors," and of the rest of the state apparatus as being ultimately answerable to them just as the employees of a small business are ultimately answerable to the boss. Government is not a business, however. Executive command is the *opposite* of democratic accountability through proper channels. As one royal commission of inquiry pointed out, "The notion of civil control ... should not be confused with control exercised by public servants. Indeed, this latter state of affairs undermines the traditional and necessary responsibilities of Parliament." These words, penned by the Somalia Inquiry that investigated the Canadian military, apply with equal or greater force to civil control of the police.

The Public Morality of Government Personnel

In our system of government, then, a good deal turns on the collective conscience of individuals holding public office. Wherever constitutional democracy thrives, its essence is found in the hearts and minds of those who work in government, in public institutions, and in the police forces. At the end of the day, it is their internal – moral – sense of constitutionalism upon which our freedoms rest. Decent government requires that individuals in power *daily* decline certain possible courses of action because they are improper, immoral, or illegal. The rule of law rests ultimately on the commitment and integrity of politicians, bureaucrats, and police at all levels. Its only foundation is *their* sense of constraint and public morality, and their willing adherence to its principles.

There are probably many strong temptations to short-circuit democratic practice, however. Inevitably things will go wrong. Like police officers, bureaucrats and politicians will fail to meet the highest standards of constitutional and legal propriety. In fact, our legal and constitutional systems assume that things *will* go wrong from time to time. Any other assumption could be based only on the existence of a class of politicians, police, and bureaucrats who are superhuman in their understanding, foresight, discipline, and propriety. Because no such class of saints exists, our legal and political systems seek out failure to investigate wrongdoing, to find ways of exposing wrongdoing to public scrutiny, and to remedy wrongs when they occur. The ultimate objective of all this, of course, is to prevent future wrongdoing.

Where people fail, other mechanisms come into play. These informal and formal means of exposing wrongdoing to public scrutiny, of establishing facts authoritatively, and, in appropriate cases, of offering remedies (whether political or legal in nature) include:

- a free press
- the courts
- public inquiry processes (including everything from royal commissions to the RCMP Public Complaints Commission to other minor tribunals)
- Parliament.

Each of these forums of accountability is assessed in detail in one or more chapters of this book. Some key points merit emphasis here, however, for the APEC affair raises a number of concerns regarding the adequacy of these bulwarks of liberty.

A Free Press

A free press is the first – and one of the most important – of the accountability mechanisms in any democratic society. It is the precondition to the creation of an informed public, the sine qua non of liberal democracy. The bare knowledge that decisions will be exposed to public scrutiny, that abuses will be revealed, imposes a powerful constraint in and of itself.

It is obvious, however, that if the press is to act meaningfully as a check on power, it must operate independently of political control. A free press requires that journalists be free from political influence. If they are not, they become mere mouthpieces for the powerful, agents of official propaganda. Equally, the press cannot serve as a check on exercise of arbitrary, unlawful, or unconstitutional power if reporters limit their ambitions to attending prearranged "photo-ops" and dutifully reporting neatly packaged material doled out by government press flacks. A vigorous, democratic press requires motivated journalists, a spirit of critical inquiry, and resources sufficient to sustain investigative journalism. All these are necessary if our media are to look behind the spin doctors. The institution of a free press requires that at least some of the newspapers, magazines, television networks, and radio stations that journalists work for provide them with the resources they need in order to fulfil these important functions and shield them from both unjustified attacks on their integrity and unwarranted legal assault.

Because a free press is so fundamental, the extraordinary circumstances surrounding the removal of award-winning CBC journalist Terry Milewski from coverage of APEC-related events and the "coincidental" efforts of the cabinet to render the Canadian Broadcasting Corporation formally subservient to its wishes are cause for concern.

The CBC is one of the most important media outlets in the country. It is the only one that has routinely dedicated significant resources to investigative reporting, which is why it, with Milewski, became the lead news organization in reporting the substantial issues raised by the APEC affair. Yet disturbing relationships of power lurk in the background, as CBC Ombudsman Marcel Pépin made clear in his report on the Milewski case:

> The CBC is a public corporation whose journalistic independence is guaranteed by legislation, but which nonetheless comes under the indirect authority of the Prime Minister. A complaint from the Communications Department of the head of government therefore takes on unusual importance for the public and all media, so much so that many commentators have even seen in this an indirect threat to the independence of the CBC.

In this context, the stunning effectiveness of the Prime Minister's attack on a journalist must be a cause for concern.

Courts and Tribunals

Although the press serves important functions in free and democratic societies, it does not offer direct remedies to aggrieved persons. This is the role of other, more formal institutions.

In particular, citizens injured by government wrongdoing rely on an effective, accessible, functioning, and independent court system for final recourse. One terribly important role of the courts is to act as referee between individuals and the state.

In many cases, however, the resources of the court system and the expertise of its personnel are not fully up to the task of investigating complicated cases. Recognizing this, the Canadian system of government, like those of other developed democracies, has attempted to fill the "accountability gap" by creating specialist tribunals or inquiries, large or small. In general such tribunals have more specific mandates than the common law courts, and greater expertise in particular areas. The RCMP Public Complaints Commission, for example, looks only at matters related to allegations of RCMP wrongdoing. Tribunals typically have greater investigative powers than the judges of the common law courts. The courts are supposed to hear only the evidence introduced by parties before them; if parties cannot afford to muster relevant evidence or if they choose, for reasons of their own, not to introduce it, judges can do nothing to compel its production. Tribunals, on the other hand, can exercise their expanded investigative powers on their own initiative.

Courts and tribunals share an all-important defect, however. It is summarized in the thought, often expressed by lawyers, that the legal system provides "the best justice money can buy."

Cynical? Perhaps. But any informed observer knows that if the promise of "equality before the law" is to be more than empty rhetoric, at least a rough equality of legal resources is needed. Money may not buy justice in Canada, but it does buy word processing services, lawyers, office space, accountants, computers, paralegal workers, expert witnesses, databases, investigative teams, research, photocopiers, paper clips, and the rest of the resources used to lay factual foundations and develop winning legal arguments.

Consider a fundamental flaw in the legal processes in a case such as the APEC affair: the Canadian federal government has no prosecutor or investigator who is fully independent of Ottawa's innermost circle of power. Ottawa has no mouse who can bell the cat. Within the federal government system, decisions on whether to bring criminal charges against police officers or staff in the Prime Minister's Office – perhaps even a minister – are made either by the RCMP (whose top brass are accused of wrongdoing in the APEC affair) or through other processes operating in the federal Department of Justice or in the Solicitor General's Office. Not to put too fine a point on it, both the ministers and the top Mountie owe their jobs to the Prime Minister and to the party apparatus he heads. They depend upon his goodwill for the continuation of their salaries, for ongoing influence, and for any patronage appointments they hope to receive when they retire from politics or policing. Although they may be individuals of the greatest integrity, these relationships of power must weigh heavily upon incumbents in these offices.

When a case does come before a court or tribunal as a result of individual initiative, another problem arises with existing accountability mechanisms. In all of the APEC-related proceedings, the PMO and the RCMP – two mighty institutions if ever there were such – enjoy virtually unlimited resources. The government's pockets are deep, and its legal juggernaut confronts a diverse group of more-or-less impoverished complainants. Although the issues raised are of profound public importance and those accused of wrongdoing enjoy virtually unlimited access to public funds, the complainants have no such resources.

After a series of highly embarrassing events, including the resignation of the Solicitor General of Canada and then of the entire RCMP Public Complaints Commission panel that first began hearings into the APEC affair, the government of Canada at last agreed to provide some public funding to complainants before the PCC. The resources and the legal firepower of the latter remain puny, however, compared with the army of lawyers who appear daily for the government and the RCMP – not an ideal situation.

The same imbalance of resources plagues litigants in the civil courts. When those cases come to be heard in courts of law, the government and the RCMP will again enjoy virtually unlimited legal resources. Only very, very large corporations or the wealthiest of individuals can match the government on this score. In court, as in other spheres, the "haves" tend to come out ahead, regardless of the qualities of the women and men who serve as lawyers, judges, and court officials.

In theory an independent commission with inquisitorial powers might redress such imbalances on its own. The RCMP Public Complaints Commission, however, is small, modestly staffed, and modestly funded. Although the integrity of Commissioner Ted Hughes is beyond reproach, his Commission faces serious challenges in investigating allegations of wrongdoing by the most powerful man in the land. If like its predecessor the Hughes tribunal encounters resistance rather than the fullest possible cooperation from the powerful institutions under investigation, it is by no means clear that the PCC's resources would be up to the challenge. It is significant that Commissioner Hughes's investigation has no source of funding that is independent of Ottawa's control.

It is worth recalling too that not so long ago and not so very far away, other, better-staffed commissions have been worn down and undermined by the people they were supposed to investigate. For example, Mr. Chrétien's government gained experience in first muting and then shutting down an embarrassing inquiry when the Somalia Inquiry moved from considering problems of military governance under the previous Conservative government to looking into apparently unseemly events that took place on the Liberal watch.

Parliament

In our parliamentary democracy, the House of Commons and the Senate are accorded pride of place in protecting the constitution and remedying wrongdoing by ministers, including prime ministers. Our system of government requires that ministers of the Crown be "responsible" to an elected Parliament for all of their activity – and that Parliament act on behalf of the people of Canada, not as servants of the executive branch. Theory and practice diverge markedly here. Theory holds that any minister can be dismissed immediately by Parliament, and that a prime minister is accountable daily to the legislature during Question Period. In theory the prime minister is the servant of the House and the members are our delegates. In practice, however, party discipline gives a majority prime minister almost total control. Prime ministers command MPs, and even seemingly powerful cabinet ministers, much more often than they answer to them. The theory of responsible government may well be at odds with the practices of modern executive government.

The instability of facts and the messiness of real-world parliamentary government conspire to make it unclear what the political outcome of the APEC affair will be. One great jurist observed that "all facts are guesses." Much turns on what will be taken as proved at the end of processes that include the RCMP Public Complaints Commission, the courts, and parliamentary proceedings.

Taking theory first, the question arises as to what constitutional convention would require in a worst-case situation, for example, if there were conclusive evidence that the Prime Minister or his senior staff personally ordered the police to prevent embarrassment to foreign dictators and that law-abiding Canadians were arrested as a result. Constitutional convention is clear: *any minister who engages in serious misconduct with respect to his office is constitutionally, morally bound to resign.* This is the key doctrine of responsible government, and responsible government is the centrepiece of our constitution. This is no ordinary theory, but the core of democracy. It does not matter whether wrongdoing resulted from the personal actions of a minister or from the actions of the minister's senior staff: the minister is equally responsible to Parliament either way. The buck stops on his or her desk.

The deployment of police for political purposes strikes at the heart of the constitution, the Prime Minister has no special status, and in such circumstances his resignation would be in order. So much is clear. This is how political accountability is *supposed* to work in Westminster-style democracies.

Quite a different question arises, however: what would the House of Commons *in fact* do if confronted with such a situation? Like the United Kingdom (but unlike the United States), Canada has no formal mechanism for displacing a leader who has engaged in "high crimes and misdemeanours," to borrow the American phrase. Unlike the UK, we have no durable party apparatus capable, in proper circumstances, of providing a power base for MPs and ministers that is outside the Prime Minister's control.

Everything turns on the attitude of a House of Commons in which MPs are subjected to party discipline even more rigorously than in the UK. Donald Savoie, a noted political scientist who worked in a non-partisan capacity on the first Chrétien government's transition team, has concluded that in Canada, power is more centralized in the prime minister's office than it is in any other democracy. We lack the checks and balances of the United States. We lack the effective parliamentary and party systems of the British. We have no independent and elected second chamber equivalent to the Australian Senate. Others have observed that backbench government MPs perform as "trained seals" – standing and clapping on cabinet command, exercising no independent judgment, and achieving little beyond providing a picturesque backdrop for the Prime Minister and his inner circle. One recent newspaper article went so far as to speculate that Pierre Trudeau had it wrong when he asserted that backbench MPs are "nobodies" once they leave Parliament, but only because Trudeau failed to anticipate a time when they have become "nobodies" *on* Parliament Hill as well as off it.

This may, however, be too jaundiced a view of Canadian members of

Parliament. We simply do not know what individual Liberal MPs might do at the end of the day. Backbench Liberals are of crucial importance because it is only government-side members who matter in majority parliaments. "Trained seals" cannot rise to constitutional duty, but it is surely highly uncharitable and unfair to dismiss the entire Liberal caucus as clapping automatons responsive only to PMO command. Party discipline might indeed undermine fealty to core constitutional principle, but government members – even perhaps ministers – might rise to duty if confronted with a clear, fundamental constitutional violation. It would be hard to predict, and all enormously speculative, of course.

Other Legal Ripples

If the political and constitutional outcomes are hard to forecast, so too are the "lesser" legal consequences. If there turns out to be provable wrongdoing with regard to the arrangements leading up to the APEC summit, the rule of law would require that the appropriate legal consequences follow *regardless of the status of the wrongdoer*. In theory, police officers, bureaucrats, ministers, political staff, and the Prime Minister himself would all bear personal responsibility for their wrongdoings. If it is a violation of criminal law to assault, handcuff, and confine one individual without lawful cause, it would be both a criminal offence and a civil wrong to organize things so that an entire police force participated in such activities without lawful cause.

Canadian law has no doctrine making police officers, political staff, or ministers who participate in wrongdoing immune from the ordinary consequences of wrongful behaviour. Any official who triggers an essentially unlawful mission could face either criminal prosecution or a civil suit or both. The consequences could be ruinous for individuals.

Such considerations are of course highly hypothetical. They are, however, at the core of the problem in Canadian civics that lay behind the sound and fury and well-known news images generated by the events of November 1997 and their aftermath.

The remainder of this book considers in depth the constitutional principles involved, the adequacy of existing accountability mechanisms, questions surrounding the appropriate role of police, and finally the character of the changing international arena that put APEC on the public agenda in Canada in the first place.

PART 2:
CONSTITUTIONAL FUNDAMENTALS

Cabinet has now joined Parliament as an institution being bypassed. Real political debate and decision making are increasingly elsewhere ... The Canadian prime minister has little in the way of institutional check, at least inside government, to inhibit his ability to have his way.

> – Donald J. Savoie, *Governing from the Centre: The Concentration of Power in Canadian Politics*

The brutal fact is that our Parliament has long since lost control of government. That rests with the PM, who has the power to appoint the Governor-General, chief of the military, head of the RCMP, all the judges of the Supreme Court of Canada and all other senior judges, all the Senators, members of the CRTC, head of the CBC, Governor of the Bank of Canada, the cabinet, ambassadors, etc., etc., etc. He signs off on every budget and gives advance approval on every piece of legislation (except exceedingly rare Private Members' bills) passed by Parliament. The practical effect is no checks, no balances.

> – Gordon Gibson, *Globe and Mail*,
> 14 September 1999

2

Free Speech, Democracy, and the Question of Political Influence

ANDREW D. IRVINE

Freedom of speech and freedom of peaceful assembly lie at the heart of what it means to live in a democracy. Without the ability to express ideas of all kinds freely, and without the ability to meet together to hear contrary and often controversial points of view, citizens are not able to exercise their sovereignty over government. Free speech, it is rightly said, is the most powerful weapon we have against tyranny.

If our rights to free speech and peaceful assembly are to be anything more than mere platitudes, however, they have to be the kinds of rights that cannot be overridden at the mere whim of either individual police officers or our political leaders. As George Orwell reminds us, "If liberty means anything at all, it means the right to tell people what they do not want to hear."

Recently we have seen just how fragile these fundamental rights and freedoms are, and just how easy it is for them to be restricted. During the 1997 APEC summit at the University of British Columbia in Vancouver, not only did some peaceful protesters have their paper and cloth signs forcibly removed, others were arrested or threatened with arrest simply for refusing to take their signs down. Still others were intimidated by police officers into signing guarantees that they would give up their right to free speech for the duration of the summit. That these events took place in the public areas of a Canadian university campus makes them all the worse. Universities have long been recognized as centres of free speech, relying as they do on the open exchange of ideas for the advancement of knowledge.

Some of the many allegations that have been raised over the way the Royal Canadian Mounted Police handled the student protests at the APEC summit are that the RCMP:

1 threatened to arrest students unless they removed their protest signs, and that they did arrest at least one student for refusing to do so

2 forced protesters who were detained to sign, as a condition of their release, an undertaking to give up their free speech rights for the duration of the APEC summit

3 forced students to restrict their protests to specific zones far removed from the view of visiting dignitaries and their motorcades, and that they did so contrary to prior agreement with the university

4 removed a Tibetan protest flag that was flying outside designated security areas in order to placate Chinese students and visiting Chinese dignitaries

5 withdrew the press accreditation of two reporters because of their political views rather than for reasons of security

6 used unnecessary and excessive force, including the unnecessary use of pepper spray, while attempting to control demonstrators

7 failed to supervise armed foreign security forces properly, which may have compromised the safety of Canadian citizens and dictated which student groups were or were not allowed to continue their protests

8 treated some protesters inappropriately while in custody; for example, strip-searching the women but not the men who were arrested

9 infiltrated and engaged in surreptitious surveillance of non-violent and law-abiding political protest groups in the weeks preceding the APEC summit, without just cause

10 may have sacrificed the rights and liberties of Canadian citizens in order to advance a number of purely political objectives of the Prime Minister's Office (PMO), if it acted outside its lawful authority.

November 1997 therefore represents something of a watershed for civil liberties in Canada. If it turns out that the free speech rights of Canadian citizens were inappropriately compromised, then, as Canadians, we cannot afford to be complacent about even the most basic of our civil liberties.

What went wrong at the APEC summit? If the RCMP had not instituted the practice of pre-emptive arrest, would this have decreased security in any significant way? If protesters had been allowed to display their signs along motorcade routes (rather than only in small, officially designated areas), would this have made conflict between protesters and police officers less likely? By resorting to the use of pepper spray, did the RCMP in fact hamper, rather than promote, security along important motorcade routes? And if it turns out that unjustified restrictions were placed on student protesters, was this for political rather than security reasons?

Of the ten issues listed above, the first five are primarily about freedom of speech. The next three are primarily about the appropriate use of force in protecting visiting dignitaries and in dealing with student protesters. The ninth concerns the use of potentially illegal surveillance methods, and the tenth is about whether politicians, or civil servants acting on their behalf, attempted to influence police policy for political ends.

We are thus left with the four important questions:

1   Did the RCMP inappropriately compromise the free speech rights of Canadian citizens?
2   Did the RCMP use unnecessary and excessive force, or other inappropriate methods, while trying to control student protesters?
3   Did the RCMP engage in inappropriate police practices, such as the illegal surveillance of non-violent political protest groups?
4   Did the RCMP allow itself to be influenced, at least in part, by political directives from the PMO, rather than by security concerns, while carrying out its mandate to protect summit delegates?

While most of the news media and editorial comment since November 1997 have concentrated on the second of these questions, all four are important. Specifically, if Canadian citizens are not permitted to speak freely in public – or to become involved in non-violent political protest groups – without fear of surveillance or intimidation, this strikes at the very core of the democratic ideal. Similarly, if the RCMP allowed itself to be used by the PMO for political ends, this is not something to be dismissed lightly. People across the country need to be assured that Canada's chief law enforcement agency cannot be used for partisan political purposes. We need to know that the RCMP is not inappropriately restricting the most fundamental rights of Canadian citizens. Democracy itself is in peril whenever the police are used not to protect citizens' rights or to enforce the law but to violate those rights in order to advance ordinary political objectives.

Many of the thousands of documents tabled before the hearings of the RCMP Public Complaints Commission (PCC) into the APEC affair are of interest in this context. For example, among the many internal RCMP e-mail messages sent in November 1997 before APEC delegates arrived in Vancouver, there is a significant exchange between RCMP Inspector Bill Dingwall and RCMP Superintendent Trevor Thompsett. After discussing several security issues surrounding the various summit sites, including the Museum of Anthropology (MOA) at UBC, Inspector Dingwall e-mailed Superintendent Thompsett as follows:

> If they hang banners towards the MOA, are they going to be visible through the trees? Could we erect some sort of draping to cut off the view? Secondly, they are only leasing the building and I suppose that we could make the argument that the exterior of the building is not being rented and the University, as landlord, could remove them.

Thompsett replied as follows:

> Common sense tells us we do not want banners nor would the PMO's office. Having said that, banners are not a security issue. They are a political issue. Who is looking after that? If they are not going to be permitted, what is the authority for removing them and who is going to do it? Shooting from the hip here but taking them down is touching with someone else's property that is not a security concern.

We see here both a recognition on the part of the RCMP that free speech and private property rights are distinct from security issues, and a reference to the apparent influence of the PMO.

A second document also concerns security issues at UBC. In a letter to Prime Minister Chrétien dated 19 November 1997, UBC president Martha Piper warns that overly restrictive security arrangements may serve to increase rather than decrease the chance of conflict:

> I am writing to you to express our concern about a proposal to seriously limit the opportunity for members of the University community, particularly students, to have a sense of involvement in the upcoming APEC Economic Leaders' Meeting on the campus of The University of British Columbia.
>
> In planning the AELM, we had reached an agreement with the RCMP on a "line of sight" gathering place where interested students, including some who are opposed to APEC, could see and be seen, however briefly, by the APEC leaders.
>
> Now, regrettably, as we enter the final planning stages for the AELM, officials from your office have decided to reduce significantly

the area available for line of sight access to the APEC leaders. This contravenes the University's commitment to its community, violates a prior agreement, and increases the risk of a serious incident arising out of over-crowding and frustration in a very confined space.

In his reply of 20 November, the Prime Minister's director of operations, Jean Carle, does little to address President Piper's concerns, and denies the existence of any prior agreement with the university.

A third document is found among several dossiers compiled by the APEC Threat Assessment Joint Intelligence Group, and is entitled "APEC TAG Daily Bulletin for 1997-11-24." In addition to a series of photographs of various protesters and potential protesters, we find the following comment:

> Two members of the media attending UBC last night as invited observers were noted to be overly sympathetic to the APEC Alert Protesters. Both subjects have had their accreditation seized. The first subject is Dr. Joan RUSSON federal leader of the Green Party. Second subject Dennis PORTER's accreditation states he is a journalist employed by Working TV.

Deciding which journalists may or may not be accredited based on their political views is a practice more characteristic of totalitarian regimes than of any healthy democracy. A fourth document again comes from the RCMP. Entitled "Conditions for Undertakings before an Officer in Charge," it contains a list of promises (or undertakings) to which protesters who were arrested had to agree in order to be released before the start of the APEC summit, including:

> I will not attend within 100 metres of any venue or site where officials of foreign governments participating in the Asia-Pacific Economic Cooperation may be in attendance between the dates, November 18th, 1997 and November 26th, 1997.

and

> I will not participate or be found in attendance at any public demonstration or rally that has gathered together for the sole purpose of demonstrating against the Asia-Pacific Economic Cooperation or any nation participating in the so named conference.

Signing the above undertakings would mean not only that political protesters could not travel freely throughout Vancouver but also that for the duration of the APEC summit they would not be allowed to voice their opposition publicly to Canadian government policies of any kind. The unconstitution-ality of such undertakings was confirmed shortly after the summit when an RCMP spokesman admitted that it had been a mistake for the RCMP to demand undertakings of this nature.

These documents support the view that the fundamental rights and freedoms of many Canadian citizens may have been compromised during the APEC conference. Equally important, these and other documents clearly provide prima facie evidence that there may have been improper attempts on the part of the PMO to advance its political objectives through the RCMP, and that at least some members of the RCMP recognized the importance of distinguishing issues of free speech from those of security. The documents seem to indicate that the PMO wanted to strike a balance between the rights of expression of students and the desire of local and vis-iting dignitaries not to be embarrassed by unflattering protest signs. This, of course, raises two more questions:

1   Is there a balance to be struck between the political interests of the PMO, and of other government officials and visiting dignitaries, and the fundamental democratic rights of Canadian citizens?
2   At what point does political involvement by the PMO or other govern-ment officials in the affairs of the RCMP become political interference?

To answer the second question first, we need to keep in mind the boundaries that politicians are required to observe in their dealings with Canadian law enforcement agencies. After all, the involvement of the PMO in security arrangements may initially appear to be innocent enough. The Prime Minister and his office obviously have a legitimate interest in the safety of visiting leaders and other dignitaries. If, however, the PMO attempted to have the RCMP suspend the rights of protesters without com-pelling security reasons for doing so, this clearly crossed the line between legitimate political involvement and improper political interference. Such violations of the rule of law are a hallmark of the police state. Canadians of all political persuasions need to be assured that the RCMP will not allow itself to be used by politicians in this way. Adherence to the rule of law by those who govern us is ultimately our most fundamental defence against police-state tactics. Unless the law can be seen to apply equally and fairly to all citizens without political interference, we will have abandoned one of the cornerstones of Canadian democracy. Governments have fallen for less.

As for the first question, the idea that there is a proper balance between observing the rights of Canadian citizens and using the police to achieve political objectives needs to be categorically rejected. The idea that the rights of Canadian citizens are something that can be reduced or eliminated upon the demand of even the highest of government officials is one that no police officer should ever entertain.

This is not to say that there cannot arise circumstances in which a proper balance will need to be struck between the rights of Canadian citizens and the safety of local and visiting dignitaries. Even so, as Superintendent Thompsett was quick to observe, there is all the difference in the world between a government's political objectives and genuine security concerns. In short, unlike genuine security concerns, the political discomfort or embarrassment of local or visiting dignitaries is never a legitimate reason for restricting the rights of expression of Canadian citizens.

Related to these issues is the question of whether the RCMP conducted illegal surveillance on non-violent political protest groups. Events such as APEC summits inevitably raise important matters of national security, both for Canada and for other countries. Presumably it was for this reason that high-profile members of various protest groups were placed under police surveillance before the summit and that pictures of potential protesters were duplicated and circulated among security personnel.

In any healthy democracy, however, law-abiding citizens must be free to associate with each other for political ends without having the blunt instruments of state power follow their every move and thought. State surveillance undermines the openness that is essential for the democratic deliberative process to operate effectively. Too often it also leads to other serious abuses of power.

Canadians know this all too well. In the late 1970s, the McDonald Commission of Inquiry Concerning Certain Activities of the Royal Canadian Mounted Police found that the RCMP had infiltrated many non-violent public interest organizations, including political parties. It also found that the RCMP had compiled dossiers on tens of thousands of Canadian citizens, and that it had engaged in "dirty tricks" to discredit various political groups. As a result of its investigations, the commission concluded that it was necessary to remove responsibility for national security intelligence gathering from the RCMP.

This decision was based on evidence found by the commission that police officers lacked the training and judgment necessary for doing the delicate job of security intelligence gathering in a way that properly respected the basic democratic rights of Canadian citizens. For this reason the Canadian Security Intelligence Service (CSIS) was created in the early 1980s, with a mandate that explicitly excluded the covert surveillance of groups involved in "lawful advocacy, protest or dissent" unless it could be proved on independent grounds that they posed a significant security threat.

The events during the 1997 APEC summit thus raise questions not only about the appropriateness of the RCMP's behaviour but also about its mandate and jurisdiction – questions that were supposed to have been resolved by the McDonald Commission and the creation of CSIS. Specifically, we need to know what evidence the RCMP had, if any, to justify its surveillance of non-violent protest groups. We need to know what role police informants played in these groups. We need to know whether the police attempted to manage the activities of these groups or to discredit them. We need to know whether the RCMP shared any of the intelligence information that it gathered on Canadian citizens with security and intelligence agencies from other countries. Finally, we need to know the current status of the dossiers that were assembled on law-abiding Canadian citizens. Could information in those dossiers still be shared with other national and international agencies? Are all of these dossiers eventually going to be destroyed unless there is evidence of criminal wrongdoing?

In light of such concerns, it is crucial that Canadians discover whether there was a systematic effort to block the exercise of their basic freedoms, an effort that could have begun with the Prime Minister and his staff and that could have extended through the senior ranks of the RCMP. It is for the same reasons that the work of arm's-length investigative bodies such as the Public Complaints Commission is crucial for the functioning of a healthy democracy. If the Canadian public is to have confidence in both its politicians and its police officers, there must be effective methods of civilian oversight that are independent of both the police and the government of the day.

Reviewing these concerns makes it apparent that the issues raised by the APEC affair go well beyond the actions of a few police officers pepper-spraying protesters. These issues are important because it is ultimately the freedom that citizens have to meet and speak openly about controversial issues without fear of government reprisal that distinguishes democracy from other forms of government. China, the old Soviet Union, the former East Germany, and many other countries all serve as examples of the latter. As Mr. Justice Peter Cory of the Supreme Court of Canada has commented:

> It is difficult to imagine a guaranteed right more important to a democratic society than freedom of expression. Indeed a democracy cannot exist without that freedom to express new ideas and to put forward

opinions about the functioning of public institutions. The concept of free and uninhibited speech permeates all truly democratic societies and institutions. The vital importance of the concept cannot be over-emphasized.

In other words, as a country's civil liberties are weakened, its claim to being a democracy is correspondingly diminished.

Of course, any comparison between a healthy democracy such as Canada and totalitarian countries such as China and the former Soviet Union needs to be made very carefully. Canada is a long way from descending into a totalitarian police state. Even so, no country is immune from the many pressures and tendencies that give rise to totalitarianism, and it is by remaining indifferent to apparently small and incremental increases of state power that citizens eventually lose their most cherished freedoms. Even citizens in countries such as Canada cannot afford to become complacent about their most fundamental rights and liberties.

A point of comparison arises with the old Republic of South Africa. Regardless of whether we think of pre-1994 South Africa as a democracy with an extremely limited franchise or as a democracy in name only, by the 1980s that country's government had instituted more than 100 laws restricting the movement of ideas. These laws were not introduced overnight all at the same time. South Africans did not wake up one morning and decide that they wanted to live in a police state. Instead, each incremental increase in censorship was introduced gradually and in response to a perceived need.

In some respects South Africa's censorship laws were remarkably powerful: newspaper and magazine articles were censored, journalists and writers were detained, editors were prosecuted, and papers were closed. Yet even in those dark days many censorship laws were largely ineffective. Speeches by political leaders were smuggled in and out of prisons and around the country, and it became a badge of honour to possess them, no matter how dry or boring they might be. Legal challenges to censorship were mounted, editorials against apartheid were published, and many government policies were ridiculed, until even this became illegal. When one edition of a newspaper was banned, the paper changed its masthead, publishing the same material under a new name, free from the banning order. Rather than publish an illegal photograph of a violent police action, another paper printed a "connect-the-dots" version instead, together with explicit instructions to readers that they were not to connect the dots.

Blank spaces were also banned, as was obliterated text. Both had been used by the *Weekly Mail* to indicate the extent of state censorship. As Anton Harber, a founder and co-editor of that newspaper reports, "The authorities realised that nothing frightened the public more than white spaces in newspapers: vivid imaginations filled the spaces with reports far worse than those that had been removed." Hence, there was the absurdity of making it illegal to print nothing!

Other policies were equally comical yet frightening. The Key Point Act made it an offence to photograph or publicize so-called "key points" around the country. At the same time, the list of sites that had been designated by the government to be "key" remained classified. Thus the only way for a newspaper to discover whether it was in possession of an illegal photograph was to publish it, and then wait to see whether charges were laid.

During this time, the amount of material censored by government was phenomenal. The peace sign was banned, as was the book *Black Beauty*. The American film *Roots* was banned for the reason that "a substantial number of blacks would, judged on the probabilities, substantially experience great or greater hate against the white [race] as a result of seeing this film."

Reading this, we may feel relief that censorship of this kind does not and cannot occur in Canada. Yet this is not so. Even though censorship in Canada is not as common, and the degree of social injustice prompting protests is not nearly as high, as in many countries, the ease with which protest signs were removed during the APEC summit shows just how easy it is for governments and police officers to overstep their legitimate authority. If we as citizens allow governments to take away our free speech rights whenever there is a perceived need to do so, we will be left with little more than a privilege that can be revoked at will.

But perhaps this overstates the situation in Canada today. Perhaps, unlike the old South African government, Canadian governments can be trusted to censor only that speech that deserves to be censored. Unfortunately, as the APEC affair has shown, such trust is bound to be misplaced. Not only do government agencies have a poor record with regard to censorship but our abdication of this responsibility to the state is equivalent to throwing away the very building blocks of democracy. By allowing the state to tell us what speech is or is not permissible, we give up our authority over government. Unless citizens are allowed to debate even the most controversial of issues openly and without fear of government reprisal, it is impossible for them to exercise their sovereignty over government.

To take a related example, in any society that wants to eliminate hate, it is important to know who the hatemongers are. Before electing candidates to our local school boards or to the prime minister's office, we will want to know their views on economic and educational policies, on evolution and multiculturalism, on immigration, and on race. It is essential. Because censorship laws regularly push this type of information underground, such laws are typically accompanied by increased state surveillance. At the same time, when this information does *not* go underground, it is often given even greater prominence in the media and in the public consciousness than it deserves. There is nothing like a banning order to increase the sales of even the most mediocre of books!

In other words, censorship laws typically are inefficient in achieving their goals or else they tend to frustrate society's need to know who the hatemongers are, what role they play in our communities, and what type of influence they have on public policy. Free speech allows hatemongers to identify themselves for all to see and obviates the need for increased state surveillance.

There is more. Not only are censorship laws both inefficient and contrary to the principles underlying democracy but they also effectively divide a country's population into first- and second-class citizens. If university professors and opposition members of Parliament are allowed to debate Canada's role in APEC openly and publicly but students and others are not, we will have effectively set up the type of division between citizens that no healthy democracy can long support. Free speech is something we extend to the young as well as the old, the foolish as well as the wise. Once we begin to decide who may or may not be granted the privilege of free speech, we begin the slide towards a dictatorship of either the political left or the political right. Supporting a constitutionally protected right to free speech means that we have to tolerate words and ideas with which we may passionately disagree. This is simply the price we pay for living in a healthy democracy.

The issues raised by the APEC affair are thus of central importance for all Canadians. Like the 1970 October crisis, the events of the APEC affair show just how fragile some of our most fundamental rights and freedoms can be. For anyone interested in the preservation and promotion of democratic values, it is important to discover whether the free speech rights of Canadian citizens were compromised during the APEC summit. It is important to discover whether the RCMP used unnecessary and excessive force, and whether it engaged in inappropriate police practices, such as the unjustified surveillance of non-violent political protest groups. And it is important to learn whether Canada's chief law enforcement agency allowed itself to be influenced, at least in part, by political directives from the PMO – rather than solely by security concerns – while carrying out its mandate to protect summit delegates.

If we, as citizens, are prepared to allow the police or the government to tell us what we can and cannot say, or what we can and cannot read, or what government policies we can and cannot publicly support, we will have given up a lot more than a desire to discover what may or may not have happened to a group of student protesters one rainy November in Vancouver.

We will have given up a fundamental cornerstone of democracy itself.

5

"Relax a Bit in the Nation": Constitutional Law 101 and the APEC Affair

MARGOT E. YOUNG

In November 1997, Prime Minister Jean Chrétien was questioned about the report that the RCMP had pepper-sprayed peaceful protesters outside the APEC Summit meetings at the University of British Columbia. Dismissing the question, the Prime Minister responded with a joke: "Pepper, I put it on my plate." Later when asked about his apparent indifference to the pepper-spraying, Mr. Chrétien provided the following explanation: "So I made a joke. You know me. I tried to get you to laugh. Relax a bit in the nation, I say."

The Prime Minister's advice is to relax, to be less uptight about the questions raised by the RCMP's treatment of protesters at the 1997 Asia-Pacific Economic Cooperation summit in Vancouver. We take too seriously this sort of event, he implies, including our Prime Minister's joking response to it. I wish to suggest that this is bad advice, and (one is forced to observe) somewhat self-serving. Already Canadians are inadequately alert to abuses of power, slow to voice suitable dismay at authoritarian excess within the Canadian state. Our political culture is too often marked by complacency and a failure to examine and critically sustain the larger political and constitutional commitments that should underlie the sort of constitutional democracy we aspire to have.

The purpose of this chapter is to set out some specific constitutional elements of immediate relevance to the APEC affair (leaving aside the more familiar issues of freedom of expression and association). By doing so I hope to provide both a sense of the constitutional context in which the complaints against the RCMP and allegations of improper political influence have occurred, as well as some critical commentary on the constitutional principles themselves and their relevance to the politics of democratic constitutionalism.

The next section is a basic constitutional primer, detailing the structure and elements of Canada's framework of constitutional law that are important to this dispute. The rest of the chapter provides a more complex analysis of two key constitutional principles, the rule of law and democracy, and the relationship between them. We will see that while constitutional recognition of certain key principles may be essential to a constitutional democracy, formal adherence to these principles is not, in and of itself, sufficient to guarantee a constitutional democracy. A more complicated story needs to be told, setting up a tension that, while certainly challenging and not relaxing, is healthy for democracy.

Canada's Constitution

The alleged involvement of the Prime Minister's Office (PMO) in RCMP operations during the APEC protests raises important questions about the use of state force and the relationship between Canada's national police force and the federal government. Such questions lie properly, although not solely, within the domain of constitutional law. A constitution, after all, is the foundation in liberal democracies like Canada for the formal regulation of the relationship between the state and the individual and for the setting of the boundaries of legitimate state action, including the deployment of state-sanctioned police force. The function of the constitution, the Supreme Court of Canada has said, "is to provide a continuing framework for the legitimate exercise of governmental power" (*Hunter* v. *Southam Inc.* [1984]). The constitution is also the supreme law of the land; any law or government action contrary to its legal rules has no legal validity. It matters very much, therefore, that when the state deploys coercive force, typically through its police, such deployment is constitutional.

So, constitutional law sets out the rules and principles that govern the lawful use of state powers. To do this, it tells us what kinds of exercises of power by the various organs of the state are lawful. Constitutional law tells us what government organ can exercise legislative power (making new laws), what can exercise executive power (administering and implementing the laws), and what can exercise judicial power (adjudicating disputes over the laws). Constitutional law also sets limits on the exercise of state power. Canadian constitutional law does this in three important ways.

Because Canada is a federal state, its constitution establishes a division of powers between the federal and provincial levels of government. For example, the federal government has constitutional jurisdiction over matters having to do with criminal law, which is why our Criminal Code is a federal statute applicable equally throughout all of Canada. The provincial governments, on the other hand, have jurisdiction over health. Thus, medical plans and health regulation are the product of provincial law and vary from province to province.

Second, the Canadian constitution sets limits that apply to all levels of government through the articulation of civil liberties or rights protected within the constitution. These limits, as articulated in Canada's constitution, define the relationship between the individual and the state. Individuals thus have, for example, rights of association, expression, and equality, all of which set constraints on the state as it acts in relation to these individual interests. Arguably, as well, Canada's constitution provides for some limited community-based rights, most particularly in relation to language rights, reflecting Canada's French and English heritages.

Third, Canada's constitution contains provisions that relate directly to the status of Aboriginal peoples in the Canadian federation. These provisions constitute both part of the division of powers between federal and provincial governments as well as constraints upon the powers of both levels of government in relation to Aboriginal rights.

In many countries, a single constitutional document – "the Constitution" – contains most, if not all, of the framework for the state's constitutional law. This is not the case in Canada. Canada has no one document that contains all of its constitutional laws. Instead, a large number of documents are part of Canada's constitution. Most important among these are the Constitution Act, 1982, and the Constitution Act, 1867. The latter, renamed in 1982, used to be called the British North America Act (or the BNA Act). The BNA Act was passed by the British Parliament in 1867 to create the new Dominion of Canada by uniting three of the colonies of British North America. It is in this document that the division of powers between the federal government and the provincial governments is specified and some aspects of the various organs of government established. The Constitution Act, 1982, is actually part of another constitutional document, the Canada Act 1982. The Canada Act 1982 was passed in 1982 to amend Canada's constitution, primarily by enacting the Constitution Act, 1982. Part I of the Constitution

Act, 1982, is the Canadian Charter of Rights and Freedoms. Part II deals with Aboriginal rights. The Charter of Rights and Freedoms, of course, is the section of the constitution that establishes such individual rights as freedom of expression, freedom of association, and equality.

Other documents that are properly considered part of Canada's constitution are listed in an appendix attached to the Constitution Act, 1982. These documents include such things as a number of statutes passed by the British Parliament dealing with its former Canadian colony, statutes passed by the federal Canadian government, and orders in council. Twenty-four constitutional documents are listed in this appendix as currently in force.

Constitutions are intended to be enduring, not easily superseded. The written texts that comprise parts of our constitution are subject to special amending rules. A defining characteristic of written constitutional rules, then, is that they are not easily changed but rather can be altered only in accordance with specific rules. This is what is meant by *entrenching* a constitution – placing it beyond the reach of simple majority rule. By contrast, non-constitutional statutes can be amended through a simple legislative majority in their originating legislative assembly, and thus lack the pre-eminence and more enduring status of constitutional provisions. Until 1982, Canadian constitutional documents could be amended only by the British Parliament. Much of the constitutional negotiations preceding 1982 involved attempts to establish a domestic amending formula. Canada now has written rules of constitutional amendment that, depending upon the changes being made, require such things as the agreement of the federal government and seven of the ten provinces representing over 50 percent of the Canadian population. The amending procedures are contained in the Constitution Act, 1982. Clearly, amendment of a constitutional document is significantly more difficult than ordinary legislative alteration. This attests to the profound role such documents play.

While Canada's constitution is largely a written one, albeit found in many documents, it also contains important elements that lie outside documents formally considered part of the constitution. These are constitutional rules or standards of political behaviour that are not spelled out in the documents considered part of Canada's constitution. Such constitutional elements are identifiable through a knowledge of judicial pronouncements on what our constitution provides or through an understanding of the traditions, history, and conventions of Canadian and English parliamentary governments. Much of the discussion in this chapter will focus on a few important examples of these constitutional elements.

For now, it is important to realize that any attempt to map out the full range of Canada's constitutional rules would have to look not only at such things as statutes passed by the British and Canadian Parliaments but also at inherent powers possessed by the federal Parliament and by provincial legislative assemblies; underlying foundational principles; statements resulting from judicial consideration of constitutional cases; historical powers that attached to the British Crown and are now in a very limited fashion distributed between the federal and provincial governments; and non-legally enforceable constitutional rules called conventions. This is what is meant by the oft-repeated statement that Canada has a constitution that is both written and unwritten.

Not all parts of Canada's constitution are legally enforceable. For example, constitutional conventions – rules of constitutional behaviour not elaborated in specific provisions of any constitutional document – while equally, if not more, important than many written constitutional laws, cannot be enforced by the courts. They do, nonetheless, form an integral part of our constitutional system, although their coercive power lies in their normative, political force, not their legal enforceability. Contravention of a constitutional convention is a serious matter, although it occasions a political crisis rather than legal sanction; it is an unconstitutional act even though it has political consequences rather than direct legal ones. The role played by the courts in relation to conventions, while not involving enforcement, is still important, as it is the courts that have on occasion recognized and articulated the nature of individual constitutional conventions.

The rest of this chapter focuses on two unwritten elements of Canada's constitution, principles that, in the words of the Supreme Court of Canada, "inform and sustain" the constitutional text. These are the principles of the rule of law and of democracy, both of which are implicit and essential parts of the conceptual architecture of the constitution: its "lifeblood," according to the Supreme Court. These principles can give rise to substantive constitutional obligations – of general or specific nature – that constrain government action and shape judicial adjudication of constitutional disputes. The extent to which the Supreme Court's invocation or understanding of these principles is desirable or even adequate is a question to which I return briefly at the end of this chapter.

The Rule of Law

The Supreme Court of Canada has stated that "the principle of the rule of law is clearly a principle of our Constitution." The Court has also noted that the rule of law "lies at the core of our political and constitutional tradition." It holds this fundamental place because of three aspects of Canada's constitution, all of which provide important illustrations of how elements of Canada's larger constitutional structure are linked to Canada's written constitutional texts.

The most obvious source of the constitutional principle of the rule of law lies in the preamble to the Charter of Rights and Freedoms, which states: "Whereas Canada is founded upon principles that recognize the supremacy of God and the rule of law." *

A preamble is not equivalent to the actual provisions of the statute but rather constitutes an interpretative guide and introduction to the statute (whether constitutional or not) that it prefaces. This constitutional preamble tells us that the more explicit constitutional structures of Canada rest upon the principle of the rule of law, and that, therefore, the principle of the rule of law must be given expression in our rules of constitutional law.

The second basis for importing the principle of the rule of law into Canada's constitutional structure lies in the much earlier statute, the Constitution Act, 1867. The preamble to this act states that the new nation was to have "a Constitution similar in principle to that of the United Kingdom." It is generally accepted that this phrase imports into Canadian constitutional structure the foundational principles and postulates of British constitutionalism. Since the rule of law has long been understood to be the very basis of constitutionalism in the United Kingdom (an element arguably dating to the time of the Norman Conquest), the principle again enters the Canadian constitution by a similar preambular, albeit more indirect, route. Other important aspects of Canadian government also enter our constitution this way. For example, the roles of the prime minister and cabinet, and many of the political processes of Parliament, owe their Canadian constitutional status in part to this reference to British constitutionalism.

The third aspect of Canada's constitution that gives the rule of law a fundamental place is even more indirect and abstract than the second, and is difficult to grasp without an understanding of the principle itself. Suffice it to say that the Supreme Court of Canada has held the principle to be implicit in the nature of a constitution:

> The founders of this nation must have intended, as one of the basic principles of nation building, that Canada be a society of legal order and normative structure: one governed by rule of law. While this is not

set out in a specific provision, the principle of the rule of law is clearly a principle of our Constitution. (*Reference Re Manitoba Language Rights* [1985])

Incidentally, this statement illustrates well the central role the judiciary itself plays as a source of constitutional law. It reinforces the point that knowledge of what the courts, particularly the Supreme Court of Canada, have said about the constitution, how they have interpreted its written provisions and understood its spirit and history, is essential to gaining a full picture of Canada's constitutional structure. Moreover, because the Supreme Court of Canada is the highest court in Canada, its statements are especially important in determining Canada's constitutional structure.

What Is Meant by the "Rule of Law"?

A range of meanings have been associated with the term *rule of law,* with considerable academic and legal debate over the values and institutional circumstances that it captures. The principle as it has shaped Anglo-Canadian law was first systematically elaborated in the writings of nineteenth-century jurist A.V. Dicey. Canadian courts, however, have focused primarily on a few aspects. Recently, the Supreme Court of Canada has confirmed the following:

> The "rule of law" is a highly textured expression ... conveying, for example, a sense of orderliness, of subjection to known legal rules and of executive accountability to legal authority. (*Reference Re Secession of Quebec* [1998])

The Supreme Court continues:

> At its most basic level, the rule of law vouchsafes to the citizens and residents of the country a stable, predictable and ordered society in which to conduct their affairs.

For our purposes here, the idea can be boiled down to two simple notions. First, the rule of law requires that individuals be protected from arbitrary power: "the law is supreme over officials of the government as well as private individuals, and thereby preclusive of the influence of arbitrary power" (*Reference Re Manitoba Language Rights* [1985]). Governmental actions that are not authorized by law are contrary to the rule of law. State officials must act in accordance with recognized standards, identified in advance, not simply in line with political whim or personal wish.

The principle of the rule of law thus speaks strongly against governmental action dictated by the arbitrary likes, dislikes, and purposes of public officers. It means, essentially, the absolute supremacy of law, notably constitutional law. All acts of public power must ultimately be justifiable by and have their source in law. More specifically of relevance to constitutional law, all acts of the government, including the executive branch (the Prime Minister's Office, for example), must adhere to the constitution. The rule of law means government according to the terms of the constitution, not according to the political or personal wishes of those who hold power.

Second, the rule of law means that all persons – ordinary citizens or members of the government – are equally subject to the law: in other words, one law for all.

Democracy

The Supreme Court of Canada has found the principle of democracy to be a fundamental value in Canada's constitutional law: a baseline for the framing of Canada's constitution and subsequent actions of Canada's elected representatives. Indeed, so obvious has it found the constitution's assumption of constitutional democracy that the Court has wondered whether explicit inclusion of this principle in a constitutional text would have seemed to the framers of the constitution to be redundant, even, the Court says, "silly." Instead, "the representative and democratic nature of our political institutions was simply assumed" (*Reference Re Secession of Quebec* [1998]).

Thus, the principle of democracy is considered by the Supreme Court as part of Canada's constitutional structure by virtue of what the Court understands Canada's political history and culture to be. Note, however, that this principle is no less a part of our constitution than other principles explicitly articulated in the texts that comprise its written portions.

This short chapter cannot possibly do justice to the debate over the meaning and requirements of democracy and the adequacy of Canadian constitutional understandings of the principle, but it can provide some sense of how Canadian constitutional law has recently understood the concept.

The Supreme Court has stated that the principle of democracy has both a substantive and an institutional (or procedural) aspect. Its substantive side speaks to the values that characterize a free and democratic society: respect for the inherent dignity of the human person; commitment to social justice and equality; religious accommodation; respect for cultural and group identity; and faith in the social and political institutions that enhance individual and group participation in society.

The Court's picture of the institutional aspects of democracy is not particularly ambitious. Democracy, the Court states, supports certain structures or procedures associated with a democratic system, such as the election of provincial, federal, and territorial representatives by popular franchise. Thus, the Canadian Charter of Rights and Freedoms guarantees the right to vote in regular elections. Democracy means that government rules with the consent of the governed. In addition, the Court has held that to function well democracy requires a "continuous process of discussion": "A democratic system of government is committed to considering those dissenting voices, and seeking to acknowledge and address those voices in the laws by which all in the community must live" (*Reference Re Secession of Quebec* [1998]).

Rule of Law and Democracy

While these two principles stand separately within Canada's constitution, they are also considered to have significant interconnection. The Supreme Court has held that the rule of law is essential to a democratic political system, as it creates an orderly and stable framework for political decisions and for the expression of the electorate's will. Democratic institutions must rest securely on a legal foundation that is respected and observed. Equally, democracy is necessarily conjoined to the rule of law. A political and legal system must, to claim legitimacy, reflect the aspirations of the people, which is what the democratic character of such a system seeks to ensure. While the Supreme Court is quick to caution that legal systems need reference to other moral values besides democracy, it has emphasized the co-dependency between the rule of law and the principle of democracy.

The APEC Affair and the Constitutional Principles of the Rule of Law and Democracy

The Rule of Law and Police Suppression of Charter Rights
Since this topic is dealt with at length in other chapters, it is sufficient here to simply point out the problematic character of any police action that violates the constitution in either intent or effect. Such an action would be a clear contravention of the rule of law. It would be a particularly serious violation of constitutional principle if the police were to engage in unconstitutional activity at the explicit request of the executive branch of the government (the Prime Minister, another minister, or bureaucrats in a government ministry). The rule of law, after all, includes as a fundamental postulate the principle that no one – not government officials or police officers acting in their official capacity – is above the law. The same law

applies equally to all. For government agents (police, civil servants, political officials) to disregard the law is to fundamentally undermine our legal system. Making the executive branch and the police subject to the rule of law is a central means by which liberal democracies like Canada seek to constrain the state's potential for oppressing its own citizens.

Democracy and the Politics of Policing

If true, the allegations of PMO involvement in directing how the RCMP dealt with protesters at the UBC campus during the APEC summit raise a number of constitutional issues that touch directly on the principle of democracy. Simply put, the primary concern is for the political independence of the police.

In 1981, the federal Commission of Inquiry Concerning Certain Activities of the Royal Canadian Mounted Police considered the proper relationship between the police and the government, noting that there is a subtle balance to be struck. On the one hand, it is essential that police be accountable for their conduct. This accountability is to Parliament through the minister in the federal government whose responsibilities include the RCMP, currently the Solicitor General. The Solicitor General, in turn, is responsible to Parliament (a function of the principle of responsible government, another unwritten constitutional principle), with the result that the police are ultimately accountable to the democratically elected civilian authority: the legislature. The essential principle at stake is that the police are not are a law unto themselves, but rather are accountable to the legislative branch of government for their conduct. In the final analysis, then, it must be the government (through both its executive and legislative branches) that is in control of and responsible for the police.

The connection between the political accountability of the police and the principle of democracy is obvious. As the coercive arm of the state, the police force represents the concentrated coercive power of the state, an aspect of state authority that the process of democracy constrains and purports to render legitimate. A completely independent police force lacks the important check on police abuse of power that accountability to a democratic political process is structured to provide. Indeed, it was precisely a concern about such police independence from accountability that catalyzed the 1981 commission of inquiry.

The democratic principle of police accountability to the legislature should never, however, be confused with the authoritarian and anti-democratic practice of police responsiveness to ministerial command. This distinction is a tricky but important one. The latter involves political involvement in police operations that is constitutionally illegitimate. Here the allegations surrounding the APEC affair gain cogency. Police cannot simply become a tool of the government. There must be a sphere of police independence from political influence if there is to be confidence that the government remains subject to law and to the enforcement of law. Politicization of the police bodes ill for the evenhanded and democratic deployment of state power.

The extent of necessary police independence and the relevance of the particular policing context in which this question is raised are often not clearly understood or agreed upon. Students of this question dispute what counts as improper political interference (see the chapter by Philip Stenning in this volume). In its report, the 1981 commission of inquiry stated that only the special powers of the RCMP should be exempt from the direction of the minister. This means that the minister could not direct the RCMP in its exercise of the powers of investigation, arrest, and prosecution. The minister should, the commission reported, have the right to be informed of any operational matters, including those in individual cases, if important questions of public policy are raised. In such cases, although the minister may give guidance to the police, the minister should not have the power to direct them.

Some scholars have argued that improper partisan direction of the police involves personal advancement or sympathy, or anything that relates to the political fortunes of a political party or the government in power. Thus, broader political considerations that invoke a wider public interest associated with the public at large rather than any specific political group or faction might be legitimate grounds for governmental direction. Others disagree with this distinction between partisan politics and broader non-partisan political considerations, arguing that such a distinction is unworkable or unsustainable. What is clear, however, is that the issue of political direction of the police is critically important for a democracy, and is thus intimately connected to our constitution's protection of Canada's democratic character. Regardless of possible justifications for the PMO's directions to the RCMP in the APEC affair (if it did give such directions), the constitutional nature of the ensuing examination of the issue is clear.

If the PMO did in fact improperly issue directives for treatment of the APEC protesters, say, to avoid embarrassing visiting leaders, significant concerns arise regarding the politicization of the RCMP. It is, after all, fundamental to the principle of democracy that the government not use the police to coerce citizens in order to advance the government's own political objectives. A police force under the direction or control of the government cannot credibly enforce the law against the government, and it can be used against those who oppose the government. Indeed, the most extreme abuse of power in a democracy is to use state power to clamp down on opposition to the government. Dictators and their police states behave in this way; democracies do not.

It is worth noting, as well, that because of the intimate relationship between the rule of law and the principle of democracy, threats to the rule of law, such as intentional disregard for constitutional provisions and principles by police and politicians, also weaken our democratic commitments. The challenge for a constitutional democracy like Canada is to ensure that, while the police must remain politically accountable, police activities are carried out in a non-partisan manner. To do otherwise would risk compromising the constitutional principles of democracy and the rule of law.

None of this discussion, of course, answers the question of whether the actions of the RCMP and the government during the APEC protest violated the constitution. It does, however, make the point that the questions surrounding the state's response to the protest clearly have constitutional implications. Any discussion of the legality of the response must acknowledge this.

A Larger Political Perspective

Two additional observations remain. The first is that Canadians already tolerate significant deviation from the principles of the rule of law and democracy. Our collective commitment to these principles is often quite shaky. Even if one accepts uncritically these constitutional notions as articulated by the Supreme Court, one can question how well they describe our political system. Moreover (and this is the second and more controversial point), it is not clear that these principles, as they are generally understood within our constitutional system, will do for us all that we appear to believe they will.

Canadians and their governments are not always quick to investigate potential police abuse of power. A range of examples illustrate this point. In 1995 the Ontario Provincial Police shot at and killed a member of a group of Native protesters occupying Ipperwash Provincial Park. To date, no provincial inquiry into this shooting death has been called, despite condemnation of this refusal by the United Nations Human Rights Committee. Similar potential police misconduct may have characterized the Gustafsen Lake dispute in British Columbia in 1995. Here, too, the events have remained largely uninvestigated, and media coverage dipped sharply as time passed. More recently, in the spring of 1999 Aboriginal protesters at the Manitoba legislature were pepper-sprayed and treated roughly by legislative police and security guards. And, a year after the APEC protest, street kids in Victoria were pepper-sprayed by by-law enforcement officers who were attempting to apprehend a pet dog. Neither of these last two events has evoked a national response similar to the one that greeted the APEC pepper-spraying and arrests. Concern about each of these other events remains largely limited to the communities from which the individuals involved came. This despite the fact that all these events raise questions about appropriate use of coercive force by the state and police adherence to law. Several of the events also touch on issues of improper political influence.

Why such selective inquiry into potential violations of important constitutional principles? To begin with, it is no coincidence that most of the pepper-sprayed and arrested individuals in the APEC affair were university students, collectively a more privileged group than the Natives and street kids involved in the other incidents. One of the most prominent among these individuals was a third-year law student, an aspirant to a mainstream and affluent profession, able to communicate his personal outrage in the legal and constitutional terms of the powerful. Contrast this with the pepper-sprayed street kids. In a community where business and political leaders consider the presence of these kids a municipal blight, there was little public response and few social or legal resources that these individuals could muster to protest their treatment. Thus, the social, political, cultural, or even economic status of the different actors in these confrontations clearly mattered. When those who hold positions of power or influence in society – such as journalists, politicians, professors, and lawyers – can identify or empathize with the affected individuals, such individuals get their attention and concern, and the engagement of the general public usually follows. It was also extremely fortunate, from the perspective of the APEC protesters' ability to engage public and media concern, that the police pepper-sprayed a CBC cameraman while his camera was running. The authority of the news footage was an effective foil to the presumptive authority that police officers have in the recounting of contested events, and led to wide public acceptance of the protesters' version.

The other examples detailed above show that the public response to the RCMP treatment of the APEC demonstrators cannot be the product solely of straightforward outrage at police tactics. Otherwise, the Canadian public and media would be equally outraged and motivated to political and legal protest by other instances of rough police treatment. There is no doubt that we are somewhat selective in the urgency of our response to potential abuses of police power, despite what a straight reading of our constitution might say about our collective principles. Public concern appears to track the socioeconomic status of the victims. The more like us they are, they more outraged we are at their mistreatment. The more marginalized the victims are, the less bothered we are about questionable police tactics.

Moreover, in one aspect at least, the APEC scenario jars our sense of the usual in police activity, thus seizing the public's attention. This claim can be explained as follows. Police powers are inevitably deployed in a fashion determined by prevailing ideology, as the police participate in both the production and perpetuation of dominant social and moral norms. One can understand this, at least in part, as a function of the discretionary nature of police activity. The choices made by individual officers – about how and when to pursue their law enforcement obligations – and the policies promulgated by police management are a product of particular ways of understanding and of viewing the world. Very seldom are police out of step with prevailing norms or the status quo. We may characterize the police community generally as, say, conservative, but their orientation is still located on the continuum of established and mainstream political values. Note that this argument does not point to the kind of partisan political influence that explicit directions from the Prime Minister's Office represent. That kind of political influence is not inevitable; its remedy lies in insistence on certain legal and institutional structures. Rather, the argument made in this section discusses the sociological fact that all of us usually act in ways that make sense to our larger ideological understanding of the world. And the police – both the individuals who comprise the Force and the institutional structures and practices in which individual police officers are situated – tend to have understandings of the world that are consonant with (not in opposition to) understandings of the world that reflect conventional or traditional perspectives.

The result is that policing practice reflects and reinforces the prevailing dominant understandings of Canadian society, to the discomfort – both mild and extreme – of those whose social or cultural location lies outside the mainstream. Those whose lifestyle or social position fits within the mainstream have a different pattern of potential entanglement with the police from those who are more marginalized within society or the economy. Police treatment of the less privileged, affluent, or mainstream is rougher, more punitive, and more authoritarian. This is simply to say that the practical experience of different segments of the population with the police is very uneven: those at the bottom of the social hierarchy experience the heaviest police responses. This is generally true regardless of whether the action to which the police are responding is legal political protest or some illegal act. Thus, part of our shock at the APEC events may be explained by the fact that we are more used to seeing that type of police force brought to bear against marginalized targets (like the street kids in Victoria), not against privileged Canadians.

The failure of the Canadian public and the political system to respond appropriately to all incidents of potential abuse of state power – particularly those where already unempowered groups or individuals are the targets – stems from a collective lack of critical engagement with the principles of the rule of law and democracy. For such an engagement to occur, we would have to question a number of things that we currently take for granted. How impressive is our formal commitment to democracy, given, say, the rather attenuated participation in political or public life that our system offers most Canadians? Indeed, one wonders whether the missives from the PMO to the RCMP about the APEC summit were unusual. Perhaps such communications are commonplace, unusual in these circumstances only because they were publicly revealed. Certainly the Prime Minister's staff has tried to present the APEC affair as "business as usual" – a defence of their actions that demonstrates a surprising blitheness about the possible counterdemocratic implications of such actions.

If the involvement of the PMO in the RCMP APEC operations was aberrant, is it because in most situations the police reinforce the status quo (including the current maldistribution of social, cultural, and political resources) so unerringly anyway that directions from the PMO are unnecessary? The implications for democracy in this line of inquiry are challenging and disturbing but also important. A number of remedial foci emerge. For instance, a police force more representative of Canadian society, particularly of historically unempowered groups such as Aboriginals, women, and racialized minorities, that was at an organizational and individual level more engaged with questions of equity and respect for all persons might be part of the answer. And a legal system shaped by the meaningful involvement of a wider and more diverse group of Canadians might generate laws less skewed in favour of the interests of the already powerful. Recall the words of the Supreme Court of Canada – no bastion of radical thought – that democracy requires more than procedural guarantees. It also involves substantive commitments to things like social justice, equality, and the enhancement of individual and group participation in society.

Without better political participation from and empowerment of those groups currently marginalized within Canadian society, the laws that form the basis of the rule of law hold little promise of delivering full justice and equality – the substantive principles of democracy. Without greater democratic participation, the principle of the rule of law is simply, in the words of one commentator, "a bit of ruling class chatter." Formal adherence only to the rule of law offers merely the pretence of a just legal and political system without delivering the substance.

It may be that respect for the rule of law is a necessary condition for a democracy, but it is far from a sufficient condition. Unaccompanied by a critical watchfulness as to substantive conditions of equity and justice, touting the principle of the rule of law too easily leads to smugness: a relaxation of political watchfulness for some and a convenient subterfuge for others.

Conclusion

The discussion of the previous section does not imply that situations such as the APEC affair should not be investigated. They should. The questions they raise relating to abuse of state power need to be taken seriously. But the lesson to be learned is opposite to the one that Prime Minister Chrétien has urged upon us. Canadians are far too relaxed about police exercise of coercive force and political control of the police. Clearly, more active engagement with the questions raised by incidents of this sort is needed, including a more sophisticated understanding of the relationship between the police and politics, a more critical and watchful stance towards the principle of the rule of law, and an insistence on a principle of democracy that is realized in both form and substance. Contrary to Prime Minister Chrétien's advice, a little more tension around these issues would be much better for the nation.

4

The APEC Protest, the Rule of Law, and Civilian Oversight of Canada's National Police Force

DONALD J. SOROCHAN, QC

Whereas the Provinces of Canada, Nova Scotia, and New Brunswick have expressed their Desire to be federally united into One Dominion under the Crown of the United Kingdom of Great Britain and Ireland, with a Constitution similar in Principle to that of the United Kingdom.
– Preamble to the Constitution Act, 1867

Whereas Canada is founded upon principles that recognize the supremacy of God and the rule of law.
– Preamble to the Canadian Charter of Rights and Freedoms

Only in a police state is the job of a policeman easy.
– The character Ramon Miguel "Mike" Vargas, played by Charlton Heston in the 1958 movie *A Touch of Evil,* written by Orson Welles

At the November 1997 Asia-Pacific Economic Cooperation (APEC) summit in Vancouver, Canada hosted seventeen leaders of Pacific Rim nations. The leaders included then President Suharto of Indonesia, Premier Li Peng of China, and President Bill Clinton of the United States. Before the summit, it was known that there were active protest groups internationally and in Vancouver that were opposed to the policies of one or more of the leaders or to the concept of APEC itself. An international counterconference of 300 delegates from non-governmental organizations and social movements from across the Asia-Pacific region, most of whom were critical of APEC, was to be held in Vancouver during the leaders' summit.

The views expressed in this chapter are strictly those of the author. These views are not to be regarded as expressions of the policy of any of the writer's present or former clients, including the British Columbia Police Commission, the Royal Canadian Mounted Police Public Complaints Commission, or the governments of Canada or British Columbia.

Before the summit, the government of Canada was concerned that a refusal by any of the leaders to attend would be an embarrassment to Canada. The government went to considerable lengths to encourage each leader to come.

The RCMP and the Vancouver Police Department were responsible for providing security for the conference. Because the APEC delegates were internationally protected persons, the police had special security responsibilities pursuant to treaty obligations. The implementation of the security measures and police treatment of protesters have focused public attention on significant issues relating to the rule of law, the role of the police in a democratic society, and the importance of oversight mechanisms for the police.

The Rule of Law

The preamble to the Canadian Charter of Rights and Freedoms acknowledges that Canada is founded upon principles that recognize the rule of law. Current discussions of the rights and freedoms of Canadians tend to focus on the Charter, which was enacted relatively recently, in 1982. The fundamental constitutional footing of the rule of law, however, predates the Charter, its predecessor, the Canadian Bill of Rights (1972), and even the founding of our country.

The importance of the rule of law, along with other original freedoms that arise from positive law, such as freedom of speech and religion and the inviolability of the person, are reflected in the preamble to Canada's founding constitution, the British North America Act, 1867 (now the Constitution Act, 1867), as core values of the "constitution similar in principle to that of the United Kingdom." The British constitutional concept of the rule of law requires that government should be subject to the law, rather than the law subject to government. This is the fundamental common law principle enunciated in *Entick* v. *Carrington* (1756).

The principles of constitutionalism and the rule of law, which lie at the root of Canada's system of government, are observed by the Supreme Court of Canada in *Roncarelli* v. *Duplessis* (1959), to be "a fundamental postulate of our constitutional structure." In that case, the Premier of Quebec was held to have no immunity against a claim for damages when the Premier caused injury to a private citizen by wrongfully interfering with the exercise of the statutory powers of a provincial commission. The Supreme Court also noted in *Reference Re Resolution to Amend the Constitution* (1981) that "the 'rule of law' is a highly textured expression, importing many things which are beyond the need of these reasons to explore but conveying, for example, a sense of orderliness, of subjection to known legal rules and of executive accountability to legal authority." At its most basic level, the rule of law vouchsafes to the citizens and residents of the country a stable, predictable, and ordered society in which to conduct their affairs. It provides a shield for individuals from arbitrary state action.

The rule of law means that everyone is subject to the ordinary law of the land. This is so regardless of public prominence or governmental status. It requires the law to be applied equally to all, without fear or favour and in an evenhanded manner between government and citizen. It ensures that all are equal before the law. The rule of law is not the law of the ruler. There is no exemption from the ordinary law of the state for agents of government, and no one, no matter how important or powerful, is above the law.

The rulers of the state – the government itself; the Prime Minister and other ministers, powerful bureaucrats; the police and armed forces – have no powers except those provided by law. The people, because the will of the society is set forth in law, should be ruled by the law and obey it.

At times laws may be unjust or there may be an inadequate enforcement of just laws. Citizens have the right and duty to work for the repeal of unjust laws and the proper enforcement of just laws through due process of law. The right of freedom of expression recognizes that a citizen may in good conscience participate in public demonstrations designed to expose injustice.

Where the demonstration results in an act of civil disobedience, where the person committing the act claims that no one ought to obey the law being challenged and offers reasons for everyone to object to it, those breaking the law must be prepared to pay the consequences, under law, for such disobedience. No society can tolerate its citizens breaking the law because imperfections in the law cannot justify an attack upon the core structure of our society – the rule of law. Ultimately the rights of individuals and proper standards of justice in a society ruled by law must be established by the government through legislative processes.

The Rule of Law in an International Context
Internationally, the rule of law has come to be known as a set of principles defined by the Conference on Security and Cooperation in Europe (CSCE) attended by all the European countries, Canada, and the United States in Paris (1989), Copenhagen (1990), and Moscow (1991). The participating states affirmed their determination to support and advance those principles of justice that form the basis of the rule of law. In this context, the rule of law is not merely a formal legality that assures regularity and consistency

in the achievement and enforcement of democratic order.

The broader principles of justice recognized by the conferences include the following:

- There will be free and democratic elections.
- There will be a representative form of government in which the executive is accountable to the elected legislature or the electorate.
- The government and public authorities have a duty to comply with the constitution and to act in a manner consistent with law.
- There will be a clear separation between the state and political parties.
- Military forces and the police will be under the control of, and accountable to, civil authorities.
- Human rights and fundamental freedoms will be guaranteed by law.
- There will be free access to the legislation adopted at the end of a public procedure.
- All persons are equal before the law and are entitled without any discrimination to the equal protection of the law.
- Everyone will have an effective means of redress against administrative decisions.
- Judges will be independent, and the public judiciary service will operate impartially.
- The independence of the legal profession will be protected.
- There will be a clear definition of powers in relation to prosecution in criminal procedure.
- Any person arrested or detained on a criminal charge will have the right to be brought promptly before the judge or other officer authorized by law to decide the lawfulness of the arrest or detention.
- Everyone will be entitled to a fair and public trial.
- Everyone will have the right to defend himself or herself in court in person or through prompt legal assistance, which will be given free if the person does not have sufficient means to pay for it.
- No one will be charged with, tried for, or convicted of any criminal offence unless the offence is provided for by a law that defines the elements of the offence with clarity and precision.
- Everyone will be presumed innocent until proven guilty according to law.
- Domestic legislation will comply with international laws relating to human rights, including guarantees for the freedom of information and communication, travel, thought, conscience and religion, right of peaceful assembly and demonstrations, associations, private property, etc.

The application of the rule of law in an international context has also been strengthened by the creation of an international criminal court to deal with crimes committed during the conflicts in the former Yugoslavia and Rwanda. The concept of this type of court to remove the cloak of impunity from perpetrators of serious internationally recognized crimes is an old one. Efforts to establish such a court date back to 1945. After years of work by the United Nations International Law Commission, a subsidiary organ of the UN General Assembly established in 1947 to make recommendations for the progressive development and codification of international law, a United Nations Conference on the Establishment of an International Criminal Court was held in Rome in June 1998. The conference resulted in the drafting of a completed convention on the establishment of a permanent international criminal court, a significant step forward in enforcing the rule of law internationally.

Enforcing the Rule of Law

The rule of law cannot be said to exist without compliance with the laws and an expectation within society of such compliance. A rule that has the formal appearance of law is not law unless there are enforcement mechanisms to ensure that the rule works as a standard for the community.

Enforcement mechanisms are essential to the operation of the rule of law to ensure that no authority will act above and beyond the law or exercise powers beyond lawful authority. Primarily the rule of law is enforced by an independent judiciary served by an equally independent and vigorous legal profession. Lawyers, as guardians of the law, play a vital role in the enforcement of the rule of law.

The police also play a vital role. A dictator may rely upon the police and the military to impose rule by laws enacted to preserve a reign of tyranny. Hitler, for example, was a skilful exponent of the theory of rule under law since almost all of his actions were justified under his "Law for the Relief of the People and the Reich." Some of the countries whose leaders attended the 1997 APEC conference value "order" over liberty and have detailed legal structures to ensure order, including laws against "hooliganism" or embarrassing those who rule the state.

Developing democracies have demonstrated that the rule of law and the resulting liberties of the citizenry cannot succeed in a state without a principled, independent, and non-corrupt police force. The development of the police in common law countries as a "citizen police" has been significant in ensuring the enforcement of the rule of law in Canada. While some developing democracies do not share the common law foundation in their legal history, they will benefit from this common law concept, which is now being reflected in the development of international human rights principles.

The Historical Development of a "Citizen Police"

Historically, the common law police officer and the common law constabulary developed as a "citizen police." In contrast, the police of civil law countries of the time tended to be officers of the state or, in some countries, adjuncts to military forces. Even though territorial police forces in Canada, such as the North-West Mounted Police (now the Royal Canadian Mounted Police), were organized on a more militaristic structure (modelled after the Royal Irish Constabulary) than the municipal police forces (which were modelled primarily on the London Metropolitan Police), both types of forces were essentially "citizen police," reflecting Sir Robert Peel's stricture:

> The police at all times should maintain a relationship with the public that gives reality to the historic tradition that the police are the public and that the public are the police; the police are the only members of the public who are paid to give fulltime attention to duties which are incumbent on every citizen in the interest of community welfare.

The concept of the common law "citizen police" did not originate with Sir Robert Peel and the legislation that created the London Metropolitan London Police in 1829. It evolved administratively, both before and after 1829 as a reaction to the European continental systems of the eighteenth century, which relied upon large standing armies and networks of spies run by the government of the day to control the populace.

The police forces in most modern European countries have developed traditions that recognize the rights and liberties of their citizenry. On the Continent the route to this recognition began with the codification of concepts of natural law and the declarations of inalienable rights. In Canada, we have benefited from both the common and civil law developments of our founding nations, which acknowledge the rights and liberties of all.

In considering present-day policing issues, it is useful to consider the common law roots and the early relationship between the community and police. The common law peace officer had three elements as the focus of duty, which remain the core elements of policing in Canada today. They are: (1) to maintain order, (2) to prevent crime, and (3) to detect and apprehend criminals. These three aspects of the common law duty are further clarified in "Nine Principles of Policing" as described by a leading author on policing, Charles Reith, in his book *The Blind Eye of History: A Study of the Origins of the Present Police Era*. The principles are as follows:

The first principle: to prevent crime and disorder ...

The second principle: to recognize always that the power of the police to fulfill their functions and duties is dependent on public approval of their existence, actions and behaviour, and on their ability to secure and maintain public respect.

The third principle: to recognize always that to secure and maintain the respect and approval of the public means also securing of the willing cooperation of the public in the task of securing observance of law.

The fourth principle: to recognize always that the extent to which the cooperation of the public can be secured diminishes, proportionately, the necessity of the use of physical force and compulsion for achieving police objectives.

The fifth principle: to seek and preserve public favour, not by pandering to public opinion, but by constantly demonstrating absolute impartial service to law, in complete independence of policy, and without regard to the justice or injustice of individual laws; by ready offering of individual service and friendship to all members of the public without regard to their wealth or social standing; by ready exercise of courtesy and good humour; and by ready offering of individual sacrifice in protecting and preserving life.

The sixth principle: to use physical force only when the exercise of persuasion, advice and warning is found to be insufficient to obtain public cooperation to an extent necessary to restore order; and to use only the minimum degree of physical force which is necessary on any particular occasion for achieving of police objectives.

The seventh principle: to maintain at all times a relationship with the public that gives reality to the historic tradition that the police are the public and that the public are the police; the police being only members of the public who are paid to give fulltime attention to duties which are incumbent on every citizen, in the interest of community welfare and existence.

The eighth principle: to recognize always the need for strict adherence to police executive functions, and to refrain from even seeming to usurp the powers of the judiciary of avenging individuals or the state, and of authoritatively judging guilt and punishing the guilty.

The ninth principle: to recognize always that the test of police efficiency is that absence of crime and disorder, and not the visible evidence of police action in dealing with them.

An important foundation for the rule of law is the principle that a police officer investigating a crime is not acting as a government functionary or as the servant of anyone save the law itself. The police officer occupies a public office initially defined by the common law and now set out in various statutes.

When investigating crime the police are independent of the control of the executive arm of government. Even the Attorney General, often referred to as the chief law officer of the Crown, has no authority to direct the police in their conduct of a criminal investigation. When performing such duties, the police are answerable to the law and to the law alone. If it were otherwise, the government, through the Attorney General, could grant immunity from enforcement of the law to members or supporters of the government by directing or controlling a police investigation.

While the rule of law requires the police to be able to act independently from the control of government in enforcing the law, it is equally important for the state to ensure that the police do not abuse the considerable powers they have been given. Who polices the police to ensure that they continue to act in accordance with the principles governing them as a citizen police?

Processes to Ensure Accountability of the Police

Accountability through the Courts
The rule of law requires that everyone, including the police, be equally subject to the ordinary law of the land administered by the ordinary courts. The availability of the courts to provide remedies to citizens who complain of police misconduct is, of course, the ultimate safeguard to ensure control and accountability of the police in a society governed by the rule of law. The courts examine police conduct in several different contexts:

• in civil actions against a police officer
• in criminal charges brought against police alleged to have committed crimes
• in considering whether evidence in prosecutions ought to be excluded because of police misconduct
• in determining whether remedies under the Canadian Charter of Rights and Freedoms ought to be granted for the breach of constitutionally guaranteed rights.

An example of judicial control of the police resulting from an accused person seeking a remedy for a breach of Charter rights is the case of *R. v. Campbell.* In this 1999 decision, the Supreme Court of Canada held that the police had no immunity from the application of the Narcotic Control Act that would permit them to sell drugs as part of a "reverse sting" operation to apprehend drug traffickers who would deal with them. The Court held that the rule of law required specific statutory provisions authorizing the police to conduct such operations. Otherwise, the police could grant themselves immunity to break the law if they believed that the ends justified doing so.

While judicial oversight will always be available, court action is not the most desirable method of resolving differences between citizens and the police. Civil litigation is incredibly expensive and time-consuming, and only the wealthiest of complainants can afford to use it to advance a complaint. Civil litigation is primarily designed to provide monetary compensation for loss rather than address the merits of citizen complaints.

The adversarial nature of litigation is also not conducive to bringing about an accommodation between the police force, the complainant, and the community. Indeed, parties to litigation often feel further aggrieved because of the litigation process itself.

Internal Disciplinary Proceedings
Police forces in common law countries invariably have internal disciplinary procedures to enforce codes of discipline. Through such procedures, constables are accountable to and controlled by their superiors. Usually such proceedings are conducted in private. Internal discipline would be a more effective instrument of accountability if the proceedings, or at least their results, were public. Some professional bodies formerly kept their disciplinary proceedings confidential but have found that the public's confidence is enhanced considerably when these proceedings are opened to the public and the discipline imposed is published.

Internal discipline is often concerned with matters that are more important to the police hierarchy than to the citizen. For example, most citizens would not find it necessary to fire a constable who, against his chief's orders, wore his police hat while playing in a rock band. On the other hand, most citizens would be astonished to learn that an officer convicted of the aggravated assault of a prisoner, and sentenced to nine months' imprisonment, was not fired. Both of these outcomes resulted from internal disciplinary proceedings in British Columbia.

Citizen Complaint Procedures

While the internal disciplinary process is essential to the proper functioning of a police force, the process is really a tool of police management. Neither it nor judicial scrutiny provide an effective and affordable remedy for the citizen who is aggrieved by the actions of a police officer. It is the citizen complaint procedure that provides an effective mechanism to ensure that the police are accountable to, and therefore controlled by, the public.

It is vital, however, that the public perceive the police complaint process as being meaningful – that is, a process that fairly and publicly addresses the concerns and grievances of members of the public. Without this perception, it is likely that complainants will attempt to have their grievances resolved by political action or media pressure rather than through a review by an independent agency that, in the public interest, has a duty to examine the complaints. While media and political questioning of the exercise of police power are themselves important safeguards, the integrity of the police force is likely to be damaged when issues of police misconduct are raised in the media without complete information and without an impartial method of addressing and resolving the complaints.

It is in this context that the roots of the "citizen police" must be recalled. The second principle of policing referred to earlier – "to recognize always that the power of the police to fulfill their functions and duties is dependent on public approval of their existence, actions and behaviour, and on their ability to secure and maintain public respect" – requires a system for ensuring a full inquiry into a citizen's complaint. Such a process must be accessible to members of the public without technical roadblocks, and, while ensuring fairness to all concerned, must be a process that impartially and fully inquires into the citizen's complaint and possesses sufficient powers to ensure that the complaint has been fully investigated.

Until 1975 there was no formal citizen complaint process for municipal police forces in British Columbia. The catalyst for reform of municipal policing was the 1971 Dohm Commission of Inquiry into the Gastown Riot in downtown Vancouver and the allegations of police abuse in suppressing the riot. The Dohm report recognized the need for a civilian review mechanism for police complaints. The 1974 British Columbia Police Act established a formal complaints process that guaranteed citizens the right to have their complaints dealt with at first instance by the municipal police board, and provided for an appeal to an independent civilian agency, the British Columbia Police Commission.

Other provinces also developed citizen complaint mechanisms. In the parts of Canada west of Ontario, the RCMP serves as the federal, provincial, and often the municipal police force. Attempts by provincial governments to have provincial police commissions provide a mechanism for citizen complaints against RCMP officers were thwarted by the Supreme Court of Canada decision in *Alberta (A.G.)* v. *Putnam* (1981), which held that the federal government has exclusive legislative authority regarding mechanisms for addressing complaints against the RCMP.

The history of events that resulted in the creation of the RCMP Public Complaints Commission (PCC) illustrates the need for such a commission. A series of events and scandals caused detrimental publicity. To maintain public confidence in the Force, the federal government appointed royal commissions of inquiry to investigate specific scandals and to make recommendations to prevent future controversies.

The RCMP Public Complaints Commission

The RCMP Public Complaints Commission was established in an effort to reverse a serious erosion of public confidence in the Force. This lack of confidence was the result of considerable evidence of police misconduct, misconduct that was never properly investigated by the RCMP.

Two commissions of inquiry – the 1976 Marin Commission of Inquiry Relating to Public Complaints, Internal Discipline and Grievance Procedure within the Royal Canadian Mounted Police, and the 1981 McDonald Commission of Inquiry Concerning Certain Activities of the Royal Canadian Mounted Police – determined that it was of fundamental importance that there be an independent body with powers to investigate citizen complaints of alleged misconduct by the RCMP.

The McDonald Commission report included an extensive survey of RCMP misconduct and documented eleven types of practices and activities by the RCMP that were not authorized or provided for by law. In the opening chapter of this survey, the McDonald Commission noted that:

> The common thread which we have detected running through these incidents is that of a willingness on the part of members of the RCMP to deceive those outside the Force who have some sort of constitutional authority or jurisdiction over them or their activities. We have come to this conclusion reluctantly and regretfully because in our view it might well be the most serious charge which we are levelling against the Force in our report. Nevertheless, we are convinced the practice existed. We have received evidence that federal ministers of the Crown responsible for the RCMP were misled by the RCMP and that on other occasions

relevant or significant information was intentionally withheld from ministers.

In Chapter 2 of Part X, "Complaints of Police Misconduct," the McDonald Commission made the following recommendation:

> We believe that an external review body is necessary to monitor how the RCMP handle complaints, and in certain circumstances, to undertake an investigation of its own. Indeed, the major recommendation in this chapter will call for the establishment of the Office of Inspector of Police Practices.

And (p. 988):

> [The legislation] should give the Inspector the authority to launch any investigation he deems necessary to fulfill his mandate. Thus, the Solicitor General should not be able to prevent the Inspector from investigating a matter in which the Solicitor General might be implicated. Finally, it should be understood that the Inspector would have access to the Prime Minister on matters where the integrity of the Solicitor General is at question.

The earlier Marin Commission had also looked into the need for an independent body to deal with public complaints about acts of members of the RCMP. It stated:

> The principal requirement of any credible reviewing authority is that it enjoy the confidence of both the public on whose behalf it is acting and the Force whose actions it is reviewing. Such confidence is only possible, in our opinion, if this authority is visibly independent of the Royal Canadian Mounted Police and responsible directly to Parliament rather than to the government of the day.

It also made the following recommendations:

1 An independent authority, to be known as the Federal Police Ombudsman, should be established by the Parliament of Canada.

2 With respect to public complaints the Federal Police Ombudsman should be responsible for:
   (i) ascertaining that all complaints are investigated in an appropriate manner;
   (ii) recommending such remedial action as he believes necessary at both the individual and organizational level;

(iii) providing a review of any particular complaint or the proceedings followed by the Force in its response; and

(iv) serving as an authority with whom a complaint may be
lodged.

3   The Federal Police Ombudsman should have all the authority
vested in a Commissioner appointed pursuant to the provisions of
the Inquiries Act.

4   The Federal Police Ombudsman should have the authority to
appoint tribunals to hold hearings convened for the purpose of
determining the merits of a complaint.

5   The Federal Police Ombudsman should report to Parliament at
least annually but should be authorized to report at any time and
to publish any report, if he deems it to be in the public interest.
...

10 The Federal Police Ombudsman should be required to undertake
an analysis of data relating to public complaints with a view to
detecting and isolating problems which can be brought to the
attention of the Royal Canadian Mounted Police together with his
recommendations for remedial action.

11 The Federal Police Ombudsman should have the authority and
power to recommend change in the disposition of a complaint;
restitution or compensation; and whatever action he considers
appropriate.

In commenting on the authority of the proposed Federal Police
Ombudsman, the Marin Commission stated:

In our opinion, the Ombudsman should have all of the authority vested
in a Commissioner appointed pursuant to the provisions of the
Inquiries Act. Without full powers of inquiry, the Ombudsman would
be unable to fulfill his role as a watchman on behalf of Parliament.

In 1986, the legislation that followed upon the recommendations of the
McDonald and Marin Commissions added Part VII to the Royal Canadian
Mounted Police Act and created the Royal Canadian Mounted Police
Public Complaints Commission. The parliamentary debates of the legislation clearly show that Parliament intended to create an entirely independent agency with powers of review independent of the RCMP
Commissioner's powers. All political parties supported the reform. The
provinces where the RCMP served as the provincial force also supported
the establishment of the Public Complaints Commission, although several

would have preferred to make the RCMP subject to existing provincial complaints commissions.

The concept of accountability by the Force to an outside agency or, worse yet, the Force being subject to any sort of direction from such an agency was repugnant to many in the RCMP management structure. Their view was that the Force should be allowed to reform itself from within. The rank and file of the Force also opposed being subject to the imposition of discipline by outsiders.

The RCMP lobbied vigorously and succeeded in significantly weakening the legislation that ultimately created the Public Complaints Commission. The independence of the PCC was weakened when the legislation was incorporated into the Royal Canadian Mounted Police Act rather than being given its own statute. More significantly, the legislation did not provide for the PCC to report directly to Parliament, as many ombudsman offices do. While the PCC does report to Parliament, it does so through the Solicitor General of Canada, a federal cabinet minister with whom the PCC also has a budgetary and reporting relationship. The PCC chair and members are appointed by the federal cabinet rather than by an all-party committee of Parliament.

RCMP lobbying also succeeded in limiting the jurisdiction of the PCC. Unlike many citizen complaint bodies, the PCC cannot impose discipline on an officer complained against even if it finds that the officer has committed the most egregious misconduct. The RCMP has also taken the position that it is not required to disclose to the complainant, the PCC, or the public the discipline that the Force has imposed upon an officer complained against. The legislation does not directly allow the PCC to order the disclosure of such information.

The PCC has the power to review the conduct of members of the RCMP, including its management, and the power to scrutinize how the Force handles complaints. It has no power to issue any directive or order to the Commissioner of the RCMP or to the Solicitor General. It may, however, make findings of fact and recommendations to both the Commissioner of the RCMP and Parliament.

Notwithstanding the limits of the legislation, the PCC has the duty and power to report to Parliament and to act as a "parliamentary overseer" of the Force. As a mechanism for ensuring the accountability of police to the citizenry it serves, the PCC is a significant instrument in the enforcement of the rule of law. It is unfortunate that some aspects of the way the PCC handled complaints about the conduct of the RCMP and its members during the APEC summit caused many to question the commission's usefulness. Some of the criticism stemmed directly from a weakness in the legislation that created the PCC – the failure to institutionalize its independence from the government and the Solicitor General.

The RCMP Public Complaints Commission and the APEC Complaints

Since the RCMP Public Complaints Commission was established in 1986, it has handled thousands of complaints. Most have involved the day-to-day differences that arise between citizens and police officers, such as allegations of rudeness, abuse of authority, use of excessive force, illegality of arrest, and neglect of duty. The commission has done its work without a great deal of fanfare but has succeeded in actually enforcing the principles of civilian oversight and police accountability.

In addressing some complaints, the PCC has gone beyond the specific grievance and examined the conduct of the member of the RCMP in the context of the Force's framework of regulations and the training of its members. One example of this was the commission's inquiry into the treatment of a sexual assault victim who was taken into custody as a material witness and transported in an appalling manner across the country. Another example was the inquiry into the use of carotid neck holds and the policies and training related to this type of force.

The APEC affair requires the PCC to address all these types of complaints, and there is some overlap between categories. The "normal" complaints of inappropriate conduct by police officers include allegations relating to:

- whether or not the police targeted potential troublemakers for arrest
- whether or not various arrests were performed lawfully
- whether lawful protest and the exercise of free speech was impeded contrary to the Charter of Rights and Freedoms when signs and flags were removed or protesters were moved out of sight of the meeting delegates
- the reasons why certain arrested persons were released only on undertakings restricting their right to protest
- the use of pepper spray and whether such use was justified and appropriate
- whether or not more force than necessary was used by the police
- whether or not it was appropriate treatment for the arrested women to be strip-searched at the Richmond Detachment.

The complaints that raise issues about RCMP policy include allegations relating to whether:

- the RCMP went beyond the requirements of its duty to protect internationally protected persons
- the RCMP allowed the Prime Minister's Office to become inappropriately involved in security and policing arrangements.

In addition, certain complaints raise the more fundamental question of whether the RCMP acted in accordance with its role as independent enforcer and defender of the rule of law. Such complaints include allegations relating to:

- what part the Prime Minister's Office played with respect to the abuses complained of
- whether the federal government inappropriately used the RCMP for political purposes rather than law enforcement and preservation of the peace
- whether police force was inappropriately used against protesters to prevent them from embarrassing the visiting delegates, considering that in Canada there is no law against embarrassing anyone.

Where Did the Public Complaints Commission APEC Hearings Go Wrong?

At the time of writing (May 1999), the Public Complaints Commission APEC hearings are still under way. They are now presided over by Mr. E.N. (Ted) Hughes, QC, who was designated the single member of the PCC, replacing the three-member panel initially assigned to inquire into the complaints. Mr. Hughes is a highly experienced former judge and British Columbia Conflict of Interest Commissioner who has also conducted several inquiries into highly controversial matters in several Canadian jurisdictions. He is a man who brooks no nonsense.

There was enough nonsense going on in and around the proceedings before the first panel to try the patience of even the most experienced and patient of judges. Members of the PCC rarely have that type of experience when appointed to the commission. It must be remembered that the concept of the commission is that of *citizen* review of complaints, not judicial review of complaints.

For good and valid policy reasons, it is not desirable for the judiciary to have supervisory control over the police other than in the exercise of judicial functions referred to earlier in this chapter. The American principle of the separation of powers, with the checks and balances that exist because of the distribution of powers between the legislative, executive, and judicial branches of government is also applicable in the Canadian and

English common law context. In my view, it is inappropriate for the judiciary to have any ongoing administrative supervisory role over the police. Such a function belongs with the executive branch of government.

My objections to the principle of judicial supervision of police are not shared by others, however, as evidenced by the recent amendments to the British Columbia Police Act that involve provincial court judges in the citizen complaint process. This departure from the principles of civilian oversight over law enforcement was the result of much lobbying by the BC municipal police unions, who (wrongly, in my view) believe that their members will fare better before a judge than before a civilian panel. Some countries have "judicial police" controlled by the judiciary. The experience of those countries, which are not governed by the common law concept of the rule of law, illustrates that these relationships are not satisfactory to either the police or the judiciary.

During the hearings before the initial PCC panel, there were many cries for a judicial inquiry. Stand-alone judicial commissions of inquiry, such as the Dohm, McDonald, and Marin inquiries mentioned earlier, have addressed incidents of police misconduct in the past. They had an identical recommendation: that there should be a standing commission to consider all complaints relating to police on an ongoing basis. It is rare that there is sufficient public or political interest in complaints against the police to justify establishing a royal commission.

Taking away high-profile cases from the PCC and referring them to judicial inquiries would undermine the ongoing authority of the commission. In the case of the APEC complaints, it would also ignore the statutory requirement that the complaints be examined by the PCC in any event. It is inconceivable that there should be two parallel inquiries into the same event.

Given the problems facing the initial panel, which led to the resignation of its members, the PCC's resolution of the problem it faced was, in my view, preferable to appointing a stand-alone judicial inquiry. Within the commission, high-profile cases or cases involving volatile parties may require the assignment of a more experienced panel than "normal" complaints. These types of cases are also more effectively and economically handled by a single commissioner rather than a panel of three. With respect to the APEC complaints, the legislation was sufficiently flexible to allow the appointment of Mr. Hughes, or someone with his experience, when it was required. The ongoing hearings before Mr. Hughes are proceeding in an organized and principled way.

The members of the initial panel were also unfairly and inappropriately attacked by opposition politicians and other commentators because they were appointed, as the legislation requires, by order of the federal cabinet. One of the weaknesses in the legislation establishing the PCC (which was enacted by a Progressive Conservative government) is that the chair and the members of the commission are appointed by an order in council of the federal cabinet rather that by Parliament itself. The same, however, is true of most of the independent tribunals at the federal level.

Similar bodies at the provincial level (police commissions and municipal police boards) have members appointed by the provincial cabinet. It is consistent with the rule of law that the democratically elected government of the day may make such appointments in accordance with statutes enacted by Parliament or by a legislature.

In many situations commissions have members who have been appointed, over the years, by governments of different political parties. Individual commission members, like society as a whole, have their strengths and weaknesses and their individual points of view. My experience in twenty-five years of practice with police commissions whose members were appointed by governments of every conceivable political stripe has been that members of these commissions are fiercely independent of government and any government influence in the performance of their duties.

Far more significant than the manner of their appointment is the legal advice that commission members receive. The importance of an independent commission counsel who understands that it is counsel's role to ensure that all relevant evidence touching on the complaint is put before the commission cannot be overstated.

One of the great weaknesses of British Columbia's old citizen complaint process (replaced with a new regime in 1998) was that the police board counsel at the initial complaint hearing before the municipal police board was often the municipal solicitor, whose principal concern was that the municipality avoid civil liability. Counsel with that kind of objective cannot possibly ensure that all relevant information is put before a police board. When the provincial police commission insisted that municipalities appoint independent counsel to advise the police board during complaint inquiries, the quality and fairness of the inquiries improved considerably.

One of the controversies that plagued the initial APEC hearing panel was the issue of funding for legal counsel representing the complainants. The PCC has no independent access to the public purse. Whether or not this is a weakness in the legislation is a matter of considerable debate.

The question of the extent to which even the courts are subject to the financial resources (including judicial salaries) made available by the government was considered by the Supreme Court of Canada in the *Reference Re Remuneration of Judges of the Provincial Court* (1997). The Court held that Sections 96 to 100 of the Constitution Act, 1867, only protect the independence of judges of the superior, district, and county courts. Section 11(d) of the Charter protects the independence of a wide range of courts and tribunals, including provincial courts, but only when they exercise jurisdiction in relation to offences. The PCC does not exercise any such jurisdiction.

The Supreme Court of Canada has held that these constitutional provisions are not an exhaustive and definitive written code for the protection of judicial independence in Canada. Rather, the Court held that judicial independence is an unwritten norm, recognized and affirmed by the preamble to the Constitution Act, 1867, referred to at the beginning of this chapter.

The Court recognized, as a general constitutional principle, that the financial security of judicial institutions means that the salaries of judges can be reduced, increased, or frozen, either as part of an overall economic measure that affects the salaries of all or some persons who are remunerated from public funds, or as part of a measure directed at provincial judges as a class. However, to avoid the possibility or appearance of political interference through economic manipulation of the judiciary, a body, such as a commission, must be interposed between the courts and the other branches of government. The Court held that, although recommendations of such a body are non-binding, they should not be set aside lightly.

Nothing in the cases dealing with judicial independence supports the proposition that a tribunal, such as the PCC, has any authority to spend public funds not allocated to it by government. The controversy surrounding the initial refusal of the government to fund counsel for complainants did not revolve around legal niceties, however. Rather, the public recognized that issues of fairness were involved when the complainants were pitted against a small army of well-paid lawyers representing the police officers and government officials involved in the hearing.

Public concern about unfairness increased when then Solicitor General Andy Scott, who had made the decision rejecting the funding application, was forced to resign his cabinet portfolio when an opposition politician reported overhearing him make statements suggesting that he had prejudged the issues before the commission. When Mr. Hughes took over the inquiry, the new Solicitor General, Lawrence MacAulay, approved the provision of funding, at Mr. Hughes's recommendation.

While this decision was clearly correct with respect to the APEC inquiry, the implications of providing legal counsel for *all* proceedings before the PCC are considerable: unless the government vastly increases funding for the commission, there would have to be fewer hearings or longer delays in the consideration of complaints. In most instances, commission counsel can ensure that all relevant evidence is put before the commission. In other cases, however, providing counsel to the complainant may facilitate hearings to the extent that their overall costs are reduced beyond the cost of the legal representation.

Conclusion

The controversy surrounding the APEC Inquiry has raised many issues relating to the rule of law. Most commentary has focused on the threat to the rule of law by the actions of the police and the government. It is regrettable that, amid all the sound and fury surrounding the hearings, the importance of the RCMP Public Complaints Commission as an instrument for enforcing the rule of law appears to have been overlooked by many.

When I attended a meeting of police oversight officials just before the implementation of the RCMP Public Complaints Commission legislation in 1985, the delegate representing the eastern Northwest Territories described the legislation, which had been watered down as a result of lobbying by the RCMP, as "typical federal legislation – designed to fail." As it turns out, however, a review of the complaints handled by the commission throughout its existence shows clearly that it has succeeded more than it has failed.

The weaknesses in the legislation that were apparent when it was enacted have been re-exposed by the APEC hearings. It is to be hoped that the politicians and commentators who have been critical of the PCC during the difficulties surrounding the APEC hearings will support legislative amendments to make it a stronger instrument for ensuring the accountability of our federal police force and the enforcement of our most fundamental constitutional principle – the rule of law.

5

The Significance of the APEC Affair

JOEL BAKAN

On a cold and drizzly November day, thousands of students came out of their classrooms and dorms to try to send a message to world leaders attending the final meeting of APEC 1997 on the campus of the University of British Columbia. Many of the students were pepper-sprayed, detained, compelled to sign away their constitutional rights, and (as later came to light) strip-searched. The campus resembled a military operation. From my office in the law building, I could see chain and concrete barricades, erected the day before, and a street peopled with nervous-looking security types. Police vans sat idle along the curb, some crammed full of students, cold, wet, and gasping from the effects of pepper spray, others waiting empty for new crops of detainees. Above the fray, police sharpshooters kept watch from the roof of the Chan Centre for the Performing Arts. The students were kept so far back from the site of the meeting – which was roughly half a kilometre away from the barricades, separated by a steep hill, a number of buildings, a road, and a stand of trees – that the world leaders must have been blissfully unaware that protests were taking place. In the meantime, some of the students who might have attended the demonstration were sitting in jail – one, Craig Jones, for putting up signs along the

Thanks to Marlee Kline, Wes Pue, and Margot Young for their helpful comments on earlier drafts of this paper.

motorcade route that said "Free Speech," "Democracy," and "Human Rights"; another, anti-APEC activist Jaggi Singh, for allegedly assaulting a UBC security officer earlier.

The sheer drama of the APEC protests was enough to attract the media spotlight. Throw in violent confrontations between police and students, allegations that the Prime Minister and his office directed police actions, and a veteran CBC reporter taken off the story after being accused of bias by the Prime Minister's Office, and you have a big story – perhaps, as some have said, the most important civil rights travesty since Prime Minister Trudeau invoked the War Measures Act in 1970.

But what is the real significance of the APEC affair?

Critics of the crackdown on student protest see it as a cautionary tale about the fragility of civil rights in Canada. Their concerns are well placed. Mounting evidence points to serious constitutional breaches (although it should be noted that no tribunal has yet ruled on the matter). Free speech clearly took a beating. Legally, the kind of speech at issue – that pertaining to social and political issues – is the most jealously guarded by the courts under the constitution. "Political expression," according to the Supreme Court of Canada in *Libman* v. *Québec*, "is at the very heart of the values sought to be protected by the freedom of expression guaranteed by section 2(b) of the Canadian Charter." Restrictions on such speech cannot be justified under the Charter unless they are absolutely necessary for achieving some very compelling objective. Security of world leaders would likely have qualified as such an objective. But was such a large buffer zone between protesters and leaders really necessary? Was it necessary to have signs removed that proclaimed the core values of the Canadian Charter of Rights and Freedoms itself – freedom, democracy, human rights? Was the threat and use of pepper spray appropriate, given the high value of the speech at issue? Was security even the objective of the measures taken? Or, as some evidence suggests, was immunizing world leaders from the potential embarrassment of knowing that their presence was being protested – an objective of insufficient import to justify overriding constitutional rights – the real aim of the measures? If security was the aim, the measures likely overshot the constitutional mark. And if protecting world leaders from embarrassment was the aim, it was not sufficiently weighty to override free speech rights.

There are a host of other potential violations besides those of free speech. Section 2 of the Charter guarantees the rights to freedom of assembly and association, as well as free speech. These rights were also likely restricted by the measures to limit the scope of the APEC protest and, more particularly, by the RCMP requiring detainees (those detained in the days immediately before the APEC leaders' conference) to sign an undertaking that they would not participate in future protests.

Then there was the detention of anti-APEC activists, such as Jaggi Singh, before the day of the leaders' summit. It has been alleged that such detentions were designed to neutralize these activists on the day of the APEC meeting. The allegations are believable. Singh, for example, was detained on a charge of assault by megaphone. Apparently a security officer's ear was hurt when Singh shouted into a megaphone at a pre-APEC demonstration. The charge was later dropped. If the allegations of "preventative arrest" are proven, it will mean that the detainees' rights under Section 9 of the Charter – "not to be arbitrarily detained or imprisoned" – were breached. Detaining a person to prevent that person from exercising constitutional rights is arbitrary by any definition of that word.

Finally, there is the issue of separation of powers and especially the important line which is supposed to buffer police from political control. The defining feature of a police state is that the police are used to achieve political purposes. That is why people are concerned about the allegation that Prime Minister Chrétien directed the RCMP security operation. If in fact that operation involved more than security – if it extended to protecting the sensitivities of world leaders by immunizing them from even the knowledge of protest – then there are legitimate concerns about inappropriate use of the police.

Taking all of these together, there are strong grounds to believe that on 25 November 1997 the UBC campus became – to use the words of CBC journalist Terry Milewski, borrowed from a joint letter to the Prime Minister from members of the UBC Law Faculty – a "Charter-free zone."

The APEC affair is, however, about more, much more, than Charter violations. And people's well-placed alarm and indignation about free speech and other Charter rights may serve, unwittingly, to obscure its deeper significance. Voltaire's famous aphorism, "I may disapprove of what you say, but I will defend to the death your right to say it," was never meant to suggest that what people actually say is unimportant. Yet "content-neutrality" – the concept encapsulating his sentiment – has become so thoroughly entrenched in our understanding of free speech that the specific messages of muzzled speakers often get buried under defences of their right to speak. That is, I believe, what has happened with the APEC story. The message of the student protesters – the reason they braved the rain, the pepper spray, and the possibility of jail – has fallen from view, as the traditional civil rights narrative is told and retold. Yet the importance of the students' actions cannot be understood in the abstract. Their actual message – not just the fact their rights were violated in trying to communicate it – is key to understanding the significance of the APEC protest and the reasons it was repressed.

Identifying particular motives and messages behind the APEC protest is difficult. Different students were there for different reasons. The protest brought together a large array of groups and individuals holding divergent, even contradictory, positions. Some were protesting the suppression of traditional civil rights in APEC countries; others took issue with a broader range of rights violations; others focused on states' colonialist ambitions – China in Tibet, Indonesia in East Timor; and still others expressed more general concerns about world exploitation and oppression, and the growing power of transnational corporations. But there was, I believe, a common theme underlying these different concerns, one that is revealed by understanding something about the nature and context of APEC itself.

The Asia-Pacific Economic Cooperation grouping institutionally embodies the neoliberal ideology that dominates today's public discourse. Repeated like a mantra by governments, business, and mainstream media, it can be summarized thus: *We live in a new world order. Nation states' attempts to protect the interests of citizens through restraints on the movement of trade and investment capital, both within and between states, must be challenged. The freedom of corporations to do their thing, regardless of their nation of origin, must be the touchstone of domestic and international policy. Deregulation, privatization, and reduction of tariffs and investment barriers are the specific mechanisms for doing this. Giving business greater freedom will promote economic growth and wealth creation, and thus ensure welfare and prosperity for all.*

Business, in other words, is not just another stakeholder or interest group competing for the attention and support of the state. It is a partner of the state in promoting human welfare and social progress. Business creates jobs and wealth and provides essential services. The state's proper role is to facilitate its needs and interests and stay out of its way. What's good for business is good for all of us.

Neoliberalism's unabashed elevation of business interests over others in society marks a shift from the pluralist ideology that held sway among elites (albeit often as lip-service) roughly from the post–Second World War years until the mid-1970s. Pluralism construed the state as a neutral mediator of competing social and economic interests, including those of business.

Business did not have a privileged position within this framework but competed for state support with other interests, such as labour, consumers, and environmental and human rights groups. Pluralism, as a legitimation theory, was manifest in concrete policies aimed at protecting the public interest by curbing the power of corporations and redistributing wealth. No doubt such measures were often weak and inadequate, and business always enjoyed a privileged status among interest groups and a place at the centre of state power, but under pluralism's reign, state and economic elites felt bound to justify their actions in its egalitarian terms. Pluralism's broad conception of public interest was the touchstone of legitimacy for the exercise of power.

It is questionable whether pluralism remains even as a pretence today. Not only are the material reflections of pluralism – the regulatory and social welfare state – being gutted but the principle itself has given way to neoliberal ideology. To the extent that the latter has a legitimization theory, it is trickle-down economics – serve the needs of business and wealth will be created, and everyone will be happy and prosper. Within this framework, there is nothing at all embarrassing about a cozy relationship between business and government. To the contrary, it is required. The criticism of pro-business bias on the part of the state thus has little bite within neoliberalism. Under pluralism it at least demanded a response.

Of all global economic organizations, APEC is perhaps the most unabashed in its commitment to neoliberalism. Although other international trade and investment organizations reflect neoliberalism's dictates in their discourse and practices, they occasionally engage in more pluralist rhetoric. APEC, in contrast, distinguishes itself by its connection (actual and desired) with business. Its brochure states:

> Key features that set APEC apart from other international organizations are therefore its commitment to business facilitation and the regular involvement of the private sector in a wide range of APEC activities. Business expertise and resources can help APEC to achieve its objectives, and business is a key constituency for APEC both regionally and in individual member economies. Business already participates in many of APEC's working groups and helps shape the policy dialogue in partnership with member economy officials. APEC Economic Leaders receive advice from the APEC Business Advisory Council (ABAC) established in late 1995. Such involvement is important to ensure that APEC's work is relevant to real problems. However, a major APEC goal is to continue to expand business participation in the APEC process.

Without any felt need to justify or explain, the involvement and perspective of business are implicitly elevated over those of the many other groups whose interests are profoundly affected by the issues addressed and the policies created within APEC.

APEC further embodies neoliberal ideas in portraying the economy, and issues of economic growth and development, as things that can magically be separated from and given priority over issues of human rights, social justice, and the environment. Through this strange alchemy, it becomes possible within APEC for leaders of putatively democratic states to rub shoulders and cut deals with – indeed roll out the red carpet for – dictators. Everyone has the same goal of economic growth. How that goal is pursued, and with what effect, is evaluated solely within the internal indicators of neoliberal economics. Brutality, exploitation, human rights abuses, vast inequalities, environmental destruction – these are side issues, if they are addressed at all. "The economy" is construed as a self-contained, universal, and neutral system, operating on quasi-scientific principles. Its nature and needs are primarily technical. They transcend politics, and thus enable bad guys and good guys, enemies and friends, to work together on making the economy work better. APEC is about the economy.

These characteristics of APEC provide insight into the significance of the UBC protest against it. What united the various protesting groups was a belief that the economy *cannot* be separated from everything else. The protest dramatically disrupted neoliberalism's all-too-easy division between economics and politics, reminding world leaders (and everybody else) that people care deeply about issues deemed irrelevant by neoliberal theory. Trade and investment are *not* independent of other issues; solutions to the world's problems will *not* trickle down to its citizens if the needs of business are met – these were the messages of the APEC protest. The protest repoliticized a meeting premised on the irrelevance of politics, and signalled that, despite the best efforts of business, government, and the media to turn neoliberal ideology into "truth," there is dissent among the citizenry. More generally, it showed that large numbers of people will mobilize and demonstrate for the principles of democracy and social justice, even as the influence of these principles on elites appears to be waning.

The crackdown on APEC protesters may also be explained, at least in part, by the nature of APEC. In determining how to manage protests on the UBC campus, the police, and possibly the Prime Minister's Office, had to balance civil liberties against possible risks from protest activities. Where they placed barriers and sight lines, the criteria they established for use of force, where they would allow signs along the motorcade route – all decisions had to be made against the backdrop of concern for the constitutionally guaranteed civil rights of citizens. The Prime Minister, his officials, and the RCMP have all acknowledged this. They have all said that the rights of protesters were foremost in their minds, that they had to balance those rights carefully against competing concerns. Before something can be balanced, however, it must be assigned a weight. A value had to be attached to citizens' civil rights in the process of police and government decision making. And the events leading up to, during, and after APEC – civil rights abuses foremost among them – suggest that citizens' rights were assigned a low value.

Why did this happen? How could a university campus become a "Charter-free zone" for a day? I offer two speculative hypotheses. First, there may be a connection between the low value ascribed to civil rights by state officials and the neoliberal character of the APEC meeting. When the economy is understood as technical and apolitical, political protest is, by definition, irrelevant – akin to protesting the politics of gravity. When the public interest is defined as the advancement of business interests, protesting business-friendly economic policy as undermining public interests is oxymoronic. Neoliberal premises leave little room for political protest about economic policy. Neoliberal logic compels the conclusion that protesters are ill-informed and irrational, driven by ideology and ignorance rather than by reasoned understanding of economic science. In other words, it is possible that the apolitical pretence of APEC was itself partly responsible for officials' disregard of civil rights. Immunization of world leaders from political dissent probably seemed less problematic for meetings seen as purely economic and not political.

A second hypothesis is that the crackdown on APEC protesters relates to broader aspects of neoliberalism. Political power is maintained either through legitimization or coercion, with most systems using some balance between the two. The last few years have been marked by what appears to be a greater readiness on the part of state agencies to quell dissent with coercion, and an increasing intolerance of "unruly" citizens. The APEC crackdown joins the ranks of increasingly frequent and disturbing examples of state repression within Canada: municipal laws that ban panhandling, busking, and sign posting on public property; back-to-work legislation as the norm rather than the exception in labour disputes; crackdowns on protests by poor and homeless people; and quasi-military actions against First Nations dissidents.

A shift towards greater coercion may be related to the demise of pluralism. Although never fully entrenched in relations between state and society, pluralism's ideals of social citizenship and political inclusiveness were accepted by elites and manifest – albeit weakly – in concrete practices. Pluralism's central message was that all interests in society are entitled to equal concern. It provided a rationale and justification for the exercise of state power that could attract popular respect, even while people criticized the sincerity of its invocation on particular occasions. Pluralism was, in short, a powerful legitimization theory because of its roots in egalitarian ideals. Neoliberalism's trickle-down principle is comparatively weak as a legitimization principle, one less likely to mollify disgruntled citizens. It is explicitly unegalitarian, and seeks to immunize huge areas of state policy from public criticism by deeming them "economic." With weaker and less intuitively appealing strategies to legitimate power, coercion becomes a necessary means of maintaining it, especially where wealth and power are unequally distributed. Could this explain the APEC affair and other recent examples of state repression? Is Canada becoming more like some of its APEC partners – a blatantly repressive state enforcing a highly unequal and undemocratic society? Perhaps, and we should be worried.

PART 3:
POLICING AND ACCOUNTABILITY

As NDP leader Alexa McDonough pointed out in the House of Commons last week, government lawyers now acknowledge the PMO played a role, but maintain that the RCMP had the final say. The chain of command in government is precisely the opposite, however, and summits are no exception to the rule.

– Norman Spector, *Globe and Mail*,
30 March 1999

6

Someone to Watch over Me: Government Supervision of the RCMP

PHILIP C. STENNING

A Modern Starting Point: The Nicholson Affair (1959)

On 12 March 1959, Commissioner L.H. Nicholson of the RCMP wrote a letter to the Minister of Justice, the Honourable E. Davie Fulton, tendering his resignation as Commissioner of the Force. It was the first and only time a Commissioner of the RCMP had resigned as a result of a dispute with the government of the day, and to this day it is still regarded by many supporters of the Force as a critical event asserting and celebrating the "independence" of the RCMP from "improper political interference" by the government.

The circumstances that prompted Commissioner Nicholson's resignation were complex. The legislature of Newfoundland had passed legislation decertifying a US-based union that had been representing workers in the logging industry who were involved in a major labour dispute that threatened to seriously harm Newfoundland's economy. The expressed policy of the Newfoundland government had been to oust this union from the province and promote the establishment of a new "home-grown" union, which the provincial Premier himself was actively engaged in organizing. As might be expected, this approach provoked a strong reaction from the labour movement both inside and outside Newfoundland, which in turn led to serious violence on the picket lines. Both the RCMP, which provided policing in the province under contract, and the St. John's-based Royal

Newfoundland Constabulary were called in to restore order and maintain peace on the picket lines.

The local RCMP commander felt that he did not have enough personnel to perform this duty effectively, and accordingly asked the provincial Attorney General to request reinforcements from the Commissioner of the Force in Ottawa, pursuant to the terms of the policing contract. The relevant clause of the contract stated:

> Where in the opinion of the attorney general of the province an emergency exists within the province requiring additional members of the force to assist in dealing with the emergency, Canada shall, at the request of the attorney general of the province addressed to the commissioner [of the RCMP], increase the strength of the division as requested if in the opinion of the Attorney General of Canada, having regard to other responsibilities and duties of the force, such increase is possible.

We may pause to note that this clause explicitly gave precedence to the opinions of the Attorneys General of the province and of Canada, respectively, over those of the police themselves, in determining both whether a request for reinforcements should be made and whether such a request should be granted. In addition, the Royal Canadian Mounted Police Act contained the following provisions at the time:

> 6.(1) The Governor General may by commission appoint a Commissioner of Police, who shall be called the Commissioner of the Royal Canadian Mounted Police ...

> 10.(1) The Commissioner of Police, *under the Minister,* has the control and management of the Force and of all matters connected therewith.

> 16. The Commissioner of Police shall perform such duties as are assigned to him, and he is subject to the control, orders and authority of such person or persons as are for that purpose named by the Governor in Council. [emphasis added]

When the Newfoundland Attorney General's request was received, the Commissioner of the RCMP advised the federal Minister of Justice that fifty extra officers could be spared to respond to the request, and that they had been assembled at an airfield in Moncton, ready to be flown to Newfoundland. The Minister, however, advised the Commissioner that "while these steps were to be taken as a precaution, I was not giving authority for the plane to take off from Moncton, and that this was not to take place until I had an opportunity to consider the situation further and to consult with my colleagues with regard to it."

The Minister of Justice met with the federal cabinet later that same day to discuss the situation, as a result of which "it was decided that a state of readiness should be maintained but that reinforcements should not be dispatched at that time." It was this decision that prompted Commissioner Nicholson to tender his resignation.

The Commissioner justified his decision in the following terms:

There is no doubt in my mind as to the need and I am certain that the number of men asked for can be provided without prejudice to "other responsibilities and duties."

I realize that other issues are before you which arise from this strike but I feel most strongly that the matter of law enforcement should be isolated and dealt with on its own merits. This is the attitude the force has taken throughout. It has not concerned itself with the issues back of the strike but has merely tried to maintain law and order in the area.

I think the contract clause on this matter of providing reinforcements in an emergency is clear and I cannot escape the conclusion that failure to supply reinforcements in this instance is a breach of that clause. Bearing in mind that we have similar contracts with seven other provinces the decision of the government has a particular significance.

With these considerations in mind I feel I have no option but to ask you to accept my resignation and this I now do.

In his response accepting the Commissioner's resignation, the Minister of Justice put forward a very different view of the situation. Reminding the Commissioner that the contract clause provided that the Attorney General of Canada should have the final say as to whether the request for reinforcements should be granted, he wrote:

In reaching my conclusion on the question whether "having regard to other responsibilities and duties of the force" such increase were possible, I, of course, as you know, gave the most careful consideration to your views that additional members could and should be sent to Newfoundland without prejudice to other responsibilities and duties of the force. However, upon consideration of all the factors, including especially the importance of preserving the character and capacity of the force to discharge its duty in connection with law enforcement in all of Canada, I came to the conclusion, after consulting with my colleagues, that, as the situation existed at that time, it was not possible to send the additional men requested without prejudicing the other responsibilities and duties of the force.

A few days later, the Minister explained his decision to the House of Commons in the following terms:

> I do not accept, and the government of Canada cannot accept, that an issue of this importance – whether reinforcements should be sent under the circumstances such as existed here – can be decided on the basis of a mere mathematical calculation as to whether men are physically available. We cannot discharge our responsibility by considering only the physical circumstances prevailing and examining the need for men under those circumstances. We must also consider the overall responsibilities of the force, and our responsibility for the force, in a much wider context.

Explaining that in the federal government's view "the activities of the government of Newfoundland appear to have gone beyond the usual role of a government," the Minister of Justice went on to say:

> As I appreciate the situation, therefore, the request made by the government of Newfoundland for Royal Canadian Mounted Police reinforcements takes on the character not of a request to assist in the normal function and duty of the province in maintaining law and order, but of a request for additional help made necessary in the course of the furtherance of a project to extinguish a union from the province.
>
> We have also had to bear in mind the possibility that under these circumstances to send additional Royal Canadian Mounted Police into Newfoundland, instead of ensuring that the situation is kept under control, might act only as provocation to further incidents of violence and defiance, so there is no certainty that the sending of them would not do more to inflame the situation than to control it.
>
> After weighing all these factors, and discussing them with my colleagues, I have come to the conclusion that the arguments against sending more men at this time outweigh the arguments in favour, and I have decided accordingly, having regard to all the responsibilities and duties of the force.

Ironically and, as far as I can tell, by coincidence, on the very day that Commissioner Nicholson submitted his resignation, the Minister of Justice introduced a bill for first reading in the House of Commons that completely overhauled and replaced the existing RCMP Act. Section 5 of the new bill (which was enacted later that year as the new RCMP Act) provided that:

> 5. The Governor in Council may appoint an officer to be known as the Commissioner of the Royal Canadian Mounted Police who, *under the direction of the Minister,* has the control and management of the force and all matters connected therewith. [emphasis added]

The wording of this provision, which remains the essential one delineating the relationship between the Minister (now the Solicitor General) and the Commissioner of the RCMP, was later adopted to define the relationship between the Solicitor General and the Director of the Canadian Security Intelligence Service (CSIS), in Section 6 of the Canadian Security Intelligence Service Act, enacted in 1984. Interestingly, however, the latter section also contains the following additional provision:

> 6(2) In providing the direction referred to in subsection (1), the Minister may issue to the Director written directions with respect to the Service and a copy of any such direction shall, forthwith after it is issued, be given to the Review Committee.

[Section 7 of the CSIS Act requires the Director of CSIS to consult with the Deputy Solicitor General on "the general operational policies of the Service," and on "any matter with respect to which consultation is required by directions issued under subsection 6(2)." It also requires the Deputy Solicitor General to advise the Solicitor General with respect to directions issued under subsection 6(2) "or that should, in the opinion of the Deputy Minister, be issued under that subsection."]

The Review Committee under the CSIS Act is a multiparty statutory oversight body whose members are appointed by the Governor in Council from among the members of the Privy Council who are not members of the Senate or of the House of Commons. Before such appointments are made (on the advice of the Prime Minister), the Prime Minister must consult with the Leader of the Opposition and the leaders of each party having at least twelve members in the House of Commons. While presumably, since the wording of Section 6(2) is permissive rather than mandatory, the Solicitor General can avoid such oversight by giving oral rather than written directions to the Director of CSIS, it is noteworthy that no such requirement for external oversight of the Solicitor General's exercise of direction has been added to Section 5 of the RCMP Act.

I have recounted the Nicholson incident in some detail because it illustrates so well many of the key issues that arise in considering the relationship between the federal government and the RCMP, and also indicates that these issues have been around for a long time. As I shall show, they remain largely unresolved to this day.

The Nicholson Affair, as it has come to be known, reveals two quite different views about what the "proper" relationship between the police and the government of the day should be. On the one hand, Nicholson's view was that policing is an expert field, that policing decisions are properly left to the experts (the police), and that policing decisions can (and should) be regarded as quite separate and distinct from "issues back of" any dispute that gives rise to the need for such decisions, namely, political considerations. This view of policing leads him more or less inevitably to the conclusion that any involvement of elected politicians in the making of policing decisions is inherently improper, even when a contract for the provision of policing services specifically provides for such involvement.

Nicholson's letter of resignation can thus be viewed as a classic expression of the notion of "police independence" as an overriding (that is, overriding even express contractual or statutory provisions that appear to be inconsistent with it) principle governing the relationship between the police and the government. This concept of police independence has been described in various ways, and with varying expansiveness, in common law jurisdictions such as Canada, Britain, and Australia over the years. All the descriptions of it, however, express a similar idea: that there are certain kinds of policing decisions with respect to which it is improper for elected political authorities (such as government ministers or other police governing authorities) to give, or for police to accept from them, any direction or control, or even significant influence or input. Some versions of the "police independence doctrine" go even further than this to assert that, besides being immune from political (governmental) direction on these matters, the police are also not accountable to or through such elected political authorities for such decisions.

Denning View (1968)

One of the most often quoted modern statements of the principle of police independence is that of Lord Denning in the English case of *R. v. Metropolitan Police Commissioner, Ex parte Blackburn* (1968) (hereafter the "Denning view"):

I have no hesitation, however, in holding that, like every constable in the land, [the Commissioner of the London Metropolitan Police] should be, and is, independent of the executive. He is not subject to the orders of the Secretary of State, save that under the Police Act 1964 the Secretary of State can call on him to give a report, or to retire in the interests of efficiency. I hold it to be the duty of the Commissioner of Police, as it is of every chief constable, to enforce the law of the land. He must take steps so to post his men that crimes may be detected; and that honest citizens may go about their affairs in peace. He must decide whether or not suspected persons are to be prosecuted; and, if need be, bring the prosecution or see that it is brought; but in all these things he is not the servant of anyone, save of the law itself. No Minister of the Crown can tell him that he must, or must not, keep observation on this place or that; or that he must, or must not, prosecute this man or that one. Nor can any police authority tell him so. The responsibility for law enforcement lies on him. He is answerable to the law and to the law alone.

Lord Denning's observations were made with reference to the status of chief constables in England rather than police chiefs in Canada, and to this day the RCMP Act (as well as the contractual provision involved in the Nicholson Affair) contains provisions that are hard to reconcile with Denning's statement. Nevertheless, the RCMP, as I shall show, has consistently argued that this principle of police independence governs the relationship between the Commissioner of the RCMP and the federal government of the day, including the minister (currently the Solicitor General) charged with statutory responsibility for the RCMP.

By contrast, the view expressed by Justice Minister Fulton in his reply to the Commissioner's letter of resignation and in his subsequent statement to the House of Commons invoked a literal reading of the contractual provision, and apparently rejected any idea that the authority it conferred on the Attorney General of Canada must somehow be "read down" in light of some generally applicable principle of police independence. The implications of the term "under the Minister," which appeared in Section 10 of the RCMP Act at the time, and of the wording of Section 16, indicating that the RCMP Commissioner was "subject to the control, orders and authority of such person or persons as are for that purpose named by the Governor in Council," were not discussed in the context of the Nicholson resignation (presumably because it was accepted that the terms of the contract were clear enough on this issue). It is therefore not possible to know whether the government similarly felt that the Minister was unconstrained by any general notion of police independence in his routine supervision of the RCMP, other than pursuant to the contractual provision involved in the Nicholson Affair. It is noteworthy, however, that no member of Parliament from any political party who spoke in the debate over Commissioner Nicholson's resignation challenged the Minister of Justice's interpretation of his authority in the case, or suggested that it might not be correct, or expressed any support for Commissioner Nicholson's view of the matter. Nor was there any debate about this issue when the relevant provision of the new RCMP Act (Section 5) was discussed in Parliament three months later.

The Nicholson Affair seems to suggest that at the time there was broad political support for (or at least no significant challenge to) the Minister of Justice's assertion of his authority to direct and control a critical decision concerning operational deployment of members of the RCMP. In the Minister's statement to Parliament, however, the role of the government more generally in such a decision was, perhaps deliberately, left unclear. The Minister made it clear that he had consulted his "colleagues" on the matter, and that as a result of these consultations, "it was decided" that RCMP reinforcements should not be sent to Newfoundland at that time. There was no indication in his statement whether this decision was, or was thought to be, a collective decision (for example, by the cabinet) or an "independent" personal decision by the Minister (in his capacity as Attorney General of Canada). The Minister did state that "it is also clear that the ultimate responsibility for the decision rests on the Attorney General of Canada," and that, after weighing all the relevant considerations, "I have decided accordingly." Some notion that it is not appropriate for other members of the government, including the Prime Minister, to either collectively or individually attempt to direct or unduly influence such a decision could conceivably be inferred from these statements. On the other hand, the Minister also prefaced his explanation with the words "I do not accept, *and the government of Canada cannot accept,* that an issue of this importance ... can be decided on the basis of a mere mathematical calculation as to whether men are physically available" (emphasis added). From this, it might be inferred that the Minister thought this an issue that was properly determined by the government as a whole, rather than "independently" by the Minister himself.

Contemporaneous records indicate that in fact the situation that precipitated Nicholson's resignation was discussed at some length at no fewer than five well-attended cabinet meetings, for two of which it was the only item on the agenda. The minutes of these meetings held on 11, 12, 13, 14, and 16 of March 1959 are revealing, and provide a perspective on the government's role in the affair that is different from that implied by the Minister of Justice's statement to Parliament. They make it clear not only that the decision to refuse the request for RCMP reinforcements was a collective decision of the cabinet but also that the decision was taken against the advice of the Minister of Justice, who had urged the cabinet to accede to the request. In the end, Prime Minister John Diefenbaker's strong opposition to this course won the day.

What Constitutes "Law Enforcement"?

Among those who espouse the various versions of the concept of police independence just discussed, there seems to be agreement that it applies only to police "law enforcement decisions" and not to other police decisions. This apparent consensus is deceptive, however, because there is little agreement on which kinds of police decisions are "law enforcement decisions" and which are not. Note that Lord Denning's statement envisages that law enforcement decisions include general policy as well as more operational decisions in individual cases, and general decisions about the deployment of police personnel. Others (such as the English Royal Commission on the Police in its 1962 report) have argued that the doctrine of police independence applies only to certain kinds of "quasi-judicial" decisions (such as whom to arrest or search, and whom to charge) in particular "individual cases," and does not apply to broader questions with respect to law enforcement "policy" (such as what weapons the police should be allowed to carry); with respect to the latter, the government of the day has a right to exert its influence. Commissioner Nicholson clearly felt that the decision whether to send reinforcements was a "law enforcement decision," but, as we shall see, one of his successors chose to characterize it differently.

In applying the concept of police independence to the situation at the 1997 APEC summit, we are faced with the question of whether what the RCMP claimed to be doing there could or should be considered law enforcement or some other police function. To put it another way, are police activities to secure the protection of international leaders and their entourages (assuming, for the sake of argument, that what the RCMP did at the summit could legitimately be characterized in this way) "law enforcement" activities, with respect to which the police should be independent of political direction, control, or undue influence? Or should such activities be considered merely as "security" activities, with respect to which the police may legitimately receive direction from the government to ensure the fulfillment of its obligations towards "internationally protected persons"?

Unfortunately, as I shall show, these questions have rarely even been publicly posed in Canada during the last forty years, let alone clearly and satisfactorily answered.

The Key Questions

The confusion about the relationship between the RCMP and the federal government that surrounded and survived the Nicholson Affair may be summarized by the following questions:

1   What right, if any, does the minister responsible for the RCMP (currently the Solicitor General of Canada) have to issue directions or otherwise give instructions to the Force (through the Commissioner) with respect to policing decisions? What limitations are there on any such right?

2   Is it ever proper for other members of the government, including the Prime Minister and his office, to be directly involved in policing decisions involving the RCMP? If so, under what circumstances is such involvement acceptable, and what form can it take (for example, a decision by cabinet, mere "consultations," and so on)?

3   What right, if any, does the minister responsible for the RCMP have to be kept informed (by the Commissioner or other members of the Force) about policing decisions or activities involving the Force? What limitations are there on any such right?

4   What right, if any, do other members of the government, including the Prime Minister and his office, have to be kept informed (by the Commissioner or other members of the Force) about policing decisions or activities involving the Force? What limitations are there on any such right?

Note that (1) and (2) concern the authority of the government to give directions to the RCMP, while (3) and (4) address the issue of the accountability of the Force to the government. Much of the literature on police accountability, as well as many judicial pronouncements on the subject (including that of Lord Denning, quoted above), seems to imply that issues of control and accountability are inextricably linked in this context. That is, if the government does not have authority to direct the police with respect to certain decisions, the police are not accountable to the government with respect to such decisions. This view of political control and accountability of police allows for only two possibilities – either full control and full accountability or no control and no accountability.

Some commentators (including this author) have argued, however, that issues of political control and accountability of police need not be viewed in such stark terms, and that in certain circumstances there may be good reasons to forego political control of the police while still insisting on their full political accountability through the government. This view may be represented graphically as follows:

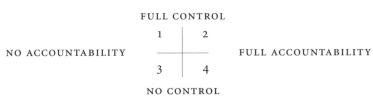

The Denning view of police independence would place police "law enforcement" decisions in quadrant 3 on the diagram – that is, the police not only enjoy complete independence from any political control (directions from government) with respect to such decisions but are also not politically accountable (through the government of the day) for such decisions; they are "answerable to the law and to the law alone" for them. This is the view that successive RCMP Commissioners have espoused since the Nicholson Affair, although not always with great consistency. As noted earlier, however, it is not easily reconciled with the express language of Section 5 of the RCMP Act.

The Minister of Justice at the time of the Nicholson Affair clearly felt that the decision in that case properly fell within quadrant 2 on the diagram – that is, the Attorney General had the authority to give directions to the Commissioner with respect to the decision, and the Commissioner was fully accountable to him for any action the Force took in the matter. As noted earlier also, however, it is not clear whether the government believed this to be a general description of the relationship between the government and the RCMP, or only one dictated by the particular language of the policing contract with respect to this particular kind of policing decision (a request by a provincial Attorney General for RCMP reinforcements).

An alternative to these two positions on police independence may be found in quadrant 4 on the diagram. According to this view, certain policing decisions ("law enforcement" decisions in "particular cases") may be considered unsuitable for political control (directions by government) but still require full political accountability (the government is entitled to be kept fully informed about them). Even within this view of police independence, however, there are two possible variations of police accountability: it may be required before the fact (the government is entitled to be informed before decisions are made or acted upon) or only after the fact (ex post facto accountability). Some commentators have argued that ex post facto accountability is preferable with respect to such decisions, as it reduces the risk that accountability will be used by government as a cover for "improper" political direction or influence.

Several incidents in which the relationship between the federal government and the RCMP has come into question since the Nicholson Affair in 1959 illustrate the difficulties of trying to resolve these issues of police independence, and make it clear that these issues remain largely unresolved to this day.

The FLQ Crisis (1970)

The role of the government in directing the RCMP was starkly raised by the FLQ crisis in 1970. It will be recalled that the Trudeau government, after full cabinet consultation, introduced emergency regulations pursuant to the War Measures Act to respond to what it characterized as an "apprehended insurrection" in Quebec following the kidnapping of a Quebec cabinet minister and a British trade representative by the FLQ (Front de Libération du Québec). These regulations conferred extraordinary powers on the police and effectively suspended many important civil liberties. Concern was expressed that the regulations were so broadly worded that the powers it conferred on "peace officers" across the country might be used by police officers outside Quebec for political purposes unrelated to resolution of the crisis in Quebec. Furthermore, since the army had been ordered into Montreal and was effectively coordinating its operations with the police there, questions were raised as to whether the police were in fact acting under political direction in exercising their powers of arrest, search, and detention under the regulations. The federal government went to considerable lengths to reassure parliamentarians that it was not attempting to direct the RCMP or any other police force in their exercise of these powers. In the legislatures of Ontario and British Columbia, however, provincial Attorneys General were pressured by opposition leaders to issue directives to police forces concerning appropriate and inappropriate use of these powers.

We shall perhaps never know for sure to what extent, if at all, political direction of policing decisions occurred during the FLQ crisis. What is clear, however, is that the crisis caused, and left substantially unresolved, considerable public ambivalence about the appropriateness and desirability of such a practice.

Anti-Separatist Policing (Early 1970s)

Events following the crisis of 1970 raised further questions about the relationship between the RCMP and the federal government. To try to ensure that the government was not caught unawares by such a crisis in the future, the federal cabinet issued a clarified mandate for the Security Service, which at that time was part of the RCMP. When it became publicly known that, ostensibly pursuant to this new mandate, RCMP officers had engaged in patently illegal activities in their efforts to gain intelligence about, and thwart the efforts of, separatists in Quebec, there were accusations that the federal government knew about, possibly even "authorized," and certainly did nothing to prevent these illegal police operations. These serious accusations were eventually the subject of a royal commission of inquiry (the McDonald Inquiry), which submitted its report in 1981.

During the course of the inquiry, Prime Minister Trudeau took the position that the government had had no knowledge of these illegal activities by the RCMP. He was publicly asked by a journalist "just how ignorant does a minister have to be before, at the very least, some responsibility is applied to the advisers who seem to have kept him ignorant?" His response was characteristically blunt:

> I have attempted to make it quite clear that the policy of this government and, I believe, the previous governments in this country, has been that they – indeed, the politicians who happen to form the government – should be kept in ignorance of the day-to-day operations of the police force and even of the security force. I repeat that it is not a view that is held by all democracies, but it is our view, and it is one we stand by. Therefore, in this particular case, it is not a matter of pleading ignorance as an excuse. It is a matter of stating, as a principle, that the particular minister of the day should not have a right to know what the police are constantly doing in their investigative practices, in what they are looking at and what they are looking for, and in the way in which they are doing it ... That is our position. It is not one of pleading ignorance to defend the government. It is one of keeping the government's nose out

of the operations of the police force, at whatever level of government.

On the criminal law side, the protections we have against abuse are not with the government, they are with the courts.

The similarity between this statement of principle and the Denning view of police independence is readily apparent. According to this view, "investigative practices" of the police fall squarely within quadrant 2 of the diagram above; that is, government ministers have no right to direct the police with respect to such practices, and the police are not politically accountable to ministers for them.

Senior officers of the RCMP claimed, however, that the government not only knew about the activities of the RCMP to thwart separatists in the early 1970s but specifically authorized them. In 1992 some evidence consistent with this claim came to light when minutes of a cabinet meeting on 19 December 1969 (a year before the FLQ crisis) were made public for the first time. The meeting had been called to discuss federal government strategy against separatism in Quebec. At the meeting Prime Minister Trudeau argued the need for a "long-term counter-action" plan against separatists, and for the establishment of a "central body" so that the cabinet "would have an effective tool to sift information and to coordinate all policies towards Quebec." He is quoted in the minutes as having said that "no modern state would allow a threat of this magnitude to its unity and integrity without mounting a consistent and coordinated defence against it." To this end, he argued that "other sources" of information (specifically, military intelligence) beyond those of the RCMP would have to be developed.

The Minister of External Affairs at the time later stated that the government "felt that the RCMP was directing too much of its attention on Communists to the detriment of the real threat to Canada from separatists." This is confirmed by the minutes of the meeting, which indicate that Trudeau compared the need for better intelligence against separatism with the earlier need for intelligence against the "menace to democratic structures" earlier posed by Communism.

The Commissioner of the RCMP and an Assistant Commissioner were both present at this 1969 cabinet meeting. The Commissioner is quoted in the minutes as having told the meeting that he would require "clear direction" from the government before embarking on the same investigative activities against separatists as he now conducted against Communists, "because of the extreme sensitivity of the problem." As for taking further action to gather information against separatists by clandestine means, the

Commissioner apparently told the meeting that this was certainly possible but that he would feel "obliged to point out the risks involved."

The McDonald Inquiry Report (1981)

These cabinet minutes were not made public during the hearings of the McDonald Commission at the end of the 1970s, and it is not clear whether the commission actually saw them. In its 1981 report, however, it took great exception to the view of the relationship between the federal government and the RCMP that Trudeau had expressed to the journalists four years earlier. The commission wrote:

> We take it to be axiomatic that in a democratic state the police must never be allowed to become a law unto themselves. Just as our form of Constitution dictates that the armed forces must be subject to civilian control, so too must police forces operate in obedience to governments responsible to legislative bodies composed of elected representatives. This important doctrine in our system of democratic government has often been overshadowed by the parallel concept that the best interests of the state are served by keeping at bay any attempts to interfere with the making of police decisions relating to investigation and prosecution in individual cases.
>
> The concept of independence for peace officers in executing their duties has been elevated to a position of paramountcy in defining the role and functions of the RCMP, thus setting the norm for all relationships between the government and the Force. We believe, on the contrary, that the peace officer duties of the RCMP should qualify, but not dictate, the essential nature of those relationships. The government must fulfill its democratic mandate by ensuring that in the final analysis it is the government that is in control of the police, and accountable for it. There is no inconsistency in asserting simultaneously that every member of the government, and above all the Minister responsible for the RCMP, has an essential duty not normally to become involved in the decisions to be made by members of the Force, including the Commissioner himself, with respect to investigation, arrest and prosecution in individual cases.

This view of police independence indicates that while the relationship between the government and the police normally lies within quadrant 2 of our diagram (full political control and accountability), an exception is made with respect to police decisions involved in "investigation, arrest and prosecution in individual cases," which are to be regarded as falling within quadrant 3 (no political control but full political accountability). The commission stated this position on police independence as follows:

> We believe that those functions of the RCMP which we have described as "quasi judicial" should not be subject to the direction of the Minister. To be more explicit, in any particular case, the Minister should have no right of direction with respect to the exercise by the RCMP of the powers of investigation, arrest and prosecution. *To that extent, and to that extent only, should the English doctrine expounded in* Ex Parte Blackburn *be made applicable to the RCMP.* Even though the Minister should have no power of direction in particular cases in relation to the exercise by the RCMP of the "quasi judicial" functions, *the Minister should have the right to be, and should insist on being, informed of any operational matter, even one involving an individual case, if it raises an important question of public policy. In such cases he may give guidance to the Commissioner and express to the Commissioner the government's view of the matter, but he should have no power to give direction to the Commissioner.* [emphasis added]

Referring to the minister's general authority to give directions to the Commissioner of the RCMP (subject to the exception just noted), the commission added "one final point" to this statement of principles:

> On no account should the Minister or his deputy give direction based on partisan or personal considerations. If the Deputy Solicitor General does so, the Commissioner should take the matter up with the Minister and if necessary the Prime Minister. If the Minister gives such an improper direction the Commissioner should speak to the Prime Minister directly.

The commission recommended that the RCMP Act be amended to reflect these general principles, but its recommendations have never been implemented by the federal government.

The Keable Inquiry and the Bisaillon Case (1981)
While the McDonald Commission was holding its inquiry, a parallel inquiry (the Keable Inquiry) was set up by the Parti Québécois government of Quebec to examine the role of various police forces during the FLQ crisis. During the course of its hearings, the inquiry's commissioner sought to compel three Montreal detectives to disclose the identity of

informants they had worked with during the crisis. The detectives demurred, arguing, among other things, that compelling them to disclose this information would constitute a violation by a government agency (the inquiry) of their independence as peace officers. When they resisted the inquiry's order in court, the Quebec courts had to decide whether this claim had any validity.

In a decision unique in Canadian jurisprudence, the Quebec Court of Appeal held in *Bisaillon* v. *Keable and Attorney General of Quebec* (1980) that, whatever relevance it might have to the constitutional position of the police in England, the doctrine of "police independence" enunciated in such English cases as the Blackburn case (that is, the Denning view) did not apply to the police in the province of Quebec, whose relationship to the government of Quebec was determined exclusively by the terms of the Quebec Police Act. The court's decision in this case was subsequently overturned on appeal to the Supreme Court of Canada, but on other grounds. The Supreme Court expressed no opinion on the Quebec Court of Appeal's view regarding the applicability of the doctrine of police independence to police in Quebec.

The Olson Case (1982)

Shortly after the McDonald Commission released its report, the question of the proper relationship between the RCMP and government was raised again in connection with the RCMP's investigation of the Clifford Olson case.

Several children had disappeared in British Columbia, and the RCMP (who police much of British Columbia under contract to the provincial government) eventually arrested and charged Clifford Olson with several counts of murder. During the initial court proceedings, it was disclosed that the RCMP had agreed to pay substantial sums of money to Olson's wife in return for Olson leading them to the buried bodies of his victims. The revelation of this "deal with the devil" (as one newspaper characterized it) caused considerable public consternation, and journalists began asking who had authorized it. They first approached the Attorney General of British Columbia, whose initial response was to remind them that the RCMP was a federal police force and that the federal Solicitor General was the minister responsible for the Force under the RCMP Act. When approached, however, the federal Solicitor General reminded the journalists that in investigating the Olson case the Force was acting, under contract, in its capacity as the provincial police force, and that in this capacity it was responsible to the provincial Attorney General. The Attorney

General of British Columbia then reminded the journalists that the RCMP were independent of government interference or control in fulfilling their law enforcement duties, and advised them to address their questions to the Commissioner of the RCMP in Ottawa. This they did, only to be told that since the matter was still before the courts, the Commissioner could not comment on the case. As a result, questions about who authorized or knew about the payments to Olson's wife were never publicly answered.

While these evasions of accountability in the Olson case arose out of the particularly complex situation of the RCMP when acting as a provincial police force under contract, the case illustrates nicely the way in which the notion of police independence can be used to avoid effective political accountability for police decision making.

The Hatfield Case (1985)

It was not long before the issue of the RCMP's independence and accountability arose again, this time in connection with an investigation of the Progressive Conservative Premier of New Brunswick, Richard Hatfield, in 1985. Acting on a tip, the RCMP found a small quantity of marijuana in the Premier's luggage at the Fredericton airport. While the case was still under investigation by the Force, Hatfield had a meeting with the Progressive Conservative Solicitor General of Canada, Elmer MacKay, in an Ottawa hotel, at which the case was apparently discussed. When the fact of this meeting became public, the federal Liberal opposition argued that the meeting had constituted an improper "interference" by the Solicitor General, for partisan purposes, with a police investigation. The Solicitor General countered that neither the purpose nor the result of the meeting had involved any improper interference with the RCMP's investigation, and that the meeting had been held purely to keep the Solicitor General informed about a sensitive criminal investigation about which there was considerable public interest (that is, the meeting was purely for purposes of accountability, not control). Note that the Solicitor General's position closely mirrored the recommendation of the McDonald Commission on this subject (quoted earlier).

The matter was the subject of further discussion at a meeting of the House of Commons Justice and Legal Affairs Committee. Liberal MP Robert Kaplan, himself a former Solicitor General, argued that while under normal circumstances it would be improper for a Solicitor General to give any directions to the RCMP regarding an individual case, "there are circumstances in which it would be right for the Solicitor-General to give an order on these matters." He argued that in this respect Section 5 of the RCMP Act, specifying that the Commissioner of the RCMP has the control and management of the Force "under the direction of the Minister," "is to be taken literally." He referred to an earlier statement by the Commissioner: "In the end, we have our independent right to conduct investigations based on reasonable grounds, and no Minister can order us not to." Kaplan commented that "if that is an accurate statement of the position, then we live in a police state. We live in a state where the police can defy a lawful order from the civilian authority."

The Commissioner of the RCMP, R.H. Simmonds, was present when Kaplan made these remarks, but did not have an opportunity to respond to them. Accordingly, he attached an addendum to a written report on the RCMP's investigation of the Hatfield case, in which he responded both to Kaplan's statements and to allegations that the Solicitor General had improperly interfered with the RCMP's investigation. He wrote that "the Solicitor-General had maintained a perfectly proper position vis-à-vis the Force throughout this investigation" and "had not in any way influenced our work or our decision-making," adding that "had he attempted to do so it would not have been accepted as it would have been an unacceptable interference with the principle of police independence and discretion." He had not found the meeting between the Solicitor General and Premier Hatfield, at a time when no charge had been laid, "dangerous or offensive insofar as our work was concerned. It had absolutely no effect on what we were doing." The Minister, he wrote, "described to me the tone of his conversation with the Premier and he, the Minister, gave me no direction."

In response to Kaplan's statements, Commissioner Simmonds wrote:

> I accept that the Minister has broad powers of direction over the Commissioner with respect to the Commissioner's *control* and *management* of the Force, and all matters connected with that *control* and *management*. However, I do not accept that the Minister's powers of direction over-ride the inherent responsibilities, authorities and powers that are given to every member [of the Force] upon appointment to the office of "Peace Officer." [emphasis in original]

In support of this position, the Commissioner cited Lord Denning's judgment in the English Blackburn case (quoted earlier). The Minister, he wrote, "is not the Attorney General responsible for prosecutions, and as, if I am correct, his powers to direct are as described, it is of little importance to me, as Commissioner, with whom he meets."

The Commissioner responded to Kaplan's "police state" comment as follows:

> The Honourable Mr. Kaplan characterizes the position that I believe to be correct as being tantamount to that of a "police state." Again, I respectfully defer. The Office of Constable, with its original powers, seems to have been most deliberately structured as outlined to ensure that the more common definition of a "police state" not be allowed to develop. The more common definition being that a police state emerges when a Government uses its police agencies as instruments of repression against the citizens of the state. It is against that very concern that the police are given a high degree of independence. Nor is it a dangerous degree because, after all, there are many ways that a capricious Commissioner can be called to account, or an errant Constable disciplined. The Commissioner is appointed "at pleasure." His estimates can be constrained, and the actions of every Peace Officer come under the eyes of the Courts.
>
> The Honourable Mr. Kaplan further takes the position that the Commissioner has no choice but to accept direction on all matters, including who he may or may not investigate or charge, and if he disagrees with the direction his option is to resign. I do not necessarily agree. The Commissioner is not appointed by the Minister, but rather by the Governor-in-Council under the Great Seal of Canada. If a Minister tried to limit the Commissioner's discretion under his inherent powers as a Peace Officer, as opposed to his responsibilities for the management and control of the Force, I believe he could just ignore such direction and let the Minister take his case to the Governor-in-Council to seek the Commissioner's dismissal. The result would be interesting to see.

The Nicholson Affair Reinterpreted

Finally, Commissioner Simmonds expressed his interpretation of the Nicholson Affair:

> The case of Commissioner Nicholson ... is not parallel. As I understand that situation the Minister of the day refused to support the Commissioner on *an administrative matter* that required the Minister's consent, that being to transfer personnel between Provinces to deal with an emergent situation. When the Minister refused to give his consent, thus severely challenging the Commissioner's professional judgment

and his leadership of the Force in the face of a crisis, the Commissioner did what most honourable men would do. He tendered his resignation. *The distinction being, of course, that the Minister did not challenge the Commissioner's authority as a Peace Officer, but rather his judgement and leadership.* [emphasis added]

Commissioner Simmonds's view that the decision in the Nicholson Affair involved an administrative matter is in striking contrast to Commissioner Nicholson's own view (quoted earlier from his letter of resignation) that it was a "matter of law enforcement." The two characterizations show how difficult it is, even among the most senior and experienced police officers, to agree on the precise and practical limits of the notion of police independence. The Hatfield case also illustrates that federal Solicitors General have not always been able to agree on this either.

The Small Case (1989)

In 1989, television journalist Douglas Small obtained a copy of the federal government's budget document the day before the Minister of Finance was to deliver his budget speech. On national television, he disclosed details of the budget proposals before they were announced to Parliament. Understandably upset, the federal government "requested" the RCMP to investigate how the document came into Mr. Small's possession. Prime Minister Brian Mulroney told parliamentary journalists that the government was determined to find out who was responsible for this "crime."

After a lengthy investigation, the RCMP charged Mr. Small with theft. At the trial, Mr. Small's attorney moved to have the prosecution stayed as an abuse of process on the grounds, among others, that the criminal charge against his client had been politically motivated. An RCMP investigator who had originally been assigned to the case testified that the investigators had concluded that charges against Mr. Small had not been warranted but that senior officers in the Force had overruled this decision, removed the investigating officer from the case, and given it to another investigator who was willing to lay criminal charges against Small.

The investigator testified that he was convinced that this decision by the Force's senior officers had resulted from improper political pressure exerted on them by the government. He thought it had been made "to please elected officials" – a conclusion denied by the RCMP Commissioner. The Solicitor General's political chief of staff, however, testified that between the time the RCMP began their investigation of the case and the time charges were laid (a period of thirty-four days) he had talked to the Deputy Commissioner of the RCMP about the case "between 12 and 15 times." Insisting that no instructions had been given, he said, "Prefacing our remarks saying we did not want to interfere in any way in the investigation, [we said] we just wanted a status report" – a characterization of these interactions that seems to reflect the recommendations of the McDonald Commission on this subject (quoted earlier).

The motion to have the case stayed as an abuse of process was unsuccessful. The judge ruled that he had not heard any clear evidence to support the claim that the charge had been laid as a result of any improper political interference or pressure. The case was dismissed on other grounds, however, and the investigator's allegations were not looked into further. This left largely unresolved the issues raised by the Small case regarding the appropriate relationship between the government and the RCMP. The testimony of the Solicitor General's chief of staff suggests, however, that the government thought it quite proper that the RCMP should be directly accountable to the Solicitor General during the course of such an investigation, provided no undue political influence or pressure is brought to bear on the police. The case also illustrates how the exercise of political authority to seek accountability can be interpreted by police as involving at least an implicit exercise of improper political influence or pressure, even if this was not actually intended.

Finally, the case raised the issue of what influence the Attorney General of Canada and lawyers in the Department of Justice might properly exert in "advising" the RCMP as to what charges would be appropriate in a particular case. There was evidence that lawyers in the Justice Department had provided the RCMP with such advice (and that it had been sought by the RCMP), but not that the Attorney General had been personally briefed about the case or otherwise involved in decisions about it. The fact that the case, although investigated by the RCMP because it involved federal government "property," was prosecuted by an Ontario provincial prosecutor and not by federal prosecutors further complicated this issue, which was also left unresolved after the case was dismissed. A somewhat similar issue would arise a few years later, in the "Airbus Affair" (discussed below).

The Marshall Inquiry Report (1989)

The royal commission of inquiry established in Nova Scotia to investigate the prosecution of Donald Marshall Jr. also addressed the question of the proper relationship between the RCMP and governments with respect to decisions to investigate and lay charges. The inquiry heard evidence suggesting a double standard in Nova Scotia, where the Attorney General and some of his officials had intervened to influence the RCMP's decisions on whether to lay charges against two members of the Nova Scotia cabinet they had been investigating, while at the same time refusing to intervene to protect Marshall from abuses of police and prosecutorial authority.

The commission concluded that the interventions of the Attorney General's officials in the cases of the two politicians had constituted improper interference with the "common law position of independence" of the RCMP with respect to decisions to investigate and lay charges in criminal cases. Its report referred to the "independent right [of the police] to commence an investigation and lay a charge," and stated that

> if the criminal justice system is to function fairly, the police must carry out their responsibilities without being influenced by extraneous considerations. Inherent in the principle of police independence is the right of the police to determine whether to commence an investigation. While the responsible ministry can set general policies with respect to all policing matters, including investigations, no police force should consider that it requires authorization from the Crown before commencing an investigation.

The commission quoted with apparent approval an earlier statement by the Attorney General of Ontario (in *Campbell* v. *Ontario* (*Attorney General*) [1987]) that "Constitutional authority in this country, and the United Kingdom, makes it plain that the decision to investigate alleged offences and to lay charges is the constitutional responsibility of the police" – a claim that, if it was intended to confer exclusive authority on the police, is not easy to reconcile with the provision of the Criminal Code that "anyone" may lay an information in a criminal case.

The Airbus Affair (1993-97)

In 1993, shortly after his appointment as Canada's Minister of Justice and Attorney General, Allan Rock had lunch with a journalist. During the course of the meal, allegations arose that former Prime Minister Brian Mulroney had, while in office, received corrupt payments in return for securing contracts for Airbus planes with Air Canada, the national airline. Rock passed this information on to his colleague, Solicitor General Herb Gray, who in turn passed them on to the RCMP. Both ministers later insisted that they had not given any instructions to the RCMP requiring them to investigate the allegations. Rock also insisted that he had not made any subsequent inquiries about the allegations or about the RCMP's reaction to the information.

The RCMP investigated the allegations but concluded that there was no evidence to support them, closed the file, and informed the Justice Department of this. About a year later, however, similar allegations were aired on a nationally televised program, as a result of which the RCMP apparently reopened its investigation. Again, both the Justice Minister and the Solicitor General claimed that this decision was made independently by RCMP investigators without any direction or influence from the government. Indeed, the Justice Minister claimed that he was not even aware that the investigation had been reopened.

In June 1995, an RCMP investigator informed an official in the Justice Department that the Force wanted a letter sent to authorities in Switzerland requesting their cooperation in an investigation of certain bank accounts there in connection with the Airbus investigation. Established procedures required that such a letter be sent by Justice Department officials rather than by the RCMP. A letter was duly drafted by the RCMP, reviewed by an official in the Justice Department, and sent to the Swiss authorities. It contained a statement to the effect that the former Prime Minister had engaged in criminal activities.

Not long afterwards, the existence of the letter and its contents were leaked and came to Mulroney's attention. Mulroney initiated defamation proceedings against the Justice Minister, the departmental official who had sent the letter, the RCMP Commissioner, and the RCMP investigator involved in the case. Both the Justice Minister and the RCMP Commissioner took the position that they could not be held liable for defamation because neither had even known about the investigation or the letter at the material time. In the case of the Justice Minister, this was confirmed by the departmental official who had sent the letter. She indicated that she had told her immediate supervisor that in her opinion neither the Justice Minister nor the Deputy Minister of Justice should be informed of the existence of the investigation or the letter of request. She stated that the decision not to involve the Justice Minister was made "to protect him against possible allegations of political interference in a police investigation" and that this "properly recognized the necessary separation of the police and policing function on the one hand and the political aspect on the other."

In response to these revelations, John Crosbie, who had served as

Minister of Justice under Mulroney, publicly called upon the Justice Minister and the Solicitor General to "accept responsibility for the careless, damaging and wantonly negligent actions and allegations of the RCMP" and resign. Crosbie argued that the Justice Minister's pleas of ignorance about the investigation and the letter indicated that "his department is not under his control and he seeks not to be held responsible for what his own officials have done despite the rules and conventions of cabinet government and ministerial responsibility." He argued that Justice Department officials had a duty to inform the Justice Minister of such serious allegations against a former Prime Minister, and that the Justice Minister should have "satisfied himself that there was sound and reasonable cause to consider that a criminal offence or offences had been committed and that the former prime minister was involved," since these allegations, if true, would become "the greatest scandal of the 20th century involving a Canadian Prime Minister."

This position is reminiscent of the McDonald Commission's advice that a Solicitor General "should have the right to be, and should insist on being, informed of any operational matter, even one involving an individual case, if it raises an important question of public policy." One may question, however, whether the Airbus letter did raise any important matter of public *policy*, as opposed to one merely of great public interest. In this connection, it is interesting to note the opinion of the Marshall Inquiry commission that "as a matter of principle, we do not believe it is appropriate for the Attorney General to become involved in day-to-day decisions affecting individual cases, *but we recognize that there will be exceptional circumstances in cases that raise public interest issues with significant implications for the public at large*" (emphasis added). The Airbus case might more easily fit this description.

The Justice Minister, however, defended the practice of insulating ministers from the conduct of criminal investigations involving other politicians, saying that if ministers were informed, "they would be blamed, regardless of how cases turned out." He was publicly supported in this view by a former Assistant Deputy Attorney General of Ontario and a prominent criminal defence lawyer, the latter arguing that "if any justice minister attempted to hinder or abort a police investigation based on his or her perceptions of the weight of the police evidence, that minister would be acting improperly."

The former Prime Minister's defamation suit was eventually settled out of court and the questions that had been raised about the proper relationship between the federal government and its police force were once again left essentially unresolved. The case was complicated by the fact that the Minister of Justice is not the federal minister responsible for the RCMP, and the argument that he ought to have been involved in some way in decision making in the Airbus case was based on his responsibility for the acts of officials in his department rather than for those of the RCMP. The Airbus Affair illustrates once again the lack of consensus, even among those with experience, about the meaning and scope of police independence and its practical implications for the relationships that should exist between the police and elected governments.

The Shirose Case (1999)

The issue of the relationship between police and governments has most recently been addressed tangentially by the Supreme Court of Canada in *R. v. Shirose* (1999). The case led to a ruling on the legality of a "reverse sting" operation undertaken by the RCMP in the enforcement of the drug laws. The RCMP officers involved were concerned that such an operation might not be legal, and so consulted extensively with senior members of the Force and sought the advice of a lawyer at the Department of Justice. When the accused who had been arrested and charged as a result of the operation challenged its legality, the officers took the position that they had relied on the advice of the Justice Department lawyer, but refused to disclose the content of the advice, claiming that it was protected by solicitor-client privilege.

In the course of its lengthy unanimous judgment, the Supreme Court discussed the legal principles governing the relationship between police and governments. The Court observed that:

> Under the authority of [the RCMP] Act ... RCMP officers perform a myriad of functions apart from the investigation of crimes. These include, by way of examples, purely ceremonial duties, the protection of Canadian dignitaries and foreign diplomats and activities associated with crime prevention. Some of these functions bring the RCMP into a closer relationship to the Crown than others.

Citing the Department of the Solicitor General Act and Section 5 of the RCMP Act, the Court went on to observe that:

> It is therefore possible that in one or other of its roles the RCMP could be acting in an agency relationship with the Crown. In this appeal, however, we are concerned only with the status of an RCMP officer in the course of a criminal investigation, and in that regard the police are independent of the control of the executive government.

At another point in the judgment, however, the Court referred to "the relationship between the police and the executive government when the police are engaged in law enforcement," and cited with approval the passage from Lord Denning's judgment in the Blackburn case (quoted earlier) in support of its statement that "while engaged in a criminal investigation ... the Commissioner [of the RCMP] is not subject to political direction." While the Court thus made it clear that Section 5 of the RCMP Act must be read and interpreted in light of this doctrine of police independence, its judgment in *R. v. Shirose* leaves it unclear whether the doctrine applies only to situations in which the police are "engaged in a criminal investigation" or also to the broader category of situations described by Lord Denning, in which the police are "engaged in law enforcement."

Conclusions: Lessons for the APEC Debate

In this chapter I have traced the relations between the federal government and the RCMP over the last forty years through a series of situations in which the relationship was in some way called into question. The relationship has been called into question most recently by the circumstances surrounding the policing of the APEC summit meeting by the RCMP in November 1997. Evidence of significant involvement by staff from the Prime Minister's Office has led to allegations of improper political interference in decision making about the policing of this event.

One would think that forty years of experience involving several disparate situations would have provided a reasonable amount of clarity and consensus about the principles that ought to govern relations between the federal government and its police force. The review undertaken in this chapter indicates that this is not the case, however. Although it is clear that some notion of police independence is thought to be appropriate, there appears to have been very little clarity or consensus among politicians, senior RCMP officers, jurists (including the Supreme Court of Canada), commissions of inquiry, academics, or other commentators either about exactly what "police independence" comprises or about what its practical implications should be for RCMP-government relations. Nor has there been any agreement about what the RCMP Act tells us about the extent and nature of appropriate government supervision of the Force, either by the minister responsible for it (the Solicitor General) or by the federal government more generally.

Interpretations of the scope of police independence range from very expansive ones (such as the Denning view) – which embrace law enforcement policy and operations as well as more general decisions relating to the deployment of police personnel and general policing strategies, and which extend to political accountability as well as to political direction and control – to much narrower ones (such as the McDonald Commission's view), which would limit the concept's application to "quasi-judicial" police decisions relating to investigation and charging in individual cases, and which would restrict political direction and control of the police, but not their political accountability, with respect to such decisions. Furthermore, there is no clear consensus as to exactly what policing activities are embraced by the term "law enforcement."

Some have argued that any political direction or control over the RCMP should be limited to the responsible minister, while others (such as apparently the majority of the federal cabinet in March 1959 and again in December 1969) seem to believe that no such limitation exists in principle.

Nor has there been agreement about what might constitute improper political influence over police decision making. Do repeated requests for information by elected politicians or their political staff members before a decision has been made by the police (as apparently occurred in the Douglas Small case) amount to unacceptable political influence over such decisions? Does a private meeting between a Solicitor General and a person who is under investigation by the police (as in the Hatfield case) constitute unacceptable political interference in police decision making? And does ministerial refusal to have any involvement of any kind with respect to police decision making in a case involving matters of significant public interest constitute an abdication of proper government supervision of the police, as the McDonald Commission and Justice Minister Rock's critics in the Airbus Affair have argued?

Unfortunately, the experience of the last forty years has provided no consensus on the correct answers to any of these questions, or to the key questions that I posed earlier in this chapter (page 96). Any persuasive assessment of the relations between the government and the RCMP during the APEC summit will need to provide some clear answers to such questions, but recent history does not provide them, and even suggests an almost wilful determination to avoid them. Perhaps we should not be surprised by this. Politics has never been a precise science and, as this review suggests, there may be considerable advantages, both to the police and to their political "masters," that things remain ambiguous.

In light of this review, however, the following might help to define proper relations between the RCMP and governments in the future.

1   Consideration should be given to amending the RCMP Act to clarify the political independence and accountability of the Commissioner of the RCMP and members of the Force vis-à-vis the federal government.

2   Ordinarily, the relationship between the federal government and the RCMP should be conducted only through the office of the Solicitor General of Canada (the minister statutorily responsible for the Force), and not through other ministers or officials. If exceptions are to be made, the circumstances in which they would apply should be spelled out publicly. For instance, security arrangements at meetings such as the APEC summit, involving foreign heads of state and other internationally protected persons, might be thought to justify such an exception.

3   The Solicitor General should exercise his or her responsibility for the RCMP only through communications with the Commissioner of the Force, and not through direct communications with other members of the Force. The Solicitor General should also be considered accountable to Parliament for any directions he or she gives to the RCMP.

4   The duties of the Solicitor General, whose office was originally that of a law officer of the Crown, should perhaps be regarded as analogous to those of the Crown's principal law officer, the Attorney General. Specifically, in his or her dealings with the RCMP the Solicitor General should be expected to act independently of direction, control, or undue influence from other members of the government (including the cabinet).

5   The Solicitor General and the Commissioner of the Force should be regarded as having a special responsibility to exercise his or her authority to protect members of the RCMP from inappropriate political or other extraneous interference or influence in the exercise of their authority as peace officers.

6   The political independence of members of the RCMP in the exercise of their authority as peace officers should not be regarded as detracting in any way from their political accountability (through the Commissioner and the Solicitor General) for any such exercise of police authority. Such accountability, however, should be exercised in a manner that will minimize the risk of it being interpreted as a cover for improper political direction, control, or influence. The Solicitor General should be considered accountable to the cabinet, as well as to Parliament, for *all* activities and decisions of the RCMP.

7   The Commissioner of the RCMP should disregard any instruction

from the Solicitor General or any other government official that the Commissioner believes is an unlawful order. The Commissioner should publicly report any such unlawful order to the Solicitor General or, if the order comes from the Solicitor General, to the Prime Minister. The Solicitor General and the Prime Minister should similarly be required to report any such unlawful order to Parliament.

While previous situations, incidents, and recommendations have not sufficiently persuaded legislators to clarify what the relationship between the RCMP and the government of the day ought to be, perhaps the APEC affair, and the public inquiry and debate in its aftermath, will spur legislators to take a closer look.

7

Hand in Glove? Politicians, Policing, and Canadian Political Culture

NELSON WISEMAN

Story Line 1

Here's one story line:

In the early 1980s an expatriate American working as a Canadian professor wrote a book called *Deference to Authority*. In the late 1990s an expatriate Briton also working as a Canadian professor wrote *The Decline of Deference*. Canada and Canadians had apparently changed. The authors' origins help us situate Canadian political discourse and institutions in relation to Britain and the United States. Canada is a hybrid of the two in a North Atlantic triangle. (Similarly, our speech and dictionaries are a combination of British and American usage and spelling.)

British Origins

The origins of English Canada lay in British-American interaction: Loyalists decamped America for untamed western Quebec (now Ontario). Consistent with the tory streak in their fundamentally liberal individualist outlook, the Loyalists opted for relatively authoritarian, hierarchical, traditional, and colonial political institutions. Mother Britain was the model, not the revolutionary and relatively more egalitarian, open, free, and rationalist political institutions of America's rebels. Centrally appointed magistrates served simultaneously as judge, jury, and politician. In Canada it would be monarchy over "mobocracy." Centralized power over checks and balances. Ascription, appointments, and royal prerogative over achievement, elections, and democratic will. Deference to authority, however, implied legitimate authority; the authorities maintained themselves within constitutional bounds. Deference needed to be reciprocated. Allegiance to the regime from those below was contingent on those above taking care of some of their interests too. "The palace is not safe," noted Disraeli, "if the cottage is not happy."

The cultural faces of the American revolutionary and the Canadian (English and French) counterrevolutionary traditions were many. Our larger and more dominant top-down churches (Anglican and Roman Catholic) were privileged, whereas America adopted the doctrine of church-state separation. The American public has always had a predilection for bottom-up fundamentalist congregations, where the individual's link to God – like the link to the presidency through direct election – is not mediated by ordained governors, magistrates, and bishops. Canada, unlike America, would have a Mild West rather than a Wild one: no shoot-outs at high noon, no vigilantes, no frontier justice, and no citizens' posses. Canada drew on the British constabulary model in creating the Mounties. They were dispatched to pacify and colonize the West. (The cabinet had a Minister of Colonization a century ago.) The Mounties ensured the "peace, order, and good government" of a nascent Canadian state whose constitution was explicitly "similar in principle to that of the United Kingdom." The Americans, in contrast, enveloped themselves in an ethos of "life, liberty, and the pursuit of happiness." Where they entrenched property rights and a legislature that could impeach the president, we entrenched Crown lands and prime ministerial supremacy.

The democratic impulse grew irresistibly in British North America. The locus of political authority shifted; the governor's prerogatives receded. By convention, the authority to determine who rules was transferred to the people. In practice this meant granting power to the leader of the largest parliamentary party. The new de facto authority – the Prime Minister and cabinet – after 1848 (a revolutionary year in Europe, an evolutionary one in Canada) appropriated the largely unchecked power of the centralized state. A century and a half later, this remains the first of three pillars of Canada's constitutional infrastructure. In theory, "responsible government" means that the executive is accountable to Parliament; in practice, tight party discipline turns Parliament into a rubber stamp for the executive whenever a party holds the majority of seats.

Federalism

From the Americans, Canadians borrowed their second constitutional pillar: the federal principle, a decidedly un-British idea. The lesson Canadians drew from the Civil War – the backdrop to the Confederation conferences – was that decentralized federalism spelled trouble, mayhem, and secession. Canadian sociology – the irrepressible bicultural cleavage – made federalism the vehicle for accommodating regional differences. The criminal law and appointments to all superior courts were assigned to Ottawa, and the provinces were assigned jurisdiction over the administration of justice. Canada has a federal legislative system, but Canada's judicial system is unitary; it is stacked from top to bottom (except for the lowly provincial courts) by the central government, that is, by prime ministerial appointment. In early Canada, foreign affairs and security rested in British hands, but Ottawa logically inherited these functions as Canada eased its way from colony to nation. The policing function is also unusual in Canada among federations. In eight of the ten provinces, the federal police force – the RCMP – is rented by the provinces from Ottawa to discharge their policing obligations. It is logical that citizens may be confused over policing when officers wearing identical uniforms work for both the federal and provincial governments. Because of RCMP excesses in the 1970s, security and intelligence functions were transferred from it to a civilian Canadian Security Intelligence Service. CSIS was largely stacked with former RCMP officers attired in civilian garb.

Charter Rights and Rights Consciousness

The third pillar of the Canadian constitution is of relatively recent vintage: the Charter of Rights and Freedoms. As the twentieth century unfolded, liberal democratic ideas gained strength and hegemony at home and abroad. Witness the Universal Declaration of Human Rights more than half a century ago. Liberal principles and the growth of "rights consciousness" contributed to legitimizing the independence and capacities of courts in checking the illegal exercise of governmental power. Liberal principles were also used to rationalize the expansion of provincial powers as a counterweight to centralized federal authority. Emergent notions of positive liberty and welfare liberalism served as counterthrusts to negative liberty and business liberalism. State instrumentality and the legal system were touted as facilitators, rather than obstacles, to the advancement of individual rights and opportunities. Legal aid, affirmative action, the recognition of group rights, class action suits, concerns for the underdog, securing fairness in legal proceedings, separating the judicial and policing functions, and broader provisions for appealing judicial decisions are all part of this positive liberal thrust.

The Decline of Deference

Canadian political culture was, once upon a time, what the elites thought and wanted. The triumph of the liberal-democratic-individualist ethos has marginalized if not extinguished the tory-conservative-collectivist streak in the political culture. At best, toryism is in remission. Political culture, like popular culture, has become much more what the masses – rather than their leaders – feel and say. The popularization and democratization of political culture implies convergence in elite and mass values and tastes. The causes and products of this phenomenon are omnipresent: the technological and communications revolutions, the spread of mass instantaneous media, welfare entitlements, the decline of nepotistic and partisan patronage, the rise of the merit principle, and expanded accessibility to higher education.

The Rise of Law

These developments have not ushered in a classless society, but they have contributed to levelling class values and expectations. Leaders and the led now eat the same junk foods and have equal access to news sources. The professionalization of politics through public opinion sampling, focus groups, mass mailings, and the recruitment of marketing consultants and public relations spin doctors has narrowed the gap between what political leaders and citizen followers think, say, and do. Symbolically and substantially we have witnessed the economic, political, and legal upward mobility of the lowly and a cultural humbling of the privileged and wealthy. The significance of the aftermath of the 1997 APEC protest in Vancouver is that the police and politicians are being called on the carpet by an adjudicative body – not the partisan sideshow of Parliament – to account for their behaviour.

Toryism's deference to authority and reciprocity has given way: everyone now feels freer to do whatever they can get away with. Public deference and state authoritarianism are no longer characteristic of Canadian life. Courteous respect is not necessarily volunteered by the citizenry nor can it be taken for granted by those at the apex of power. Contrast the present with the past, when the police were a power unto themselves, making policy. They were not content to enforce it. At the turn of the 1930s, for example, the Toronto Police Commission announced its intention to "stamp out Communism" even though being a Communist was not a crime. The police proceeded by intimidating owners of theatres and halls into declining to rent to Communist organizations. Then they denied Communists permits to meet in public parks. When they met on street corners, they were hauled into courts, convicted on trumped-up charges of "vagrancy," "creating a disturbance," and "obstructing traffic." Protests, riots, and clashes with police are not new in Canada's history. What is new is their scale and the participants. More of them are middle class, young, and well educated. This makes for a potent political brew. Even before Ontario's Conservatives introduced their first speech from the throne in 1995, students confronted police, smashed into the legislature, and wreaked havoc.

Politicians and police are now compelled to be more circumspect. At the same time, the distance between politicians and police has grown. The veils of secrecy, privilege, and solidarity surrounding cabinet deliberations and the workings of the Prime Minister's Office are fraying. A conflict-of-interest commissioner (the current head of the RCMP Public Complaints Commission) undid one British Columbia Premier. Courts, police, and media are menacing politicians in new ways. Consider the RCMP raid, with media accompaniment, on the BC Premier's home in 1999 and his subsequent fall from power. In the 1980s, the New Brunswick Premier's home was searched after marijuana was seized from his luggage on a plane carrying the Queen. An Ontario court has ordered the Premier, Attorney General, and Solicitor General to testify in a civil case involving the shooting of an Aboriginal protester by the Ontario Provincial Police. The potential appearance of the Prime Minister before the RCMP Public Complaints Commission investigating the APEC affair shows how authority has shifted from political elites to legal elites. This means a more legalized political sensibility among citizens as well as rulers. It also means a more politicized legal system. Courts, commissions, inquiries, and other such legal and quasi-judicial agencies are treading in new waters.

The media now feed public insolence rather than deference towards politicians and police. The media were once handmaidens to officialdom and purveyors of government propaganda. Now, journalists (especially since the Watergate watershed in the United States) are trained in journalism schools as attack sparrows. The operative principles are: politicians are mendacious, and the media's job is to expose this and to uncover rather than abet cover-ups. When the media see the police clashing with, restraining, or repelling Canadian demonstrators, they are often properly suspicious of official motives. The media strive to expose unjust and arbitrary official behaviour where once they applauded it. (And dramatic, confrontational scenes caught on video make for good, profitable broadcasting to boot.) A number of prime ministers in recent years concluded that the media were out to get them. One was pounced on by the RCMP on the basis of crude media innuendo and the flimsiest of evidence. Award-winning CBC journalist Terry Milewski was effectively removed from covering the APEC affair by an only slightly more subtle assertion of prime ministerial power.

Civil liberties consciousness is a positive force, the essence of a democratic order. It has become pervasive in the political culture. The largely toothless 1960 Canadian Bill of Rights, precisely because of its inadequacies, frustrated and whetted the appetite for more among lawyers and the public. The Canadian Charter of Rights and Freedoms revolutionized both the legal and the political classes. Mass public opinion embraces it as a symbol, the new sacred icon, of a common Canadian nationalism. (Quebeckers talk down the federal Charter but rally around their own charter, which is substantially similar.)

Politicians are in mortal political fear of contesting or overriding the Charter. Lawyers and citizens are keen to resort to it and judges are willing to entertain their entreaties. This has gone hand in hand with a profound change in the *Zeitgeist* of the legal community. Like the political and police systems, it is more open and accessible to outsiders. It is less of an old-boy network, less WASP, and more diverse, fragmented, and cosmopolitan in its values and composition. It is more influenced by the nuances of the humanities and social sciences. The older cohort in the legal fraternity tended to enter law to benefit from the privileges of its exclusivity. Increasingly, in the explosion of applicants to law schools, young idealists are intent on entering the system to change it and society. What were once contentious political issues resolved politically are now increasingly transformed into legal issues.

Politicians and police, beware: the end of an era – your immunity and impunity with respect to legal accountability for political acts – is at hand.

A Different Tale: Story Line 2

Here's another story line:

Nothing has changed. Go back through newspapers over the years. They reveal that police stories are the same, decade after decade. There is a lot more legal talk, legal paper, legal manoeuvring, and legal delays, but is there any more or less violence in relations between the public and the police than in the past? Today's poor, young blacks feel as threatened by

Todd J. Tubitis (MOA Collection)

E. Redding (Government of Canada photo, MOA Collection)

1. The Museum of Anthropology (MOA) at the University of British Columbia, site of the APEC summit leaders' meeting

2. Official photograph of APEC leaders sporting new leather jackets

3. Jean Chrétien and Indonesia's President Suharto shaking hands

4. Protest tents next to the Museum of Anthropology, 27 November 1997

5. Doctoral student Mike Thoms and Green College residents Jenn Baggs and Todd Tubutis display a protest banner

6. Demonstrators wearing shirts accusing
President Suharto of crimes against
humanity

7. Arrest of a demonstrator

8. Police secure a no-go zone on the
UBC campus

9. Sit-in on road before arrival of Suharto
and other leaders attending summit
meeting at UBC

CBC TV News

CBC TV News

10. Protesters are doused with pepper spray

11. Arrest of pepper-sprayed protester

Christopher Grabowski

CBC TV News

Todd J. Tubutis

CBC TV News

12. Arrest of Craig Jones. A police officer is peeling a paper sign off the sidewalk to the left of the arrest.

13. Craig Jones, arrested after displaying signs reading "Free Speech," "Human Rights," and "Democracy," has been a prominent voice expressing concern about the policing and politics of the 1997 APEC summit.

14. Cartoonist's interpretation of
the PMO's complaint against
CBC journalist Terry Milewski

CBC TV News

CBC TV News

15. The original RCMP Public Complaints
Commission panel hearing complaints
into matters arising from the 1997 APEC
summit. The panel members were (from
left to right) John Wright, Gerald Morin
(chair), and Vina Starr.

16. Gerald Morin

police as the immigrant Irish did in the nineteenth century. Is the rule of law and political accountability more or less entrenched in our consciousness and activities? In the past, police brutality was easily hidden. Now it is subject to some critical publicity. But is the behaviour of the police and their political masters substantially different, and does the public respond differently? Perhaps police excess may be compared to sexual abuse; there is a lot more reporting of it, but that doesn't mean there is more or less of it going on.

The Forgotten Somalia Inquiry: Grinding Down Public Outrage

If the APEC protest hearings drag on, the public's attention span will be challenged. Remember: the 1997 federal election came on the heels of the Prime Minister summarily terminating the Somalia inquiry. That failed to catch on as an issue in the campaign, the debates, and the outcome. The Prime Minister's mandate was reaffirmed and a few heads rolled, all in the lower ranks of the military. For the public and the media, Somalia is a fading, distant memory. Compare the Canadian Forces' behaviour in Somalia with what RCMP officers did in Vancouver. There is a lot less public discomfort with the latter. Initial outrage in the Somalia case gave way to boredom. The public's interest in the nefarious doings of its military and their political "masters" appeared inversely proportional to the droning on of the lawyers.

The APEC Summit as "Business as Usual"

To many Canadians, the police behaviour at the APEC protest did not constitute a gross violation – if a violation at all – of human rights. Perhaps there was some bad judgment, haste, and overzealousness on the part of the RCMP. Even here the record to date is unclear and confused. To other Canadians, the behaviour of police and politicians at the APEC summit confirms their long-standing view that the state and its police organs engage in the systematic repression of democratic voices. Some will relate the affair to Canada's pre-eminent cultural cleavage, noting that the Prime Minister was moulded by Quebec society before its Quiet Revolution. From this perspective, French Canadian society never understood civil liberties and, as Pierre Trudeau intimated more than four decades ago, English Canadians never went to the trouble of instructing them.

The APEC protest and media coverage made a mountain out of molehills. The protest did not expose anything new about the Indonesian regime. Official Canada's keenness to host a corrupt, nepotistic dictator with blood on his hands was certainly not novel. Canada has always maintained relationships, some cordial, with tyrants. The Prime Minister has a legitimate but not a precisely defined responsibility to provide for the security of his invited foreign guests. If protesters overstep their bounds, who should determine whether force using pepper spray or some other means (the Prime Minister has since suggested water or bats) is warranted? The Prime Minister, the police, or a 5-4 vote of judges who are appointed by the Prime Minister? It is an eternal problem.

There is something laughably quirky about APEC's summitry. The 1997 meeting was designed to be a photo opportunity, not a meeting of substance. It turned into a domestic blow, rather than glow, for the Prime Minister. It has no upside for him. The meeting's ostensible purpose was to facilitate trade, investment, and mutual assistance. The most noteworthy Canadian-Indonesian investment news that year came just months before the summit: Canadian speculators were bilked of hundreds of millions of dollars in an Indonesian gold mine scam. The protesters and their major villain both recognized the meeting for what it was; the Indonesian president was a reluctant guest. The summit did nothing for any of the leaders and their economies. It was the reaction to and confrontation at this functionally unnecessary gathering that garnered and merited public attention. It all turned out to be an engaging performance on everyone's part. The reviled Indonesian president was toppled within a year of the protest, but not because of anything remotely related to it. In one sense the student demonstrators achieved what they wanted.

Canadians as a whole have always demonstrated high levels of respect for police officers. In this they are not much different from Finns, Germans, or Americans. Canadians said so, once again, in a survey published a year after the APEC protest. The public ranked police officers third of thirteen (after small business owners and doctors) in their respect for different types of professions or jobs. Judges were fifth, behind teachers, lawyers were tenth, and politicians last. The politicians' function in the political system, it would appear, is to serve as scapegoats; police represent order, public safety, and stability. There is nothing uniquely Canadian about a citizenry with a positive, rather than suspicious, image of its police. Common to Western societies, this sentiment is probably stronger in some countries (Germany) than in others (Italy). Collectively, Western attitudes contrast with those in totalitarian states (China, Indonesia, Burma). There, "police" to many is synonymous with political repression and arbitrary state power.

The Mountie Myth

What is singularly Canadian is the myth of its national police force, the Royal Canadian Mounted Police. Only in Canada have the police been the proudest national symbol. The Mounties' Musical Ride has adorned the country's paper currency, its image has been marketed for profit by an international giant (the Walt Disney Company), and Mounties in full gaudy regalia are positioned next to visiting foreign dignitaries to signify Canadian pomp and pageantry. The Mounties' stiff-brimmed hats and garish scarlet tunics are the romanticized stuff of old movies, books, television, and tall tales. In recent years, the Mountie has become somewhat more a figure of fun and derision, but the lingering dominant image – of honesty, politeness, modesty, and bravery – persists as a source of public pride and identity. In a conflict between what a Mountie says and what a young student demonstrator alleges, the public's reflex is to side with what is perceived as the upstanding and law-abiding, law-enforcing police officer.

Precisely because the police are held in high public esteem and politicians are not, they have something to offer each other. The public is less affronted by police excess than by an imperious politician's authoritarianism. The politician may hide behind the police officer; a blanket of "plausible deniability" is woven. "Hughie [RCMP Staff Sergeant Stewart] will take the fall," opined the government's Solicitor General. Public attitudes are schizophrenic on relations between politicians and police. They do not believe that politicians should direct policing; they also do not believe that the police should have independence and want them held accountable for their actions. Police and politicians dine out on the refrain "it's a legal and policing issue" whenever controversy swirls.

The Police as an Armed Political Force?

The use of police as an arm of political administration in a liberal democracy is disquieting. It is hardly new, however, in Canadian history. Police were used by the authorities to thwart union-organizing activity among autoworkers in Oshawa, Ontario, in the 1930s, in Quebec's asbestos industry in the 1940s, and among Newfoundland's loggers in the 1950s. The RCMP's covert operations targeting the Parti Québécois in the 1970s are well documented. Yet the police and the relations between them and the political class are almost wholly absent from the standard textbooks in Canadian politics and public administration, as though this were not an issue.

In fact, of course, *maintaining appropriate buffers between police and executive power is the central issue in any liberal democracy:* a "police state" is defined as a country in which this border zone is not protected.

In theory, policy is in the realm of the politicians. Administration – in the APEC affair, the security of foreign dignitaries – is in the realm of the police, who are public servants. In practice, as students of public administration keep reminding us, the line is fuzzy. A blurred grey zone overlaps the vitally separate orbits of politics and policing, the policy-administration dichotomy. Consider the memo from a senior official in the Prime Minister's Office to the organizers of the summit: they were "to do anything" to ensure the Indonesian president's attendance; on the other hand, a "firm stand" would be taken with the Indonesians, explaining that while protests would occur, their president would be safe and secure. To the Indonesians, however, as to many around the world, "security" means avoiding political catcalls and posters. If something goes amiss in the field, as it did, the Prime Minister claims his hands are clean. When the police act heavy-handedly or in violation of the law, a "dumb cop" excuse is almost always effective in shielding politicians from *their* responsibility for what happened. Conversely, if "embarrassment" to the visitor becomes apparent and police do not counter it, the fallout can be at the Prime Minister's expense. The Soviet president was jumped from behind and could easily have been injured or killed on Parliament Hill in the 1970s. In the 1990s, the RCMP were taken to task for letting a protester so close to the Prime Minister that he literally took things into his own hands and throttled the demonstrator. And the Mounties were properly held accountable in the harrowing late-night break-in at the Prime Minister's residence.

When "What Must Be Done" Meets "What Must Not Be Prohibited"
At the APEC summit, security police were tightly sandwiched between what must be done (sparing a visitor "embarrassment") and what must not be prohibited (Canadians shouting and waving embarrassing things at him). This was a conflict between political expedience and the Canadian constitution.

Accomplishing both would have been possible if the summit's location had not been on the University of British Columbia campus. No security-conscious administrator would have recommended it, but prime ministerial hubris – his prerogative – insisted on it. A paradoxical upshot of the APEC affair – and one that can only be for the good – is that it might strengthen the independence of the RCMP in dealing with the Prime Minister and his minions.

The Political Power of Police

On the other hand, one would not want the police to assert political power in their own right. Police power and autonomy have grown over the years. Police and security forces are constantly breaking laws. Threats are not fabricated but tend to be blown out of proportion, since intelligence officers, more than others, tend towards paranoia. To be sure, policing has become more bureaucratized, requires more paperwork, and imposes more restrictions on officers, reducing their discretion. Collectively, however, police are a more potent interest group than in the past, and quite autonomous. In Toronto, the police union has organized against politicians who rebuke its members; it is using the court system to sue those who besmirch the police image. The national association of police officers lobbies government to change the criminal law. Could any other category of civil servants so attack the politicians' policy-making function or try to muzzle the citizenry and get away with it? It is akin to a deputy minister taking a public position on what government policy ought to be.

This is not in the scheme of "responsible" cabinet-parliamentary government as we have known it. Recently, a visiting British lawyer was hauled off the streets and, despite his protestations of innocence and ignorance of an alleged crime, was humiliated, strip-searched, and subjected to a rectal examination. When he complained after his release, the authorities investigated and admitted that they had snared an innocent person, but they refused to apologize.

Police power and its use for political and other unlawful purposes is as strong – and as *wrong* – as ever.

Nothing has changed.

8

Forcing the Issues:
Police Use of Force at the
APEC Protest

CONSTABLE GIL PUDER

When violent incidents such as the Rodney King beating in Los Angeles in 1991, the Robson Street riot in Vancouver in 1994, or the APEC demonstration at the University of British Columbia in 1997 generate graphic media images, the conduct of the police is often at odds with the public's perceptions of their peace officers. This dichotomy resulting from the use of force by police concerns everyone who values peaceful democracy and the rule of law. People may wonder whether the actions they observe are reasonable, evidence of systemic failure, or simply aberrant misconduct. Leaving these questions unanswered reduces the public's confidence in the criminal justice system, a result that is in no one's interests.

Responsible governments enact laws to provide social order. Citizens then expect those laws to be applied in a reasonable, unbiased fashion, by officials who exercise discretion while maintaining their professionalism. Police are unique among public servants in that they enforce a wide variety of laws and have statutory authority to do so, responding to a virtually unlimited number of circumstances that might require intervention. Most Canadians understand that their police officers need to be able to fulfil this mandate safely. Many people, however, are troubled by the use of force by police because of apprehension that such force might be used against them if they themselves should break the law.

Controlling the Controllers

Canada's police are not simply provided with statutory authority and the tools for enforcement and then left to their own devices. Mechanisms for accountability include laws, regulations, and policies designed to manage the uses of force, as well as controls that should complement each other and provide harmonious direction. Ideally, police conduct falling within this framework will meet a professional standard of care. To ensure that their actions are reasonable, officers must always consider four general restrictions placed upon their potential behaviour.

First, the use of excessive force amounts to an offence of assault under the Criminal Code of Canada. Police officers who act without lawful authority or who "go too far" expose themselves to criminal liability. Unfortunately, although criminal law is the superior authority governing policing, it provides very general and somewhat subjective guidance. Criminal law can also be very difficult to apply, given the need to establish intent and its high standard of proof (beyond a reasonable doubt). Policing thus requires rules of conduct that address some of the unique aspects of our occupation.

Second, some of the responsibility for managing enforcement practices lies with police employers, who develop organizational policy. Policies that affect the uses of force deal with the application of law, such as when to arrest for various offences. Policies can also describe the tactics recommended in specific circumstances, and the training requirements that are intended to ensure officer competency. Unfortunately, policing has a history of developing policies that are heavily weighted towards expedience, the effectiveness and/or lawful authority of which may be questionable.

Several concerns arising from the 1997 APEC protest are related to RCMP policies that led to the arrest of non-violent protesters. One central issue has become the focus of a larger, ongoing debate: how closely must police policy conform with the law? A related situation occurred during Vancouver's Symphony of Fire in 1999, when a Vancouver Police spokesperson publicly stated that all people entering downtown Vancouver would be detained so that they could be searched for liquor. This policy created the potential for police to use force if a person refused to submit to an arbitrary detention and search, or perhaps objected to the seizure of liquor lawfully obtained and carried. By using force to detain, search, or remove property in these circumstances, officers would almost certainly have been committing a prima facie assault. In such situations, individual police officers face a dilemma: just follow orders and do things they know to be potentially unlawful, or exercise discretion and risk internal reprisals.

This is a compelling reason why organizational policies that create these situations demand intervention by the courts. Protecting both citizens and individual officers requires that the uses of force remain within the bounds of lawful authority.

The third general restriction consists of police regulations, which are often enacted by governments in order to ensure that their police adhere to lawful standards of conduct. Usually appended to legislation empowering enforcement officers, regulations may be applied to firearms and ammunition, intermediate weapons, disciplinary processes, and training. Uniform policing standards within a region increase public confidence in the expected quality of service. Unfortunately, overlapping jurisdictions over provincially regulated police and federal agencies such as the RCMP inevitably create confusion.

Fourth and last, in a country noteworthy for its dynamic, diverse population, policing must constantly adapt in order to receive social acceptance. Social expectations are largely reflected in the evolution of common law. When an aggrieved person believes that he or she has been victimized by practices that violate societal norms, the person has recourse to the civil courts. Challenging the reasonableness of police use of force would result in civil litigation, and officer conduct is usually framed within the concept of negligence. Police intervention is then subjected to the test of a professional standard of care. In these cases, the courts may assign liability to the public agency and award damages to injured parties.

An example of this occurred in 1992, when an amateur photographer captured on videotape a man being wrongfully arrested by the Vancouver Police Emergency Response Team (ERT). Officers executing a drug warrant struck the man while holding him in a prone position. It was subsequently discovered that there was no evidence linking the man to any offence. After an investigation, the Regional Crown Counsel publicly explained why the police conduct was not criminal in nature: the ERT officers had no criminal intent, since they were acting in good faith upon the best information received from colleagues, and they had breached no regulation or policy. There was, however, significant public concern over an innocent person being subjected to this type of treatment, and the incident was referred to in the letter of transmittal accompanying the report of Justice W.T. Oppal's Commission of Inquiry into Policing in British Columbia. The victim initiated a civil action and subsequently received a settlement.

Even this cursory examination of criminal law, organizational policy, police regulation, and social acceptance (which combine to form an easily remembered "COPS" acronym) makes it easy to appreciate that frontline officers labour under onerous expectations. Often lost in any discussion is the reality that the police still have jobs to do and a duty to fulfil. Occasionally police work demands that force be used against another person. In these situations, including the APEC summit, exactly what should police officers be trying to accomplish?

Any task requires a goal, and the critical requirement for police is to establish an appropriate physical relationship with their subject(s). This relationship is characterized as *control*, which may be defined as "the ability to safely direct another person's behaviour, whether compliant or resistant." Using more force than is reasonable to establish control would likely be viewed as both excessive and negligent. Questions about the RCMP's use of force during the APEC protest, in particular the widespread use of pepper spray, revolve around the issue of whether control should have been established using less violent tactics. In volatile and unpredictable situations, however, walking the fine line between control and excess is no easy matter.

To help officers behave reasonably, police training attempts to teach skills that will enable officers to carry out their foreseeable duty requirements. These control tactics are "uses of force designed to gain control with the least violent reasonable means, having regard firstly to personal safety and secondly to minimizing harm to the subject." Control tactics can potentially be misused or abused, but any skill taught should meet three criteria: (1) the skill should be one that can be learned by non-expert, frontline officers; (2) the skill should be retained without excessive practice and then competently performed in stressful situations; and (3) when performed properly, the skill should result in the desired performance outcome.

Considering the mechanisms of accountability guiding police use of force, the goal of control through intervention, and the skills and equipment provided to officers, what determines the quality and nature of the police response? When an offender resists, how will officers choose whether to grapple or to use pepper spray? Should they strike a blow with their hand or a baton? Do circumstances demand the use of a firearm? Or does prudence require police to withdraw, disengaging from the situation to prevent unacceptable risks to themselves or others?

Answering these questions requires revisiting Sir Robert Peel's principle "that the police are the public and the public are the police." Police are human, no more and no less than other people, and when using force are making very human decisions. The discretionary authority vested in public peace officers means that not all lawbreakers require immediate or draconian intervention. Officers must consider the situation at hand, making hard choices about whether or not to intervene and about the most reasonable response under the circumstances.

A Demanding Situation

People in any situation evaluate factors that they perceive to be important. These firsthand analyses depend heavily upon both the perceptions of the individual and the unique nature of the incident itself.

Police must concern themselves first with their subjects' *demonstrated behaviour*, since people's actions are what necessitate lawful intervention. These actions may create risks for the officer(s), any other citizens in the immediate vicinity, and the subject(s), who may experience a police response. It would be impossible for police to prepare for each of the countless actions that they might confront. Distinguishable behaviour types can be identified, however, and many were evident in videotaped news footage of the APEC demonstrations.

Cooperation is obviously desirable from a police perspective. Some of the demonstrators at APEC were completely compliant with RCMP arrest procedures despite concerns they may have had about the lawfulness of the officers' actions. Even cooperative people, however, pose some risk. Certain offenders may cooperate, yet have a history of conduct so dangerous that officers must respond forcefully to ensure their personal safety.

The behaviour of uncooperative subjects who resist police action falls into one of two general types. *Passive resistance* is non-cooperation accompanied by little or no physical action. Examples include refusing to leave when requested, failure to follow a lawful order, and "sit-ins" or "dead-weight" demonstrations, such as protesters at APEC sitting on a roadway. On the other hand, examples of *active resistance* include pulling away from an officer's grasp, pushing to escape, grabbing people or objects to hinder police tactics, and running away. All of these behaviours were displayed by some of the APEC protesters who were videotaped breaching a security fence.

People who apply physical force towards a police officer (or towards any person) cross the threshold from resistance to *assault*. Common examples include punching, kicking, spitting, gouging, shoving, and using weapons. Once again this behaviour was evident in the APEC footage, with some protesters pushing and shoving bicycle police officers in an apparent attempt to force their way into a restricted area. Extreme assaults that are likely or intended to cause death or serious bodily harm would be described as *deadly force assaults*. Examples include choking, attack with knives and other edged weapons, use of firearms, and continuous beating with hands, feet, or blunt objects.

Since police observe behaviour in the real world, not in the abstract, officers must also consider their physical environment. The APEC summit required officers to weigh a number of factors: protected dignitaries, potential weapons, buildings and barriers, vehicle routes, crowds, and confined areas, plus many other environmental variables. Whenever possible, prudent police planning modifies the environment to improve security. An example from APEC was the construction of fences to restrict crowd movements.

There was good reason to change the APEC environment in advance, as the risk to police officers increases greatly when intervening with crowds. The APEC summit featured several such situations. Officers who encounter active resistance or assault from multiple subjects must act immediately. Police become dangerously exposed when entangled with any individual among a group of combatants, and intermediate weapons such as batons and aerosol sprays are often required. Physically intervening with large numbers of people requires strenuous exertion, and officers may need to resort to these weapons when their personal skills and abilities prove insufficient.

Whether dealing with a single person or with a crowd, police officers cannot expect to consistently overpower all offenders. Physical characteristics are not the top priority in modern police recruiting, giving way to diversity and a well-rounded skill set. Furthermore, even the fittest, most skilled officer may confront an offender with whom physical interaction is exceedingly hazardous. For these reasons, police must always compare their own physical abilities with those of their subjects, balancing their potential personal performance against the subjects' apparent ability to resist. This means evaluating variables such as size, muscularity, age, gender, skills, and weapons.

In situations such as APEC, police officers who are not in top physical condition will often need to escalate their response in order to gain control. For this reason, crowd control and emergency response teams (who because of the nature of their work regularly use force) unquestionably require regular, valid physical testing. Appropriate physical standards should be mandatory for police who are likely to use force, since physical testing is one of the few objective, unbiased methods of accurately predicting an officer's performance. Unfortunately, if RCMP officers at APEC exhibited characteristics of problematic physical conditioning, this would raise the issue of whether their physical abilities, or lack thereof, may have led them to use more force than should have been necessary.

Information sources that lead to forceful intervention is another issue that arose at APEC, largely because of the detention of students. Police officers must often act upon information that they believe to be reliable, which enables them to anticipate the intentions of their subjects. In many situations officers cannot make a thorough evaluation without considering relevant information. This information can be received from victims and witnesses, or a suspect may be recognized by the police and associated with some previous action. Officers might also have related personal experience or access to records systems. A reasonable belief that a person is predisposed to a certain type of behaviour will understandably influence police evaluations. The issue highlighted by APEC is this: exactly how reliable must information be to justify forcibly detaining someone because that person *might* commit an offence in the future?

Finally, the factors of distance and time are closely related. Inadequate time increases the likelihood of imprecise decision making, since some variables will inevitably be overlooked. The nature of police work, unfortunately, often involves responding quickly in high-risk circumstances. Similarly, close proximity to some situations increases the risk to officers, necessitating a reactive rather than carefully planned response.

The underlying theme of this discussion is that police intervention, whether forceful or not, is never lawful simply because officers have a monopoly on coercion. Police are not "licensed" to use force of any sort by virtue of their public office. A forceful response is reasonable and therefore lawful only if the situation *demands* it. The factors discussed here – demonstrated behaviour, environment, multiple subjects, physical abilities, necessary information, and distance and time – form precisely that acronym – DEMAND. After evaluating their situation, however, police officers must still choose a reasonable response.

Response Options

In the absence of police intervention, any incident will play itself out according to its own peculiar dynamics. Police responses, however, will alter the course of events, and officers will become part of the situation itself. Professionalism requires balancing the desired outcome, the likelihood of success, and the degree of force that is reasonably foreseeable. There are literally hundreds of police tactics that apply to different situations, and it is beyond the abilities of even the most expert officer to thoroughly understand all potential interventions.

As in evaluating situations, decision making is facilitated by classifying control tactics into progressive groups. Termed *response options,* these categories are based on similarity of technique and the foreseeable degree of force. Approved response options often vary between police agencies, depending on the officers' equipment and training as well as what is authorized under regulation or policy.

Police must first consider whether they can establish control at reasonable risk to personal, public, and subject safety. If the risks are unreasonable, officers must disengage wherever possible. Time, distance, cover, and assistance may all be facilitated when police disengage from a situation. After physical intervention has begun, however, disengaging can prove to be extremely difficult.

Once the police are involved, their presence can influence people's behaviour. A person's perception of police presence will include the officers' physical appearance, uniforms, and visible equipment, as well as the number of personnel and the reputation of the individual or agency. Just as police evaluate the situations they face, people evaluate the officers who respond. For example, during the "Riot at the Hyatt" demonstration in Vancouver following the APEC summit, protesters became agitated when they apparently recognized certain police officers. Projecting an appropriate police presence is an essential element in minimizing conflict.

Dialogue, however, is the first response that permits police-subject interaction. Components of dialogue include the actual words that are spoken; the tone, volume, and pitch of the officer's voice; and non-verbal communication, or body language. Police training devotes considerable time to teaching officers how to communicate tactically, as effective dialogue skills increase the likelihood of resolving conflict without actual use of force. Some of the words used by the RCMP at the APEC protests merit scrutiny. For example, an officer was videotaped announcing, "I'm going to use force." Since this statement apparently provided no alternative to force being used, one wonders what incentive the protesters had to cooperate with RCMP requests.

Fortunately, force is actually used in only a small percentage of police interventions. In these situations, *open-handed tactics* are the most common response. Characterized by body and clothing grasps, open-handed tactics include a wide range of grappling techniques. A police officer may simply overpower a subject through *physical dominance,* or coerce some level of cooperation using *pain compliance*. *Lever and joint manipulation* involves grasping a person's limbs and moving them beyond their normal range of motion, while *throws and takedowns* unbalance and ground the subject. Once control has been established, *handcuffs and restraining devices* are used to restrict a person's movement.

Open-handed tactics are noteworthy in that they almost always include the use of force by police. Officers must eventually lay their hands on people who are forcibly taken into custody, often to apply handcuffs. When police can safely gain control using an open-handed response, it is questionable whether more forceful measures are reasonable. On the other hand, certain open-handed tactics can cause serious injury when applied with maximum exertion. Powerful leverage techniques can break limbs and tear connective tissue, while neckholds have been known to be fatal. Should an open-handed tactic of such magnitude be required, police officers would be well advised to consider other options.

At the APEC summit the RCMP used pepper spray extensively. Aerosol weapons are increasingly popular in policing, and have undoubtedly prevented injuries to both police officers and subjects. These handheld sprays deliver an irritating agent, most often containing either a chemical compound or a concentrated extract of peppers. An aerosol spray provides no physical control over a person, however, and there is anecdotal evidence of people persisting in violent and dangerous behaviour despite being heavily contaminated. Even when subjects are temporarily disabled by the effects of the spray, officers must still use open-handed tactics and dialogue to gain control.

A crucial question arising from the use of pepper spray at APEC involves the intent of the RCMP officers: what were they trying to accomplish? In general, pepper spray temporarily blinds a person and causes mucous discharge, coughing, and burning pain. Any one or a combination of these effects may well distract the person from a certain course of action. If someone were actively resisting or assaulting an officer, it is obvious that pepper spray might stop or alter that person's behaviour. If the same person were cooperative or passive, however, the rationale for applying pepper spray would be questionable at the very least.

Adequate time and distance are needed for police to employ any weapon, and officers who find themselves in situations without either may still need to disable their subjects. Circumstances may require a police officer to strike a blow to gain control. When personal body weapons are used to deliver blunt trauma, officers can be said to have used an *empty-handed impact technique.* Common striking techniques include punches, kicks, elbows, knees, palm-heels, and so on. Anyone striking blows, however, needs to consider the reality that "for every action, there is an equal and opposite reaction." Because police officers place themselves at high risk of injury when they use their own bodies to strike, it is advisable for them to use an *impact weapon,* such as a police baton, whenever possible. Instruments designed for striking allow officers to increase their striking power, maintain distance from their subjects, and reduce the risk of personal injury.

Even highly skilled officers with the best intermediate weapons must occasionally respond to dangerous situations involving people who cannot be safely controlled while conscious. These cases demand that officers consider using *neck restraints,* manual pressure on a person's neck causing temporary unconsciousness. Although neck restraints are open-handed tactics that can be applied successfully with minimal exertion, there is a remote potential for fatality even when correctly performed. Neck restraints are thus recommended only for properly trained officers, in cases where there is no other reasonable option.

The term *deadly force* is most often associated with firearms but is much broader in scope. Under the Criminal Code definition – "force that is intended or is likely to cause death or grievous bodily harm" – deadly force includes other potential tactics, such as knives, repeated or severe blows to a person's head, choking, ramming with vehicles, and so on. Contrary to publicized claims from special interest and marketing groups, in many situations there really are no alternatives to deadly force. Police officers must still occasionally use their sidearms to ensure both their own safety and that of the citizens they protect.

In an overview of this nature, it is not possible to thoroughly examine specific techniques and weapons, or the unique tactics – such as service dogs, electrical "TASER" weapons, and baton rounds – employed by highly trained police specialists. Rather, the options described here typify what is available to the general duty officer. Even when specialized responses are used, however, determining whether the response is reasonable requires answering a fundamental question: did the situation *demand* it?

Performing Actions

Evaluating a situation and selecting a response determine what will be done. During intervention, however, police officers must act. To gain control reasonably, they need some method of measuring their likelihood of success. Learning what happens during the execution of different techniques is really a function of training, enabling officers to accurately forecast their own performance. Once again, several factors need to be considered.

All forceful responses require physical abilities, the relevant attributes of individual police officers that indicate their performance potential. Body composition, cardiovascular fitness, flexibility, muscular strength, and endurance are all health-related components of fitness that have been traditionally measured in police training. Using force also involves agility, balance, coordination, power, speed, and reaction time. These skill-related components of fitness have been identified as being directly related to performance potential in control tactics. In many situations a more physically able officer is able to perform more efficiently and achieve control using a less violent response.

Once again, the problematic characteristics exhibited by some RCMP officers at APEC raises the issue of occupational standards in policing. Of particular concern are those members of specialized units who are regularly called upon to use force. Workplace physical standards must meet the criteria of a bona fide occupational requirement, recently described in the 1999 Supreme Court of Canada ruling in the matter of *British Columbia (Public Service Employee Relations Commission)* v. *BCGSEU* (1979):

> A three-step test should be adopted for determining whether an employer has established, on a balance of probabilities, that a prima facie discriminatory standard is a bona fide occupational requirement (BFOR). First, the employer must show that it adopted the standard for a purpose rationally connected to the performance of the job. The focus at the first step is not on the validity of the particular standard, but rather on the validity of its more general purpose. Second, the employer must establish that it adopted the particular standard in an honest and good faith belief that it was necessary to the fulfilment of that legitimate work-related purpose. Third, the employer must establish that the standard is reasonably necessary *to* the accomplishment of that legitimate work-related purpose.

Fortunately, standards developed from empirical analyses of the physical demands of arrest and control have been available for some time. The Police Officers' Physical Abilities Test has been used for over a decade in BC municipal policing. It is incumbent upon police employers to ensure that officers deployed for high-risk interventions are physically competent, given the nature of their foreseeable duties.

When police execute their skills (in this discussion I refer to them as *control tactics*), the efficiency of the movement contributes heavily to the outcome. Skill development can be easily understood in the context of firearms or pepper spray: will officers hit what they aim at? This principle has implications for any use of force, however, and is directly related to training. Skills are, of course, developed through practice.

The stress of responding to many situations often causes police officers to experience physiological arousal. This can affect performance in a variety of ways. A simple gross motor movement, such as swinging a baton, can be enhanced by arousal, but a complex fine motor skill, such as shooting a firearm while moving, can be seriously degraded. High levels of arousal can also cause the phenomenon known as *perceptual narrowing*, in which an officer's ability to cognitively process information becomes tightly focused, resulting in loss of detail. This "tunnel vision" is often experienced by police officers involved in critical incidents.

An intuitive understanding of the effects of physiological arousal during crises appears to have developed in policing, as evidenced by the practice of supervisory and command officers distancing themselves from actual physical involvement. It is simply too difficult to make sound, rational decisions when one is highly aroused. This raises a question of why RCMP officers with supervisory responsibilities were physically engaging protesters at APEC, particularly in situations where there *appeared* to be numerous subordinates available. The importance of separating the police duties of supervision and interaction is well supported by scientific research into human performance.

Conclusion

Using force is a complex activity. The enormous number of factors that influence this form of police intervention are interwoven in many ways. Undaunted, however, police more often than not rise to the challenge of restoring peace in contentious situations. This does not mean that they require special treatment or consideration, but rather that any process of determining whether the use of force is reasonable should not be taken lightly.

In a presentation to the Policing in British Columbia commission of inquiry, a representative of the BC Civil Liberties Association observed that "at the end of the day, in a democratic society, it's the citizens who decide how much force is necessary." Everyday people provide evidence in court and sit on juries, make representation to police boards and commissions, and vote for the officials who make laws and regulations governing police conduct. Citizens must themselves decide the measure of force necessary for police to secure public order, ensuring both the safety of the officers and that the force used is reasonable. Striking such a balance could well be a task requiring the wisdom of King Solomon. When making hard choices, Canadians must avail themselves of the facts, consider their responsibilities, and choose well.

PART 4:
PUBLIC ACCOUNTABILITY IN A FREE AND DEMOCRATIC SOCIETY

The real problem was the reaction of Mr. Milewski's bosses ... Their job was to protect their reporter once they were assured his work met professional standards (which it did). Instead, CBC executives bent under the PMO pressure ... What was even more distressing was the relative silence of his colleagues. "Milewski is right," a CBC producer, who insisted on anonymity told the *Globe*, "but is it worth [going to bat for him] if the government re-opens the stable funding issue for the CBC?"

> – Lysiane Gagnon, *Globe and Mail*, 27 March 1999

The real problem here is that Canada has no formal mechanism for dealing with the central accusation in this case – political interference in policing by the prime minister and/or his office ... In the United States, Congress has all sorts of investigative tools at its disposal for matters of this kind. In Canada, it's basically left up to the government of the day to determine what kind of investigation will take place ... The last thing Jean Chrétien wants is a parliamentary or judicial inquiry into his own actions. So he gives us a police inquiry that, in the words of PCC chair Shirley Heafey, doesn't have a mandate to blame the prime minister even if the evidence shows he was up to no good."

> – Jim McNulty, *Province*, 15 January 1999

9

Forces of Journalism

TERRY MILEWSKI

The fourth estate in a society of laws has a somewhat medieval role. Like a town gossip, the news media have no troops. Beyond the power to amuse and to inform, they have little more than the power to shame – to embarrass miscreants by telling tales in the court of public opinion. In theory, this means the media can hold the powerful to account. In practice, the telling of the tale often makes little difference. The dogs bark, and the caravan moves on.

Occasionally, however, the dogs draw blood. In such cases, the victims may find the impulse to "shoot the messenger" irresistible. Where APEC and the Canadian Broadcasting Corporation were concerned, the government of Canada succumbed to this impulse. On 16 October 1998, the Prime Minister's spokesman, Peter Donolo, famously called upon the CBC to put a stop to my work – to "ensure that it is not continued." A summary of the case may shed light on the limits of media power in the age of spin.

Media Coverage of the APEC Summit
What distinguishes the case of the 1997 APEC summit is that, at first, the dogs did not bark at all. The visiting leaders assured us that the Asian economies were going to be fine. On the periphery, some students clashed with police. It was routine stuff, and the media gave it little attention.

Susan Delacourt of the *Globe and Mail* noted this on 17 October 1998 in an article headed, "Why the media failed to get the APEC story." She suggested that street protests are rarely taken seriously, that the big guns of the media were trained on the official events, and that reporters assigned to the Prime Minister may have been too "cozy" with their subject. "The hottest political story this season was rated as a 'meanwhile' when it actually happened," she wrote. "What's newsworthy in 1998 should have been newsworthy in 1997, right?"

Indeed, in a curious reversal of roles, the summit organizers seem to have been more aware than the media that their restrictions on protest could prove newsworthy. Six weeks before the leaders arrived, on 12 September 1997, Prime Minister Jean Chrétien's top APEC official, Robert Vanderloo, recorded in a memorandum the sentiments of the Prime Minister's communications director, Peter Donolo:

> PMO has expressed concerns about the security perimeter at UBC, not so much from a security point of view but to avoid embarrassments to APEC leaders ... The response (as suggested in fact by Donolo) is that we have to find a balance that meets both concerns (we do not wish student demonstrations and efforts by the gov't to suppress the freedom of expression to become a major media story).

The RCMP was concerned about the same issue. In an e-mail message on 20 November 1997 – five days before the summit – Inspector Bill Dingwall told Director of Security Superintendent Wayne May that removing protesters from a camp near the summit site might best be accomplished after dark. "Media are aware and no doubt they will be covering extensively," Dingwall advised. "Will also need to examine options of limiting media coverage should the decision be made to remove them (during the quiet hours, moving in buses, moving media back, etc.)."

The arrests were, indeed, carried out at night, and media coverage was, indeed, limited. I know. As one of the journalists assigned to cover such peripheral stories, I completely missed it.

I had better luck, however, when the leaders finally arrived at the University of British Columbia on 25 November. Thanks to the superb work of CBC cameraman Robb Douglas, we were able to provide an informative look at the conduct of both protesters and police. Robb's videotape of Staff Sergeant Hugh Stewart blinding him and his camera with pepper spray became emblematic of the summit. It was even more famous than the Prime Minister's remark at a press conference that evening: "For me, pepper, I put it on my plate. Next!"

Many of the assembled journalists laughed at this, and the story of the protests would normally have died the next day. Instead, it emerged that we'd all missed something. Three days before the summit, law graduate Karen Pearlston had reported that police told her they had "orders from the Prime Minister's Office" that protest signs were not allowed by the motorcade route. Students arrested at the protest camp had been asked to sign undertakings that they would not demonstrate as a condition of release. Law student Craig Jones spent fourteen hours in jail for refusing to give up signs saying "Free Speech," "Democracy," and "Human Rights." The latter sign was laid out in small pieces of paper on the sidewalk – and Jones produced a photograph of an RCMP officer picking up these pieces of paper as he was being arrested. Nearby, history graduate Mike Thoms reported that police had seized a bedsheet bearing the words "Dictators Not Welcome at UBC."

Either this bedsheet was a weapon or there was a story here. Two days after the summit, we revisited it. Karen Pearlston described her encounter with police:

> The police officer told me that it was on orders from the Prime Minister's Office that there should be no signs and no people along this stretch of the roadway. And the other thing that the officers told me was that if I continued to put up signs that they would arrest me. And when I asked on what charge, one officer said to me "we'll make something up."

December 1997: More Questions

Pearlston's account was crucial to what followed. RCMP spokesman Sergeant Russ Grabb denied any political involvement: "The Prime Minister's Office did not direct or provide us instructions in that regard." A statement from his superiors went further: "The Prime Minister's Office was not involved in RCMP security arrangements." Peter Donolo denied that the PMO gave any orders to keep protest signs out of sight, and added that he saw no reason why the RCMP would order anyone to take down signs outside the security perimeter. As our story noted, though, that was exactly what had happened.

Citing an inquiry into these events, the RCMP then ceased to comment on them. Two weeks later, on 9 December, we reported on Craig Jones's decision to sue the RCMP, and summarized the two sides of the story thus:

> The RCMP's version of events is that they were not concerned about the content of those signs, but about their potential to be used as missiles

which might have been lobbed over a nine-foot security fence, which was placed right here. Jones says there is no way he could have thrown the coat-racks that he used to hold up two of his signs over the fence. And he says other forbidden signs were on bedsheets which could not have been used as weapons.

Evidence of a political purpose in other police actions began to accumulate. On 10 December, Staff Sergeant Lloyd Plante lent credence to a complaint by Jaggi Singh that he had been arrested in order to stop him from leading demonstrations. Staff Sergeant Plante, in charge of the UBC detachment, said, "We wanted to remove him from the scene before he had the opportunity to incite some sort of disturbance" (*Province*, 11 December 1997). The same day, my colleague Neil MacDonald reported from Ottawa on questions about the placement of the designated protest area:

> A spokesman for Jean Chrétien said such decisions are up to the RCMP. He said the PMO was involved in the discussions, but he would not say why it would have wanted the protest line moved ... But the question is this: if security decisions are the exclusive domain of the RCMP, why would the PMO have any say in what to do about a legal protest?

"Charter-Free Zone"

I was then assigned to prepare a short documentary on the subject. I called it "Charter-Free Zone" – a phrase stolen from a protest letter sent to the Prime Minister by members of the UBC Faculty of Law. Hours before the documentary was broadcast on 18 December, we obtained a copy of an earlier protest letter, sent to the Prime Minister by UBC president Dr. Martha Piper. It was dated 19 November – six days before the summit – and it accused the PMO of violating its contract with UBC by imposing tighter restrictions on protests than those agreed to by the RCMP.

Asked to account for this letter, Peter Donolo again offered no reason why the PMO took a different view of the security requirements than the RCMP. He confirmed, though, that the PMO had sought to move the protest area back. It was then clear that the Prime Minister's Office was, indeed, decisively involved in the security arrangements.

In a little over two weeks following the summit, the events of 25 November had been reported on CBC television five times. The December documentary went much further, however. The piece suggested that civil liberties seemed to have been "cancelled" to spare the visiting leaders embarrassment – particularly President Suharto of Indonesia, who had threatened to boycott the summit. It described the arrests of Jaggi Singh and Craig Jones, among others, and summarized some unanswered questions put to the PMO and the RCMP. A few extracts follow:

[*The National*, 18 December 1997:]
The Prime Minister's Office confirms that its officials did want the protest areas moved back. But the PMO has not answered the question, why? ... What is known is that people like Craig Jones tried and failed to make a visible protest at APEC. Jones was arrested when he refused to remove signs from the motorcade route saying "free speech" and "democracy."

CRAIG JONES: I mean there was no expression of concern about the security or anything else. It was simply him saying "we can't have our signs there" and me saying "oh yes we can."

...

MILEWSKI: The RCMP declines to comment on this now, but claimed at the time that the signs were a security risk.

SGT. RUSS GRABB / RCMP SPOKESMAN: A decision was made to ensure that all motorcade routes were safe from placards or signs that could have been used to have been thrown in front of a motorcycle officer or onto the windshield of a motorcade vehicle.

MILEWSKI: In that case, says Jones, then how come the Mounties never even looked at his backpack lying on the ground?

JONES: It stuns me to think – I mean I couldn't leave a pack unattended in a train station in London without, you know, the bomb squad being there, poking at it with shotgun-armed robots. And here we are with 18 world leaders going by, and there is no interest in the backpack.

MILEWSKI: Only in the signs?

JONES: Only in the signs, yes.

...

MILEWSKI: In the end, of course, it'll be up to the courts to decide whether the RCMP had proper legal grounds for its actions, and whether anyone's civil liberties were violated. But for now, as long as both the RCMP and the Prime Minister's Office refuse to comment, several unanswered questions remain: if the security plan was good enough for the RCMP, why was it not good enough for the prime minister's office? Did the Prime Minister offer any assurances to visiting leaders that demonstrators would be kept out of sight? And if he didn't, why were they kept out of sight?

Reaction to the documentary was minimal. The urgent topic at that time was Christmas shopping. In a year-end interview, the Prime Minister told Craig Oliver of CTV: "We have given them a chance to protest and the signs were all along the road ... And I am proud that we had organized it in such a way and that it was – everybody behaved very well." There the matter rested – for a while.

January and February 1998: The E-mail Messages Fly

Before and after Christmas and into the New Year, I pressed for answers and compared notes with Craig Jones, among others. It is our e-mail correspondence during this period that later attracted an allegation by the Prime Minister's Office that I "secretly conspired" against the government. I mention it here to emphasize the sequence of events. The questions, the lack of answers, and the strategy of Craig Jones were as public as they could possibly be in November and December of 1997. The notorious e-mail messages on these subjects were written in January and February of 1998, weeks after the same matters were broadcast to the nation. As a secret conspiracy, this left much to be desired.

Just as the sequence of events went unremarked, so did the content of Jones's own e-mail messages, although they were made public just when mine were. For example, on 27 November, the day I met him, Jones was already accusing the RCMP of telling "blatant lies" about his arrest. Evidently he was not waiting for my advice – although he was giving me plenty. On 11 December, he sent me a message saying, "the question is, if (the RCMP) had determined that the closer site was satisfactory, on what basis did the PMO object to this?" Absurdly, it was later suggested that I had improperly disclosed this question to its author, in my own message of 9 January – a month after Jones disclosed it to me and the CBC disclosed it to the nation.

Similarly, Jones's comments in our December documentary left no doubt that he believed the RCMP showed little interest in security issues when they arrested him. As quoted above, he said that "it stuns me" that the police showed "no interest" in his unattended backpack – "only in the signs." It was later suggested that he got this idea from me, in a message dated 18 February 1998 – two months *after* he expressed it on TV.

September 1998: New Developments

Meanwhile, a clock was ticking: the RCMP Public Complaints Commission (PCC) was gathering official documents on the affair. Nine months after the summit, this search produced an intriguing prospect for a journalist: dozens of lawyers, police officers, and complainants had access to these hitherto secret documents. I obtained many of them from a variety of sources. As a result, a series of reports were featured prominently on *The National*, starting on 8 September. That first story noted in part:

MILEWSKI: Ever since APEC, the Prime Minister's office and the RCMP have both insisted that all the arrests were strictly for security reasons, that there was no attempt to stifle dissent and no political interference with the police. Now, CBC News has obtained extensive documentary evidence that the opposite is true. They are internal government documents from the Prime Minister's Office and the RCMP showing that they were determined to keep a lid on protests even if they had no legitimate security grounds for doing so.

...

The RCMP also had orders from the Prime Minister to shut down a perfectly legal protest camp near the summit site. Internal RCMP memos record that "PM wants the tenters out ... PM wanted everyone removed." The RCMP complied, demanding that the students promise not to demonstrate ... As another RCMP memo noted "we do not want banners nor would the PMO's office. Having said that, banners are not a security issue. They are a political issue. If they are not going to be permitted what is the authority for removing them and who is going to do it?"

...

Law student Craig Jones put up "free speech" signs and was thrown in jail without charge.

CRAIG JONES: Our government bargained away the constitutional rights of Canadian citizens for no other reason than to appease the embarrassment concerns of President Suharto of Indonesia.

MILEWSKI: But tonight, in Montreal, the Prime Minister insisted he was only concerned about Suharto's physical security.

CHRETIEN: I did not talk to the police myself but I wished that it was to be done in order. And there were areas for protesters and areas where there were not protesters to maintain order.

MILEWSKI: The RCMP also continued to claim that it was motivated by security, not by politics. But that's going to be very hard to square with these new documents, which go before a public inquiry next week. There, some of the students involved hope to subpoena the Prime Minister and to prove that this was not about keeping a dictator safe, but about keeping him happy.

In the days that followed, a second documentary and a series of news reports provided further details. One suggested that some of the arrests at APEC – such as Jaggi Singh's – had "a political purpose." Another said that the government had allowed armed Indonesian bodyguards on the UBC campus, knowing that they had threatened to shoot protesters. In a third, former Indonesian ambassador Benjamin Parwoto said from Jakarta that he had assured the Prime Minister that Suharto was not concerned about security, but only about "embarrassment." This contrasted with the Prime Minister's own statement that President Suharto had been "preoccupied with his security."

A significant fact, in view of the subsequent complaint against the CBC, is that the PMO made no challenge of any kind to any of these reports.

To make matters worse, on 2 October our first documentary won a Gemini award for producer Carmen Merrifield and me. We should have remembered that pride goeth before a fall.

October 1998: The Release of the Jones-Milewski E-mail Messages

The controversy arising from these revelations was intense. Other news organizations quickly picked up the story and the opposition parties made it their principal focus in the House of Commons. There were allegations of "doormat diplomacy." Events at the Public Complaints Commission inquiry then took a curious turn.

On 25 September, the counsel for RCMP officers, George MacIntosh, sought and obtained an order from the PCC requiring Craig Jones to provide the commission with any documents he had relating to APEC. Jones handed over many documents and a high-capacity computer disk containing some 780 e-mail messages. Commission counsel Chris Considine, however, had no time to review the material, as he had done with other evidence. He proposed that MacIntosh be allowed to review the messages, on the understanding that he would share with other parties those he wished to use. This did not happen. Instead, on 9 October, a selection from the e-mail messages was tabled at the inquiry by MacIntosh. Principally, he had chosen Craig Jones's messages to and from me.

A remarkable feature of this package was that, although my own messages were selected, edited, printed, and disclosed by MacIntosh, his cross-examination of Craig Jones focused on Jones's messages, not mine. Equally remarkable was the fact that, when Jones objected to their distribution, MacIntosh offered no resistance, remarking, "That would be too late, wouldn't it?" It was a revealing exchange (13 October):

CRAIG JONES: ... The purpose of this process, of course, was to allow us the opportunity to challenge the admissibility or relevance of any particular piece of this correspondence before it was put to the panel. I have a letter from – from Mr. Considine to Mr. Macintosh that he copied to me, in which that – that arrangement appears to be confirmed ... I do not believe that it's proper for this panel to accept all of these e-mails into evidence as one, without reviewing them as to the relevance and admissibility of these things; and I object to Mr. Macintosh's doing this ... Mr. Chair, may I also ask that these documents not be released to the members of the media, as I believe Mr. Macintosh has already done?

GEORGE MACINTOSH: Well, Mr. Jones, if I had done that, Sir, that would be too late, wouldn't it?

Jonathan Oppenheim, another complainant whose e-mail messages were thus exposed, also objected:

JONATHAN OPPENHEIM: ... And a real concern that – that the RCMP and the Federal Government think that it's okay if someone makes a complaint to start delving into their private lives, and I think it sends a very clear message to Complainants, that if you lodge a complaint, you're gonna be under personal attack on issues that have nothing to do with – with the mandate of this Inquiry.

I had cause to reflect on this remark in the days to come. Jones's lawyer, Joe Arvay, weighed in, too:

JOSEPH ARVAY: I think Mr. Jones' concern is that Mr. Macintosh has chosen to make an exhibit, and is now part of the public record, documents that he never used.

The commission agreed, and, without objection from MacIntosh, my messages were stricken from the record of the inquiry. It was, as he said, too late to strike them from the *public* record – not that the assembled journalists seemed to care one way or the other. Indeed, even though the messages were tabled on live television, before a large press corps, nobody found any news in them. The national media didn't mention them at all, and there was only a passing mention in the *Vancouver Sun,* buried in a story about Craig Jones's testimony regarding his signs.

It's interesting to note that the RCMP's lawyers – the firm of Farris, Vaughan, Wills, and Murphy – were simultaneously acting for the two Southam papers in Vancouver – the *Sun* and the *Province.* The *Sun* story, written by Jeff Lee and published on 10 October 1998, was notable for its reference to a section of the e-mail messages that had not been publicly released, suggesting privileged access on the part of the author. This was confirmed six months later, on 17 April 1999, when Lee told a convention of the Canadian Association of Journalists that he had obtained the messages selected by MacIntosh "one or two days" before they were tabled at the inquiry. He added that, in retrospect, he felt he had been used to undermine my credibility. True or not, the fact that he was given the selected package of messages certainly suggested a desire to obtain publicity for them, even if they served no purpose at the inquiry.

As it turned out, though, the *Sun* story barely touched on the issue. If the purpose of the disclosure was to generate controversy, it failed – on the first attempt.

The *Province* Story of 14 October

A second attempt was made five days after the initial release, on 14 October. It came in the form of an unsigned news story in the *Province,* and was credited to "Southam Newspapers." This story, unlike its predecessor in the *Sun,* was prominently featured on page 3, and dealt exclusively with the e-mail messages. It set the tone for what followed by asserting at the outset that I had "been advising one of the protesters."

The point of the piece was to insinuate that Craig Jones was not thinking for himself but was coached by me, and that there was some impropriety in our sharing information. A highly unusual feature of the story, which purported to be a news report, was that no sources were given or quoted to back up its contention, something that editors normally insist upon. In fact, the newspaper's reporter, Keith Fraser, denied authorship of the story. The anonymous writer simply asserted that I had been "advising" Jones, on the grounds that I "gave Craig Jones questions to be put to the Prime Minister's Office and discussed upcoming TV reports."

The idea that reporters should *not* discuss upcoming reports with sources was, of course, bizarre, although the *Province* was at least consistent: it did not sully itself by speaking to the subject of its story – me. The suggestion that I had given Jones some sort of secret information by discussing questions "to be put" to the PMO was equally preposterous. It refers to a message, dated 9 January 1998, in which I described unanswered questions I had long since put to the PMO and had reported on the air on 18 December 1997. In other words, both the questions and the lack of answers had been discussed publicly three weeks before the message was written. On the face of it, it's hard to know why any journalist would think it improper to tell one person what it was proper to tell a million. Besides that, if it were a sin to reveal information that might hurt one party or another, then none of my reports should have been aired.

A second allegation in the *Province* story was that my messages revealed "frequent communication" with Craig Jones "as Jones prepared his complaints." Again, the public record showed that Jones's complaints were filed on 8 December 1997 and that our first e-mail message was exchanged the following day – a product, perhaps, but certainly not a cause of the complaints that preceded it.

A curiosity of the *Province* account was that it never mentioned the person who made the e-mail messages public: counsel for the RCMP. As noted earlier, a source is something that more old-fashioned editors like to have. While omitting this highly relevant fact, the story strove to imply that Jones, like me, had been too free with information: "Confidential government documents were given to the complainants by the commission, but those who received them signed an undertaking saying they would not release them ... Milewski had a series of scoops based on those confidential documents." The *Province,* of course, had no idea who my sources were.

Even so, the *Province*'s sister paper, the *Sun,* told a similar tale the following day – which was another oddity, considering that the story was six days old, that the *Sun* had already reported it, and that nothing new had happened since then. The piece, by Jeff Lee, alleged that "Mr. Milewski provided [to Mr. Jones] a synopsis of information he obtained from a confidential document and made unflattering comments about police and federal lawyers." Three problems suggest themselves. First, the "synopsis" that the *Sun* said I had given to Jones was the one that the *Province* had accused Jones of giving to me, and contained nothing that Jones would not properly have already. As the *Province* had correctly noted, these documents had been given to all the complainants by the commission.

Second, no "unflattering" reference to any federal lawyer was evident in the messages that had been made public. There *was* one, however, that had been deleted before publication by the RCMP's counsel. Evidently, the *Sun* had been given the unedited original.

This was later confirmed by the author of the story, Jeff Lee, as noted earlier. His article, suggesting dismay that I had revealed "confidential" information to Craig Jones, expressed no dismay that I had revealed the same information, in detail, to the nation as a whole – just as the *Sun* had also done, although in somewhat bizarre circumstances.

These circumstances bear some discussion. The same day that its story appeared – 15 October – the *Sun's* editorial board condemned a "worrying traffic in confidential documents" between Jones and myself. This was odd, considering that, five weeks earlier, the *Sun* led its newspaper with the fruits of the same "worrying traffic." Lacking any of the actual documents, the *Sun*, on 9 September, had unblushingly headlined quotes taken from a leaked copy of my "synopsis" – the same one that the *Sun* labelled "confidential" when I shared it with Craig Jones. The *Sun* had never seen the documents, and neither had its source, who had merely obtained my notes. The *Sun* knew the notes were mine and gambled its front page on my credibility – crediting "CBC News" with the quotes, including those we had not broadcast. Apparently, my "traffic" in confidential documents was not so "worrying" as to stop the *Sun* from cashing in on it as soon as possible.

In short, the *Sun* got this "confidential" material from me and disclosed it – sight unseen – on its front page. Then, its editorial page condemned me for disclosing the same material, *privately,* to the person accused by its sister paper of being my source.

As strange as all this was, it remained a minor local story that was now six days old. The national media still didn't touch it. A new development was needed if any controversy was to take flight. The Prime Minister's Office provided just that, in a stirring press release on 16 October 1998.

This document was in the form of a complaint to the CBC Ombudsman, but it made no challenge to the facts laid out in my reporting, an omission of such overwhelming importance that some attempt should surely have been made to disguise it. Indeed, in a second letter, Peter Donolo made just such an attempt by claiming that the "facts" had been challenged in the first letter. Which facts these were was not revealed.

The complaint was, instead, an attack upon my motives. Its essence was that I was motivated by bias, rather than by the abundant and undisputed evidence presented. It was my good fortune, however, not to be called "biased." In the name of the Prime Minister, Donolo told the nation that I was "biassed [sic]" and had a "conflict of interest." He adopted the claims of the *Province* and the *Sun* as fact, and offered them as proof that I was "secretly conspiring" against the government with a lifelong Liberal, Craig Jones. In this way, the RCMP and the PMO engineered and exploited the publication of my e-mail messages to attack me personally.

An intriguing aspect of the Donolo letter was that it purported to be written in ignorance of what the e-mail messages actually contained. It seemed to rely solely upon the published accounts noted earlier, and added that "the e-mails revealed in the newspapers are, we understand, only a fraction of those written by Mr. Milewski which are in the possession of the RCMP Public Complaints Commission. I encourage you to contact the Commission to obtain the remainder of these documents." At the same time, the letter objected to my quoting Professor Wesley Pue on the grounds that, "according to documents tabled at the inquiry, Mr. Pue ... has been advising complainants." Since no such thing was reported anywhere, and since the only documents referring to Professor Pue were the Jones-Milewski e-mail messages, we are forced to conclude that Donolo relied on the messages that he supposedly did not have. What's more, Professor Pue had never been an adviser to any of the complainants, and none of the documents cited by Mr. Donolo suggested otherwise.

In any event, very few journalists were fooled by all this. On 22 October, under the headline "How to muzzle an irritating reporter," Naomi Klein wrote in the *Toronto Star:*

> What concerns me is the ethics of the bizarre manner in which the RCMP and the Prime Minister's Office turned these private notes into public documents. The story behind the release of the E-mails raises grave questions about whether the government and the RCMP used the commission ... to take out a journalist ... [it] looks an awful lot like a cleverly orchestrated ploy – as though the RCMP lawyer used his access to Jones' E-mail archive to target and embarrass a critical journalist ... Their only purpose has been in providing the Prime Minister's Office with what little fodder it needed to attempt to discredit [Milewski] ... When the RCMP lawyers get their hands on documents relating to Jean Chrétien's critics, the Prime Minister's Office, to borrow a phrase from Terry Milewski, sure knows how to "milk" them.

Even so, the PMO's complaint was effective, and gave national exposure to the story. Now the *Globe and Mail* had a front-page item: an unprecedented prime ministerial attack upon a journalist. Prominently featured was a 20 January 1998 e-mail message in which I argued that a rumoured allegation against RCMP Staff Sergeant Hugh Stewart was unsubstantiated, and poked fun at Craig Jones's lawsuit as "Jones vs the Forces of Darkness." The PMO tried to represent this as a solemn declaration of intent to blacken the name of an innocent government – and much of the coverage dutifully reported with a straight face that "Milewski referred to the government as the forces of darkness."

How many readers took this seriously is questionable. One cartoonist

(Gable, *Globe and Mail*, 13 November 1998) showed Darth Vader wielding a censor's stamp and telling a CBC reporter to "just carry on as if I weren't here." Another (Peterson, *Vancouver Sun,* same day) portrayed Jean Chrétien as Darth Vader, complaining, "And yet Milewski roams free!" Inevitably, my wife presented me with a Darth Vader mask to take the kids out on Halloween.

During this period, the CBC conducted an internal inquiry, and announced on 6 November that I would be removed from coverage of the APEC affair "permanently." In a letter that day to Peter Donolo, issued in a press release, the CBC endorsed the substance of my reports, but added this:

> Our journalists must abide by the principles of accuracy, integrity and fairness. Further we are obligated to avoid situations or contacts which could give rise to perceptions of partiality. Therefore, we cannot condone a reporter offering or seem [sic] to be offering advice on legal strategy to anyone involved in a story. Also, we cannot condone a reporter sharing questions submitted to one party in a story to [sic] another party in the story.

The Ombudsman's Report

The Ombudsman assigned to investigate the PMO's complaint emphatically repudiated these conclusions, however, saying that it would be "obvious" to "anyone" who read my correspondence with Craig Jones "in good faith" that I was *not* giving him advice.

The Ombudsman was a distinguished Quebec journalist, the late Marcel Pépin, who had earned an enviable reputation for fairness during a thirty-five-year career as a journalist and CBC executive. He issued a report on 23 March 1999 that demolished the complaint with such finality that the PMO immediately dropped the matter. His report says much about the illegitimacy of the government's attack. M. Pépin could not accept that our critics could silence a journalist by making him "part of the story" and creating a bogus "perception of bias." He began by considering the source:

> It is the PMO, thus the Prime Minister himself, we must conclude, who does not like the way in which ... Terry Milewski covered the APEC Summit ... Furthermore, the CBC is a public corporation whose journalistic independence is guaranteed by legislation, but which nonetheless comes under the indirect authority of the Prime Minister. A complaint from the Communications Department of the head of government therefore takes on unusual importance ... so much so that

many commentators have even seen in this an indirect threat to the independence of the CBC.

Having thus put up his guard, M. Pépin set about his demolition:

The journalist was not marching under the banners during the APEC Summit, he was not paid by Jones and his group, he did not use CBC material to promote the cause of this group, and in his reports he constantly supported his claims with documents which he showed on the screen. At no time did he lack loyalty to his employer, or abuse the prestige of his function to promote any ideology whatsoever ... And I think that Mr. Milewski was convinced that the need to ensure visitors' security was not enough to explain the action of the police force at the APEC Summit, nor to justify limitation of the exercise of the demonstrators' basic rights – where he shared the concern of Mr. Jones and his group. A community of views is not synonymous with conflict of interest.

While he was at it, the Ombudsman condemned the claims made by the *Province,* the PMO, and the CBC that I "advised" Craig Jones. This section was particularly damaging in its implications:

The Province is mistaken and commits a serious sin against the journalistic principle of accuracy ... To anyone who in good faith consulted the exchange of correspondence between Terry Milewski and Craig Jones, it would have appeared obvious that Mr. Milewski's objective was not to provide material for Mr. Jones's legal strategy ... it certainly cannot be affirmed that he was advising Mr. Jones and Mr. Arvay on their legal strategy. What he wanted, and no more, was to obtain some answers to his questions.

The conspiracy theory, the forces of darkness ... nothing was spared:

The word "conspiracy" implies a secret agreement to harm someone or an institution. It ascribes to those conspiring malicious intentions and such intentions cannot be ascribed to a journalist who is attempting by normal means to obtain information about a matter of public interest ... I am incapable of imagining any professional journalist seriously qualifying the government of Canada as the forces of darkness. I know dozens, though, who in private conversations would use this sort of expression cynically or jokingly.

The sharing of questions got the same treatment:

Some of these questions were expressed publicly in an elaborate report aired on the CBC three weeks before they were provided to Mr. Jones ... I have not found anything in the *Journalistic Standards and Practices* that prohibits this sort of procedure between a journalist and his source ... I cannot subscribe to the interpretation by CBC management, which sees in this a breach of ethics. What principle says that a reporter should refrain from giving information that belongs to him in order to obtain other information? This is an entirely new theory to me, which I cannot find any support for in the academic sources I have consulted.

Not content to merely dismiss the complaint, the Ombudsman urged other journalists not to be intimidated by it:

My finding is that Mr. Milewski's reports as a whole cannot be faulted, from the point of view of accuracy and fairness ... That he could have a penchant towards respect for basic rights and be constantly skeptical regarding official explanations does not constitute, in my opinion, a breach of conduct. No one is asking journalists to pretend they are indifferent and blasé when covering events as controversial as those concerned here. Objectivity must not be confused with dull and pale neutrality.

No one will soon accuse Marcel Pépin of "dull and pale neutrality." Sadly, his superb report proved to be his last. One can only hope that his bark, and his bite, will deter future Prime Ministers from similar attempts to "shoot the messenger." I wouldn't bet on it, though.

10

Personal Reflections on the Ill-Fated First APEC Inquiry

GERALD M. MORIN, QC

Time and time again Canadian television viewers have been mesmerized by the image of an RCMP officer drenching protesters at the 1997 APEC summit with pepper spray from a canister the size of a fire extinguisher. They watched in real time and in slow motion. Broadcasters never tired of showing the clip. Viewers appeared never to tire of seeing a thick stream of liquid pepper cascade across the camera lens. It was as though the collective eye of the country had been seared. Our security in the belief that we lived in the kindest and gentlest of democracies seemed shaken. Each commentator scrambled to be more indignant than yesterday's indignant commentator, who was more indignant than the previous day's commentator. Facile editorials filled the newspapers. Members of Parliament sought political advantage from the event. Interest groups used it as a springboard to launch their own agendas.

In the midst of this furor and finger pointing, a panel of the RCMP Public Complaints Commission (PCC) sought to conduct a fair and impartial review of the facts. What really happened? Who did what, and why? Our mandate was to inquire into and report upon:

(a) the events that took place during, or in connection with, demonstrations during the APEC conference in Vancouver, B.C., between November 23 and 27, 1997, on or near the U.B.C. Campus and subsequently at the U.B.C. and Richmond Detachments of the R.C.M.P.;

(b) whether the conduct of the R.C.M.P. involved in the events was appropriate to the circumstances;

(c) whether the conduct of members of the R.C.M.P. involved in the events was consistent with respect for the Fundamental Freedoms guaranteed by section 2 of the *Canadian Charter of Rights and Freedoms.*

We did not complete our mission. In December 1998, I resigned as chair of the panel. Shortly afterwards, the other two commissioners resigned. It is now the task of former judge Ted Hughes to answer the questions that Canadians want, and need, answered.

It is of the utmost importance that Hughes conduct his inquiry free from interference or distraction. This book may be published before he has heard all of the evidence or completed his deliberations and rendered a report. In this brief chapter, I try to provide a personal perspective that may be useful to those interested in the integrity of the complaints process while attempting to steer clear of any issue or area that might affect Ted Hughes's ability to fulfil the mandate that we could not.

These reflections are not intended to be a thorough analysis of all that transpired during the ten months that I chaired the first APEC Inquiry. My comments are not meant to be the final word, or even a complete explanation. I simply chronicle my reasons for resigning as chair of the panel. Readers may notice "holes" in the narrative:

• I do not dwell upon the well-publicized remarks of Solicitor General Andy Scott as recorded by MP Dick Proctor. While the unguarded banter between the Solicitor General and his seatmate on a plane gave Mr. Proctor and the media an opportunity to embarrass Mr. Scott, its further review here would provide little of value.

• I do not detail the allegations of RCMP Constable Russell Black that I may have prejudged the outcome of the inquiry, or my response, or the responses of others refuting the allegations. I did nothing and said nothing that could have been construed as prejudging the outcome of the inquiry. I prejudged nothing. While very distressing, Constable Black's allegations did not have a direct impact on my decision to resign as chair of the panel. I will have to touch upon the allegations, however, because PCC chair Shirley Heafey's response to them are a part of the circumstances that led to my resignation.

• Finally, I must emphasize that my comments here are my comments alone, and not the comments of my fellow commissioners Vina Starr and John Wright, or of the panel as a whole. Ms. Starr and Mr. Wright conducted themselves with dignity throughout, and the contents of our many discussions and deliberations with respect to the hearings shall remain between the three of us.

In the final analysis, I resigned because of a significant disagreement with PCC chair Heafey over the respective roles of the commission and the panel. My involvement in the APEC Inquiry began in February 1998 and ended some ten months later with my resignation as chair of the panel. The last six weeks of my tenure were fraught with tension between Ms. Heafey and the panel, and particularly between Ms. Heafey and me. The primary source of the friction was our differing perceptions of the role of the panel vis-à-vis Ms. Heafey as chair of the commission. As chair of the commission, Ms. Heafey had a role to play in the work of the panel. In the final weeks of the life of the first panel, however, I came to the conclusion that she had gone past her legitimate role and had encroached upon the decision-making role of the panel to the point that the panel's independence had been fatally compromised.

The Roles and Make-up of the Commission and the Panel

To place my concerns and comments in perspective, it is necessary to understand how the RCMP Public Complaints Commission functions.

The PCC was established by the Royal Canadian Mounted Police Act. When the commission chair deems it to be in the public interest, she can institute a hearing to inquire into a complaint, as she did in the case of the APEC affair. The commission chair then appoints a panel to conduct the hearing.

The panel is responsible for conducting the inquiry and preparing a report setting out its findings in accordance with its mandate. It is the trier of fact. The panelists are "judges," if you will. The commission chair is responsible for supervising the work and staff of the commission (which provides administrative assistance to the panel) and, with the approval of the Treasury Board, engaging professionals to assist the panel. At a basic level, she ensures that the panel has the resources necessary to carry out its work. At another level, she seeks to ensure that a consistent and coherent body of policy is developed and applied by each panel. *It is vitally important, however, that in her efforts to ensure consistency and adherence to policy she does not interfere with the independence of the panel in performing its investigative function, which involves both fact finding and the making of recommendations.* The complainants and the public must have absolute confidence that the panel is completely free from hidden or overt influence.

The APEC panel had to determine the facts through an open hearing process, and from those facts determine whether the RCMP had acted appropriately. The process is, and must be, transparent. If the panel's determinations are to be accepted as valid, all the factors upon which it bases its decisions must be known to all. Any influence from the commission chair, who is appointed by the government (which, of course, has a vested interest in the outcome of the inquiry), not only is unfair and unacceptable to the participants but would also impair the public's faith in the institution. We must be impartial and must be seen by all to be impartial.

I had been a member of the PCC for a little more than a year before the APEC Inquiry. In February 1998, Ms. Heafey asked me to sit on the APEC Inquiry panel. I declined. I felt that the panel would have to hear evidence for several months, which was too long a time for me to be absent from my law practice in Prince Albert, Saskatchewan. A week later, she phoned and asked again. Again I said no. She called a third time and said she thought the inquiry would take only three or four weeks. Although I was certain that the hearing would take much longer, at least twelve weeks, I was able to clear my schedule and agreed to serve. This was the second panel struck by Ms. Heafey since her appointment as commission chair.

Ms. Heafey and I agreed that I should chair the panel because of my significant courtroom experience. The panel chair has no greater power than the other commissioners; he or she simply directs the proceedings. The other two commissioners on the panel were Vina Starr and John Wright. Vina Starr is a no-nonsense Aboriginal lawyer from Kitimat, British Columbia. She articulates her opinions and positions fearlessly and eloquently. She backs down before no person but will consider all opinions before taking a final position. John Wright had had significant experience with complaints hearings. His experience with the complaints process, coupled with an uncanny ability to find an acceptable middle course between seemingly irreconcilable positions, was invaluable.

The Issue of Funding for Student Complainants Dominates the Hearing
In the spring of 1998, the student complainants applied to the commission for funding so that they could retain counsel to ensure that all matters were thoroughly canvassed. The hearings were adjourned until September to allow time for a decision on the application for funding and to facilitate full disclosure of documents to all of the parties.

Section 45.45(5) of the RCMP Act states that any person who satisfies the commission that he or she has a "substantial and direct interest in a complaint shall be afforded a full and ample opportunity, in person or by counsel, to present evidence, to cross-examine witnesses and to make representations at the hearing." The right to participate is clear. What is not clear is whether funding must be provided in such circumstances and, if so, who would provide the funds. The panel did not have the ability to provide funding, although Ms. Heafey, as commission chair, could do so if she had the approval of the Treasury Board.

On 21 July 1998, the panel wrote to Solicitor General Andy Scott, requesting that funding be provided to retain counsel for the students. This request was denied in September. The students did not give up, however, and made applications to the Federal Court of Canada and further representations to the panel. The public, or at least the media, focused on the issue of funding for the students, which had a direct correlation to the perceived fairness of the hearing and the way in which the panel's final report would be viewed. On 6 October the panel again wrote to the Solicitor General:

> In the eyes of the public, the scope and importance of this hearing has risen so much that public confidence in our findings and recommendations may require separately funded legal representation for the complainants. There are important fundamental issues about who we are as Canadians at stake in this hearing.

Shortly after, Ms. Heafey met with the panel over dinner and expressed her displeasure with the amount and type of media exposure that the issue of student funding had received. She stated that she "was under a lot of pressure in Ottawa." This and other comments left the impression that she had been in contact with the Solicitor General or officials from his department.

For the first time, I felt that the independence of the panel was being threatened. The panel had chosen to revive the issue of government funding for the student participation. Our responsibility was to ensure, as best we could, that the process was fair and that the final report would be seen as the result of that fair process. Now the chair of the commission was saying that she (or perhaps others) did not approve of the panel's handling of the funding issue.

My feeling of unease grew as the meeting with Ms. Heafey continued. She also took great exception to the way in which the panel's counsel, Chris Considine, was handling media inquiries. She said that she did not want Mr. Considine speaking for the panel, and that she had received a call from someone (whom she did not identify) asking, "Why am I hearing about the panel's decisions on television?"

The meeting with Ms. Heafey was most disconcerting. Had she crossed the line between her role of ensuring consistent policy and our role of determining the appropriate method by which facts could be adduced and the public kept informed? The panel office was receiving thirty to fifty media inquiries each day. This was a *public* hearing process. There had to be a response to the questions of the public that were brought to the panel through the media. Mr. Considine was in the best position to provide the information requested and had done an exceptional job of responding clearly to the media while carrying out his other duties as panel counsel. We had made the decision to keep the public informed. To silence Mr. Considine would be to silence the panel, because it is clearly inappropriate for panel members to provide media interviews.

This meeting was a turning point in the relationship between the panel and the commission chair. An attempt was made to construct a wall that would insulate the panel from interference. For example, the panel instructed Steve MacDonald (a lawyer lent to it from Ms. Heafey's office) not to communicate with Ms. Heafey or anyone else regarding any discussions relating to the hearing or any decisions that were made by or being considered by the panel. He was to report only to the panel.

On 16 October the Solicitor General again rejected the panel's request to provide funding for the students' counsel. The panel would have to meet to determine its position on this important issue. On 18 October, before we could meet, we were presented with our "position" by Ms. Heafey. I was given a handwritten "decision" (see appendix on page 168) and instructed by Ms. Heafey to "read it into the record" of the proceedings. I was informed in a written memorandum from Steve MacDonald that Ms. Heafey had retained University of Ottawa law professor Ed Ratushny, who had written the statement.

At this point, I felt that Ms. Heafey had crossed the line. In my view, she was now not only seeking to determine the way in which the panel would ensure public confidence in the process (which is arguably one of her roles) but also seeking to assume part of the decision-making function of the panel. It was my opinion that the breadth of the statement, written without consulting the panel, amounted to dictating the way in which the panel would fulfil its mandate:

• The statement that I was directed to read into the official record was premised on events that had not taken place. According to the statement, "over the past weekend the panel deliberated whether it could do any-thing further to address the issue of unrepresented parties." This was clearly untrue, as no such deliberations had been conducted by the panel.

- The panel was instructed to close the debate regarding funding for the student complainants. The statement read: "The avenue of public fund-ing for counsel for the complainants before this hearing is now closed." We had made no such decision. The apparent purpose of the directive was to end public debate. The panel was not concerned with public debate but with ensuring that the facts were determined and that the process was fair. Was the directive from Ottawa? It did not matter. It was improper, regardless of the source. It was the responsibility of the panel, and no one else, to determine whether the panel's role with respect to funding had come to an end.

- The practical effect of the statement was to instruct the panel to curtail the flow of information from the panel to the public. The statement read: "This Panel has now decided that it will adopt a similar approach for the remainder of the proceedings. Mr. Chris Considine and co-counsel Mr. Kevin Gillett will now assume the role of independent counsel and are instructed to marshal and present the evidence on behalf of the com-plainants and to advance such evidence and present argument in accor-dance with the law and the public interest and to act at arms length from the panel ... The role of independent counsel will not include any involvement in any possible 'public relations' endeavours in relation to these proceedings. Accordingly, independent counsel is instructed not to engage in any further communication with representatives of the media."

The panel could not maintain its independence and fulfil its mandate by submitting to the directive of the PCC chair. The propriety of the chair's dictating the decisions of the panel was a serious matter that had to be addressed with the chair. When the hearing resumed on 19 October, the panel did not comment on student funding or the role of commission counsel. We had resolved to meet with Ms. Heafey in the immediate future to determine whether the issue of her interference with the independence of the panel could be resolved.

The Panel's Focus Is Diverted by Constable Russell Black

On 22 October, as we were attempting to arrange a meeting with Ms. Heafey to discuss our serious concerns regarding the prepared statement, I was informed about allegations made by RCMP Constable Russell Black. Black asserted that he had overheard me make comments in the casino in Prince Albert indicating that I had prejudged the results of the inquiry process. We immediately adjourned the hearing so that this matter could be dealt with.

Despite Black's allegations, we still felt that it was imperative to meet with Ms. Heafey about our many concerns regarding her interference with the panel's independence. (The panel did not discuss Constable Black's allegations, to ensure that Ms. Starr and Mr. Wright were not "tainted.") A meeting was set for 31 October in Vancouver. I flew to Vancouver but Ms. Heafey did not attend because her mother was ill. The panel offered to meet with her in Ottawa, but she indicated that she had been in a car accident. All our attempts to meet with her in November were unsuccessful.

I was finally able to meet with Ms. Heafey in Vancouver in early December. I had received an agenda, prepared by Ms. Heafey, limiting discussion of the roles of the commission chair and the panel to half an hour. This was her response to several letters from the panel detailing specific concerns over her interference with the panel's independence. Thirty minutes was simply not enough time to explain and resolve these serious concerns.

Although the most significant issue was the panel's independence, it was not the only issue between us. After Constable Black had made his allegations, I retained the services of independent legal counsel and a private investigator to investigate the allegations. Ms. Heafey considered this inappropriate because the "media might find out." I did not care whether or not the media found out. The allegations of Constable Black reflected upon me personally and, if accepted, would have derailed an important inquiry. I had a right to defend my integrity and the public had a right to know more about the source of, and the motivation for, his allegations.

Further (and as an interesting sidebar), two things had occurred that I thought odd enough to merit investigation. First, the conference room in which the panel met had been broken into in late November, despite reasonable security precautions. Nothing appeared to have been taken or disturbed, so we thought nothing more of it at the time. Second, a few days later my car, which was with me in Vancouver, had been broken into. Because my vehicle has a built-in computer, technicians were able to determine that the car had been entered at least four times by someone who probably had sophisticated electronic equipment that could bypass the car's security system. Nothing had been taken from the car. Perhaps I was being paranoid, but where I come from, people who break into cars usually make it worth their while by taking the valuables.

I had no idea whether the two events were related or who might be responsible. In consultation with commission counsel, we had the commission offices and my vehicle swept for electronic listening devices. None were found. Interestingly, when Mr. Considine contacted a private investigator to look into the two breaches in the car and office, the company informed us that they could not work for us due to a conflict of interest. The obvious questions are who were they working for and when did that work occur.

Ms. Heafey interpreted my actions to mean that I believed the RCMP might have been involved in the security breaches. I did not believe then, and do not believe now, that the RCMP had been involved. I had no idea whether the security breaches were coincidental or indicative of something more sinister. I was simply erring on the side of caution.

It was abundantly clear when I met with Ms. Heafey that there could be no solution that satisfactorily resolved my unease over her interactions with the panel some six weeks earlier and our disagreement over the handling of the Russell Black allegations and the latest security precautions. I could not continue as chair and tendered my resignation. A few days later, Ms. Starr and Mr. Wright did likewise.

It was with great regret that I resigned from the panel. I had been privileged to serve with Ms. Starr and Mr. Wright, both of whom I hold in the highest regard. Our ability to continue with the hearings ended with the directive to read the statement written by Mr. Ratushny upon Ms. Heafey's instructions. At that point, all pretence of allowing an independent panel to control its process and fulfil its mandate ended. Subtle influence had given way to express instruction. The mere attempt to control the panel in this manner was sufficient to undermine the entire process and lead to our resignations.

Would I have been able to continue with the panel in the wake of Constable Black's allegations? I don't know. Although more than twelve months have passed since these allegations were made known to me, the sense of outrage and helplessness that I felt then remains with me. The allegations struck at the core of my being. As an Aboriginal growing up in Saskatchewan and later as an Aboriginal lawyer in the predominantly non-Aboriginal profession of law, I have always been keenly aware of the injustices wrought by those who prejudge. I know the pain inflicted by those who judge matters and people based on preconceptions rather than on the facts. Now I was accused of that which I abhorred.

The implications of the allegations were serious and multifaceted. Could I continue as chair of the panel in light of clear allegations of bias, no matter how untrue I knew them to be? Was it in the best interests of fulfilling the mandate that I step down and allow the other members of the panel to continue? On the other hand, should the entire hearing process be derailed as a result of one individual making unfounded statements? But for my resignation these questions might have been answered in the courts and through further investigation. I suspect they will never be answered now.

These questions weigh upon me and are, for the most part, unique to this particular panel and my involvement in it. More important is the question of the integrity of the complaints process. Can the public have confidence in a process where a vitally important issue, such as the one before my panel, can be influenced so greatly by one person who is appointed by the government? Ought the Solicitor General to have the final say about who should and who should not receive funding in order to effectively participate in the process? How best can the roles of the commission chair and the panel be clarified and separated to ensure the independence of the decision-makers? These are some of the questions that must be addressed if the RCMP Public Complaints Commission is to properly perform its very important function.

I leave the answers to others. As for me, I return to Prince Albert, wiser for the experience.

Appendix

The following statement was faxed to the RCMP PCC panel (chaired by Gerald Morin) on 18 October 1998 by Ms. Shirley Heafey with instructions to "read it into the record" of the proceedings. The panel declined to do so.

Opening Statement of the Panel
(Oct. 19, 1998)

On Friday, October 16, this PANEL received a letter addressed to the Chair of the Panel (Gerry Morin) from the Solicitor General of Canada, the Hon. Andy Scott, which maintained the Government's decision that funding for the complainants' legal fees will not be provided. *[The letter, together with the Panel's earlier letters should be read into the record if that has not already been done.]

The Panel now wishes to address Parliament through its enabling statute. Parliament chose not to grant the Commission authority to provide such funding.

However, a recent judgment of the Federal Court of Canada declared that the Commission "... has the authority to make a recommendation that funding be provided if it wishes to do so." As a result, this Panel did make such a recommendation which has now been denied. The avenue of public funding for Counsel to the complainants before this hearing is now closed.

Over the past weekend, the Panel deliberated whether it could do anything further to address the issue of unrepresented parties. In doing so, we have sought guidance from some of the observations contained in the Federal Court judgment referred to earlier. There, Madam Justice Reed described the following passage from the independent legal opinion on funding to be "instructive":

> "Mr. Whitehall expressed the view that the role of Commission Counsel is not as restricted as had been suggested. He also pointed out that there was nothing wrong with Commission members cross-examining witnesses. While that may be legally correct, aggressive questioning by Panel members may seriously detract from the perception of impartiality of the Panel and the credibility of its subsequent recommendations. Similarly, Commission counsel is an extension of the Panel and must avoid the perception of favouring some parties over others. It is true that an inquiry is not, essentially, adversary [sic]. But there are occasions during inquiries when aggressive cross-examination of witnesses or protection of witnesses from overly aggressive cross-examination must be undertaken by Commission counsel.

> It is difficult to maintain a perception of impartiality when taking on an adversarial role in public and then meeting in private with the Panel to discuss the proceedings. This is an inherent dilemma for Commission counsel where there is a dual role of presenting the evidence and advising the Panel. The example provided by Mr. Arvay at page 219 with respect to the Securities Commission is preferable. Counsel who presents the case to the Panel acts at arm's length from the Panel, which may draw upon its own counsel for advice as may be required. Similarly, counsel for some human rights commissions have the statutory responsibility for 'carriage of the complaint' before a tribunal panel." (Page 11)

Earlier, she had emphasized the "public interest" dimension of a complainant's role:

> "[The complainant] acts as a representative of the public interest – the public interest in ensuring that the police do not overstep the bounds of what is proper conduct." (Page 10)

She also noted that there were attractive features to the:

... suggestion that independent commission counsel be appointed to act as advocate for all the complainants ... (Page 12)

However, that option was not before her.

This model of independent counsel has been adopted by the Canadian Judicial Council in the conduct of public hearings pursuant to the *Judges Act*. Independent Counsel has been appointed to present the evidence related to a judge's alleged misconduct. Instructions are given to such counsel to act in accordance with the law and the public interest and to act at arm's length from the Panel conducting the proceedings.

This Panel has decided that we will now adopt a similar approach for the remainder of these proceedings. Mr. Chris Considine and co-counsel Mr. Kevin Gillett will now assume the role of independent counsel and are instructed to marshall and present the evidence on behalf of the complainants and to advance such evidence and present argument in accordance with the law and the public interest and to act at arm's length from the Panel. The Panel prefers to have these proceedings continue in a non-adversarial manner to the extent possible. However, where necessary, Independent Counsel will vigorously cross-examine witnesses who are represented by counsel and intervene to protect the interests of those who are not represented.

The Panel notes that Madam Justice Reed also stated:

"One has to acknowledge that there is a public relations strategy to the applicants' approach." (Page [illegible])

The role of Independent Counsel will not include any involvement in any possible "public relations" endeavours in relation to the proceedings. Accordingly, Independent Counsel is instructed not to engage in any further communications with representatives of the media.

The Panel wishes to acknowledge the valuable advice provided directly to us by Messrs. Considine and Gillett to date. However, in the current circumstances, we have decided that they can best assist the Commission and thereby advance the public interest in the role of Independent Counsel. This appointment will be more expeditious than retaining new Counsel for this purpose since they are already familiar with the proceedings. They will no longer have access to the Panel which is not available to any of the other Counsel participating in this hearing. Mr. Steven McDonell, who is present here today, has been appointed Counsel to the Panel and he will advise and assist us as may be required but will have no role in adducing evidence.

11

Raising the Dough: Funding for Lawyers at Public Inquiries

KAREN BUSBY

The inquiry of the RCMP Public Complaints Commission (PCC) into the RCMP's conduct at the Asia-Pacific Economic Cooperation conference in Vancouver in November 1997 raises a number of questions about the adequacy of existing mechanisms for ensuring government and police accountability for wrongdoing. In this chapter, I will show that unless complainants are represented by lawyers, such mechanisms, especially in complex and lengthy inquiries, are ineffective, one-sided in favour of those being called to account, and unfair to complainants. First I will outline some general legal principles governing tribunals like the PCC and the chronology of events at the APEC Inquiry that touch on the issue of funding for lawyers. Then I will describe various ways by which citizens who make complaints to tribunals such as the PCC can pay for legal representation. Finally, I will focus on the specific issue of using the public purse to pay the APEC complainants' legal bills.

A Short Story Leavened with Some Law

Some administrative tribunals, such as community panels making simple land use decisions or first-level labour grievance committees, conduct their proceedings in an informal matter. For example, witnesses might not be required to take an oath, cross-examination may not be permitted, and the hearing format may be an interview or a roundtable discussion. To help ensure informality and accessibility, some tribunals discourage, even prohibit, lawyers from appearing at their hearings. However, particularly where the parties disagree about the facts or where the outcomes of a tribunal hearing are significant (such as the loss of a job), a tribunal will sacrifice informality in order to use procedures that allow for a rigorous testing of the strength of the evidence. Because the PCC's investigations usually involve situations where the facts are contentious and the potential consequences are serious, the procedures used by this tribunal are very similar to those used in a formal courtroom, including the right to cross-examine witnesses and the right to be represented by a lawyer.

From the beginning of the APEC Inquiry, the public purse paid, directly or indirectly, to bring as many as a dozen lawyers to the table, including those representing the individual RCMP members against whom complaints were made, the RCMP as an entity, the PCC, the federal Department of Justice, and the University of British Columbia. In fact, other than the British Columbia Civil Liberties Association the only parties at the APEC Inquiry whose lawyers were *not* being paid from the public purse were the individual complainants, that is, the student protesters who said that, among other things, they had been assaulted, falsely imprisoned, strip-searched, defamed, and denied their constitutional rights of free expression and peaceable assembly by the RCMP, the federal government, and others. The students were obviously in no position to pay their lawyers and, as it became apparent that the inquiry might require months of preparation and hearings, their lawyers clearly could not continue to represent them until the end of the hearings without compensation.

The complainants asked the first PCC panel, chaired by Gerald Morin (the Morin Commission), to recommend that the federal government provide funding to the complainants for legal fees. The Morin Commission refused to do this, stating that if it made the suggested recommendation, it would compromise its duty to be impartial because it would appear to have taken on an advocacy role for only one side of the dispute, the complainants. An administrative tribunal will lose the power to decide the matters before it if can be shown that the tribunal's members are partial to or biased in favour of or against a party. An apprehension of bias, as long as it is a reasonable inference from known facts, can be sufficient to establish bias. In July 1998 the complainants commenced proceedings in the Federal Court of Canada to challenge the Morin Commission's refusal to recommend payment of legal expenses. Judge Barbara Reed rejected the PCC's bias argument and held that a recommendation that all parties, including the complainants, receive funding would not demonstrate a preference and therefore would not compromise the PCC's impartiality.

The RCMP raised a different objection in the Federal Court to the complainants' challenge. They argued that the PCC did not have the authority to make such a recommendation. Judge Reed also rejected this argument, stating that tribunals often need to request additional funds from governments in order to complete their hearings. Note that this determination flagged a problem related to bias, that of the independence of tribunals from the governments that created them. For example, what if a hearing goes on longer than anticipated, the tribunal does not have enough money to complete its job, and the government refuses to make additional allocations? This was the case with the Somalia Inquiry (concerning allegations of wrongdoing by the Canadian Armed Forces) in 1996, where the federal government refused to provide additional funding when the inquiry went on longer than planned. The tribunal was forced to close down without completing its investigation and report. Some people fear that the same problems could ultimately derail the APEC Inquiry.

In September 1998, just before the Morin Commission hearing was to begin, some of the complainants brought another application in Federal Court. This time they argued that the hearings should be suspended because the process was inherently biased in favour of the government. Judge James Hugessen held that, on balance, it was more important for the hearing to commence than to deal with a last-minute application to suspend it.

The Morin Commission made two separate requests to Andy Scott, the Solicitor General, for funding for the complainants' lawyers. Both requests were rejected, and the second rejection, in October 1998, was widely criticized in both Parliament and the media.

Shortly after the second rejection, Scott resigned, stating that allegations that he had prejudged the issues and interfered with the PCC made it untenable for him to continue as Solicitor General and could undermine public confidence in the tribunal. Within days of Scott's resignation, another batch of bias allegations arose, directed toward a rather different target. Stirred by a complaint from the Prime Minister's Office, the Canadian Broadcasting Corporation launched an investigation into reporter Terry Milewski's coverage of the APEC affair. (These allegations are discussed in the chapter by Milewski in this volume. In March 1999, the Ombudsman found that the PMO's concerns that Milewski's reporting was biased were not justified.) Then in November 1998, still more "bias" charges arose. At the instigation of the RCMP, the Federal Court ordered that the Morin Commission be stayed pending determination of whether Morin should be removed because of biased comments he was alleged to have made about the RCMP. Morin and the other two members of the panel resigned in December 1998, stating that the cumulative negative effect of the bias allegations was affecting public perceptions of the PCC's integrity. Morin also expressed his concern that the Ottawa-based chair of the PCC was meddling in the conduct of the APEC Inquiry.

By the end of December, Ted Hughes had been appointed as the sole member of a new panel (the Hughes Commission). A retired judge who had chaired other difficult inquiries, Hughes had the temperament and experience that would help him avoid and resist allegations of bias and demand some measure of independence from the government. While neither the Scott resignation nor the PMO's complaint to the CBC Ombudsman directly jeopardized the continuation of the APEC Inquiry, these events, together with the government's refusal to fund the complainants' lawyers and its perceived support for Morin's removal, fuelled speculation about the government's sincerity in professing a desire for the PCC to get on with the job. Hughes undoubtedly knew that he would need to take every precaution to ensure the PCC's impartiality and independence; any misstep would probably see either the RCMP or the government taking the PCC back to the Federal Court again.

The first matter Hughes considered when the APEC Inquiry resumed was whether he had the power to order the complainants' legal costs to be paid from the PCC's budget. Before deciding, he wrote to Lawrence MacAulay, the new Solicitor General of Canada, in February 1999, recommending that the government pick up the complainants' legal tab. MacAulay agreed to pay the legal fees incurred after Hughes's appointment for those complainants who had been directly involved in the confrontation with the police officers. I will consider the reasons for Scott's rejections of the Morin Commission's earlier requests in more detail below. In the next section I will discuss the various ways of paying for legal fees, other than direct government funding, that the APEC Inquiry complainants may have considered, and describe why they were not available in this situation.

Some Funding Recipes

Legal representation is expensive. Lawyers charge between $50 and $250 (or more) per hour, with an average hourly fee of about $150; during a trial or inquiry, they will often work fourteen-hour days. In complex or lengthy cases, more than one lawyer may be required to represent a particular set of interests. Out-of-pocket expenses such as expert witness fees, travel and accommodation, transcripts, and photocopying can add up very quickly. Allowing for preparation time, a modest estimate of the complainants' legal fees and expenses would be $500,000. Few citizens, and certainly none of the student complainants, have access to such large sums of money. So what other resources might be available to pay complainants' legal expenses in a case such as the APEC Inquiry?

Pro Bono and Contingency Fee Arrangements

Most lawyers do some legal work on a pro bono basis, that is, for little or no compensation. Obviously this mechanism works best when the matter requires only a few days, and does not work when the case, such as the APEC Inquiry, will take months of full-time work. Some lawyers work on a contingency fee basis, that is, for a percentage of the amount that the case is ultimately settled for or that is awarded by a court. Contingency fees are illegal in some Canadian jurisdictions, but even where they are permitted, lawyers will take cases on this basis only if there is a reasonable chance that a monetary award will be made. The PCC does not have any authority to recommend compensation for complainants (at best, it can arrange for the recovery of some out-of-pocket expenses), so a contingency fee arrangement between a client and a lawyer before this tribunal would not be workable.

Private Legal Defence Funds

Private or quasi-private legal funding mechanisms, such as support from charitable foundations, are very limited in Canada. Unlike the seemingly vast war chests in the United States, there are very few legal defence funds in Canada and those that exist are small and usually focused on very specific objectives. For example, the publicly funded but independent Court Challenges Program, which is probably the largest legal defence fund in Canada, has a total annual budget of just less than $3 million. It can fund only cases that raise either constitutional equality issues or minority language rights issues. To my knowledge, no Canadian legal defence fund has either the capital or the fund-raising power or the mandate to underwrite the legal fees for the APEC Inquiry complainants.

Legal Aid

In many Canadian jurisdictions, legal aid is available only for criminal matters and some family matters. Some jurisdictions fund public interest legal aid clinics, but their staffs and budgets are very small and need to be used to the greatest strategic advantage. (The public interest clinic in Manitoba, for example, has two lawyers, and clients are expected to raise some of the money needed for legal fees on their own.) Because of such limitations, the APEC Inquiry complainants were not able to obtain legal aid.

PCC Orders

A very small number of tribunals have the power to award intervener funding, that is, to require the dominant party or the party with the "deep pockets" to give other parties a sum of money for legal expenses at the beginning of the proceedings. Such power must, however, be expressly granted to the tribunal in legislation. Similarly, some tribunals could agree to pay the complainants' legal bills out of their own budget. The PCC does have the express power to pay some expenses, such as complainants' travel and accommodation. However, it does not have the power to order intervener funding and, although this question has not been clearly determined, it is unlikely that it has the authority to pay legal expenses out of its own budget.

Judges have the power to order one party to pay some of the legal expenses incurred by another party (referred to as the power to award "costs"). One purpose of costs is to encourage the parties to settle cases, so this power can be exercised only *after* the hearing is over; generally, the "winner" will be ordered to pay costs to the "loser." Where settlement is unlikely, as in the APEC Inquiry, because of the complexity of issues, the multiplicity of interests, and the need for the whole story to be publicly aired through a full hearing, the use of costs is not a suitable funding mechanism. It is also too uncertain a mechanism for complainants (and lawyers) to rely upon because they would not know until the inquiry was finished whether they would be reimbursed on this basis. Moreover, this power is available only where it has been specifically conferred on the tribunal by legislation – and it has not been given to the PCC.

Other Government Agencies

In some situations, a citizen's rights and interests can be pursued through a publicly funded, independent office designed for this purpose. For example, many governments have ombudsmen, public advocates, privacy and information commissioners, and the like. Such offices function best as negotiators or mediators between citizens and public servants on the issue of whether a particular task needs to be performed by a public servant. They usually lack coercive powers (that is, they cannot order anyone to do anything), and they do not have the resources, mandate, legal skills, or perceived independence necessary to undertake a task like client representation at a public inquiry such as the APEC Inquiry.

Sometimes the interests of the citizen and the government or agency are sufficiently similar that the government or agency lawyer can represent the citizen as well. For example, many complainants will not have their own lawyers before a human rights tribunal but will simply rely on the human rights commission lawyer to represent their interests. Obviously this kind of representation is impossible before the APEC Inquiry, as the government's interests are, in all likelihood, in conflict with those of the protesters.

In summary, from both a legal and a practical perspective, there are no funding mechanisms or other ways of accessing lawyers in hearings such as the APEC Inquiry other than government funding of the complainants' legal expenses. Given the dearth of options, can the case be made that the public purse should pick up this tab?

Bellying Up to the Bar?

In a letter dated 16 October 1998, Solicitor General Andy Scott set out three reasons to reject the Morin Commission's second recommendation that the federal government pay the complainants' legal fees: (1) the government had provided the PCC with enough money to do its work; (2) the PCC, with the assistance of its lawyers, had the necessary authority and means to carry out its mandate; and (3) the PCC had distinguished itself by treating members of the public with respect, fairness, dignity, and integrity. As discussed below, none of these reasons holds water. But Scott's letter is perhaps most telling in what it does *not* consider. The most obvious and important reason for funding the complainants is that the complexity, duration, far-ranging allegations, and implications of the APEC Inquiry are, to put it mildly, unlike those of any other PCC inquiry.

Unlike Any Other Inquiry

Most PCC inquiries have involved allegations against one or two officers by one or two complainants regarding incidents that lasted one or two hours, with, perhaps, one or two documents and one or two legal issues. Such inquiries would last only one or two days and involve one or two lawyers. In such circumstances, the complainant may be able to afford the $1,000-2,000 legal bill that might result from such a hearing or forge ahead without legal representation. In contrast, the APEC Inquiry involves fifty-two complaints against approximately thirty-nine RCMP officers. RCMP planning for the APEC meeting took place over a period of months and involved numerous documents generated not only from within the RCMP but also from outside sources, including the Prime Minister's Office. The legal issues are of unprecedented difficulty for the PCC, including those as complicated as cabinet secrecy and subpoenas to the Prime Minister himself, the institutional independence of the PCC, and difficult issues under the Canadian Charter of Rights and Freedoms. The APEC Inquiry will last for one or two years. It will involve at least a dozen lawyers and, by some accounts, more than 120 witnesses. The complainants' legal bills will probably come to about $500,000. The complexity and duration of the hearing are reason enough to ensure that the complainants have lawyers.

Scott's Reasons

One of Scott's reasons for rejecting government funding of the complainants was that the government had already provided the PCC with additional funds to do its work. By this assertion, Scott seems to imply that the PCC could pay for the complainants' lawyers from its own budget. As noted earlier, the PCC does have the power to pay for some complainant expenses, such as travel and accommodation. But the power to pay legal expenses is not expressly set out in the legislation and, while this question has not been finally determined, there is a good possibility that the PCC simply does not have this power. Moreover, the additional funds provided by the government are sufficient to cover only the PCC's expenses for the inquiry. As previously noted, there are lingering doubts, especially after what happened to the Somalia Inquiry, about whether the PCC's APEC Inquiry will be funded to completion.

Scott's second reason, that the PCC, with the assistance of PCC lawyers, had the means and authority to carry out its mandate, is also a non sequitur. As noted earlier, members of administrative tribunals must strive to be impartial, and if they attempt to provide extra assistance to an unrepresented party, they run the risk of damaging the appearance of impartiality. Similarly, lawyers for a tribunal cannot provide assistance to one side without compromising their need to appear impartial among all parties.

Much in the process used by the PCC has the trappings of an adversarial process, including giving the complainants the status of "parties," the right to counsel, and, most important, the right to cross-examine witnesses. Adversarial fact finding is premised on the idea that each party will conduct its own investigations as thoroughly as possible and then bring to the proceedings whatever evidence it can that is favourable to its cause and unfavourable to the cause of its adversaries. This process does not work well when one party does not have the skill or ability to muster or challenge evidence.

Remember that RCMP officers have extensive experience as witnesses and can therefore be difficult to cross-examine. Frankly, even the best lawyers find them to be tough nuts to crack. Those cross-examining the RCMP officers, for example, will probably need to investigate issues such as the officers' credibility and motive and whether there are pressures from within the Force to present a certain picture of the events. While members of the commission can examine, even cross-examine, witnesses, aggressive questioning on such issues by the PCC could seriously detract from the perception of impartiality and from the credibility of any subsequent recommendations. Similarly, since PCC lawyers are an extension of the PCC and must therefore avoid a perception of favouritism, they too must refrain from thorough cross-examination, especially on issues of credibility.

The APEC Inquiry has been steeped in direct and indirect allegations of bias and lack of independence from the start. The Hughes Commission can therefore be expected to take extraordinary measures to avoid further allegations. No doubt they are keenly aware that if they turn up the heat during cross-examinations, the RCMP or another affected party would immediately apply to the Federal Court to have the commission's work halted for bias. The students do not have cross-examination skills equivalent to those of the skilled litigators they face, so unless they are represented by lawyers who have these skills, no one at the APEC Inquiry will have the mandate or the ability to conduct the kind of cross-examination of the RCMP and others that will be necessary. Adversarial fact finding will be frustrated and the APEC Inquiry will become a sham.

Scott's third reason for rejecting government funding for the complainants' legal fees – that the PCC had distinguished itself by treating members of the public with respect, fairness, dignity, and integrity – also ignored the adversarial nature of the proceedings. Moreover, it failed to address the very practical impossibility of day-to-day attendance by the student complainants at months of APEC Inquiry hearings. Obviously the thirty-nine RCMP officers named in the complaints are not booking time away from work to attend each day of the PCC hearings. Nor are the politicians, bureaucrats, or university officials who have been implicated in the events giving rise to the complaints. Rather, these individuals will rely on their lawyers, who will be present every day of the APEC Inquiry, to keep them informed about what evidence has been presented and to discuss with them how to counter or support that evidence. If none of the student protesters are represented by lawyers at the hearing, they will need to be present in person throughout in order to know what has happened and to ensure that their case against the RCMP is made. Since their continuous presence is impractical (and, in any case, not very useful because of their lack of adversarial lawyering skills), the PCC would quickly become intolerably one-sided if the complainants were not represented by lawyers.

The Complainants' Duties, Rights, and Interests

The potential consequences of the PCC's hearing for the individual RCMP officers can be significant, as the PCC may make findings of wrongdoing and recommend disciplinary action. The RCMP, in various forums, has argued that because of these consequences they have personal interests at stake in the hearings that are superior to those of the student protesters. Indeed, they have gone so far as to argue that the student protesters have no direct interest in the proceedings and therefore do not need legal assistance. This argument against providing counsel underplays the diverse nature and the complexity of the students' duties, rights, and interests, including the duty to represent the public interest; the right to protect themselves against criminal charges, abusive cross-examination, and excessive invasions of privacy; and the interest in gathering evidence for civil actions.

The first time the Morin Commission was taken to the Federal Court (on the issue of its ability to make a funding recommendation), Judge Reed answered the RCMP's claims regarding the superior nature of their private rights by stating that a PCC complainant "acts as a representative of the public interest – the public interest of ensuring that the police do not overstep the bounds of what is proper conduct. The public interest is as important as the RCMP members' private interests in their jobs and reputations." Complainants have a role before a tribunal such as the PCC akin to that of the Crown Attorney in a criminal case: they are responsible for placing before the tribunal the case against the RCMP. Complainants must present and challenge evidence (although, unlike Crown Attorneys, they do not have the state's apparatus to assist them in their investigations). They must also research and present arguments on the difficult legal questions that arise in this case, such as whether the Prime Minister can be subpoenaed. These are onerous tasks and ones that complainants – *since no one else has this mandate* – must perform well if the PCC process is to be credible and effective.

Shortly after the events giving rise to the inquiry, the RCMP stated in a press release that the students were under investigation for committing criminal offences and that they had not been engaged in lawful protest. At least one protester was charged and those charges were not dropped until early 1999. At the time of the Morin Commission's funding recommendations, many other students were still facing the threat of charges. Anyone under such a threat would be foolish to give evidence about the events that gave rise to the potential charges without a lawyer present to look out for his or her interests.

Complainants who are called as witnesses are cross-examined by the RCMP lawyers. These cross-examinations can last for days and could involve wide-ranging and heated attacks on the complainants' credibility. The PCC and its counsel have only a very limited ability to raise objections on the grounds of relevancy or abuse for the same reasons that they are constrained from conducting a rigorous cross-examination: a concern that such interventions may give rise to allegations of bias. Moreover, one of the first students to testify before the Morin Commission was ordered to turn over private e-mail communications with a journalist. Other complainants could face similar invasions of privacy in the quest by the RCMP or others to challenge their credibility. Complainants who face such vigorous cross-examination or the prospect of serious invasions of privacy should be represented by lawyers to ensure that the proceedings do not become sidetracked by irrelevancies or so unfair to the complainants that they are intimidated into dropping out.

Many of the student protesters have also commenced civil actions, including class actions, against the Prime Minister and other ministers, the government of Canada, and the RCMP and its individual officers, alleging conspiracy to breach and actual breach of constitutional rights, abuse of public office, and tortious conduct, including assault, battery, false arrest, and invasion of privacy. In my view, it is perfectly legitimate for the students to use the APEC Inquiry to gather evidence for their civil actions. The Krever Inquiry into the safety of Canada's blood supply provided the evidentiary foundation for a number of contaminated blood cases, cases that would have been impossible to pursue if that inquiry had not had wide-ranging investigative powers. Similarly, the APEC Inquiry may provide the students with evidence that, practically speaking, would have been impossible to obtain during in civil proceedings. If their lawyers are absent from the APEC Inquiry, these evidence-gathering opportunities will be lost.

Just Desserts

In February 1999 Commissioner Hughes recommended to Solicitor General MacAulay that the complainants' legal fees be paid by the federal government. He focused on the unfairness of expecting the students to present a case against those who were represented by senior, experienced lawyers, the unusual nature of the APEC Inquiry, and the impossibility of the students being present day in and day out at the hearing. He concluded that providing such legal representation would "unquestionably improve the quality of the proceedings ... in every sense it will make for a more balanced and efficient process." Within two weeks, MacAulay agreed to pay, as Hughes recommended, the legal expenses incurred from the time of Hughes's appointment by those complainants who had been directly involved in the confrontations with the officers.

The complainants' inability to obtain legal services by means other than government funding, the complexity and duration of the hearings, the heightened sensitivity to allegations of bias and lack of independence, and the diverse nature of the complainants' duties, rights, and interests all pointed to the importance of the complainants having publicly funded lawyers at the APEC Inquiry. Hughes was careful to state in his letter to the Solicitor General that funding in this case should not be taken as a precedent for funding in other PCC cases. Yet there remains the question of whether lawyers should be paid for only in extraordinary situations such as the APEC Inquiry or whether such funding should also be provided in more ordinary circumstances. Given the complainants' onerous obligations at every PCC inquiry to protect the public interest, this question deserves further consideration.

PART 5:
GLOBALIZATION AND CANADIAN RIGHTS

The evidence already in shows that Mr. Chrétien wanted to be, and was, personally involved to an unusual degree in reassuring the Indonesians that their president would not be embarrassed. The summit was Mr. Chrétien's parade, and he did not want Suharto raining on it. His most senior officials – chief of staff Jean Pelletier; Clerk of the Privy Council Jocelyne Bourgon; top policy advisor Eddie Goldenberg; Mr. Chrétien's foreign policy adviser Jim Bartleman; and director of operations Jean Carle – all understood his concerns and were implementing his wishes.

– Norman Spector, *Globe and Mail*,
6 October 1998

The fact is that as the APEC Summit approached, we weren't leaning over and whispering to the Indonesians about their more repressive tendencies – the Indonesians were leaning over and shouting at us about our more democratic ones ... What is most striking about the documents is that they do not contain a single example of any Canadian government official standing up proudly in defence of Canada's democracy ... Not only does Suharto get his way on several key issues, but the Canadian government puts up absolutely no resistance – the prospect of fighting for "Canadian values" is never even raised.

– Naomi Klein, *Saturday Night*,
February 1999

12

The 1997 APEC Summit and the Security of Internationally Protected Persons: Did Someone Say "Suharto"?

OBIORA CHINEDU OKAFOR

In November 1997, Canada played host to heads of state and heads of government from countries of the Asia-Pacific region. The occasion was the Asia-Pacific Economic Cooperation conference, held on the campus of the University of British Columbia in Vancouver. Days before the summit, serious allegations began to be made regarding ill treatment and illegal treatment by the Royal Canadian Mounted Police of a significant number of people who for various reasons had chosen to protest the summit. Many of these allegations have been supported by substantial evidence. What makes the conduct of the RCMP towards the anti-APEC protesters especially disturbing was the seeming brazen suppression of lawful and peaceful dissent in a liberal democracy such as Canada.

Of specific concern to students of public international law is the way in which a particular international legal standard has been employed as both justification and authority for the RCMP's conduct. In the wake of the protests, the RCMP and the Prime Minister's Office justified the RCMP's actions by invoking Canada's obligation to take special measures to prevent attacks on the person, freedom, and dignity of every internationally protected person (IPP) within its territory. The important question raised by this official explanation is the extent, if any, to which this international norm justifies the RCMP's disregard of important aspects of Canadian constitutional law, especially the Canadian Charter of Rights and Freedoms.

The validity of specific details of the allegations of police misconduct before and during the APEC summit is for the RCMP Public Complaints Commission to assess. Here I probe the broader questions of the uses and abuses of public international law in the domestic (especially Canadian) context to further ends that often bear no relationship to those for which the norms were created.

If the allegations concerning police conduct at the APEC summit are substantiated, public international law's admirable objective of ensuring that host states both refrain from and take steps to prevent the perpetration of attacks on the persons, freedoms, and dignity of IPPs would appear to have been taken advantage of to defend conduct that would ordinarily be impermissible under Canadian law. Moreover, it appears that the actual reason for such official misconduct may have been the perceived need to save a particular head of state from the embarrassment of viewing Canadian demonstrations against his government's policies and practices.

Broader questions are also raised. Why was it so important to secure, at the cost of the serious human rights violations that accompany the suppression of dissent, the attendance of President Suharto at the 1997 APEC summit? What did the attendance of certain leaders at the meeting mean for the Canadian government and the Canadian people? Did it mean the continuation of a highly rewarding trade and economic relationship that had been facilitated by leaders such as Suharto? Was Suharto's attendance a metaphor for the inflow to Canada of the presumed benefits of free trade, economic prosperity, and an enhanced bottom line? If so, does evidence of the sacrifice of the basic human rights of many Canadian dissenters at the altar of economic benefit implicate this analysis in broader debates about the extent to which human rights may be violated in the pursuit of economic gain? Does it raise the broader issue of sincerity and posturing in the construction and practice of both public international law and international human rights law? Does this remind us that most governments – even normally responsible ones such as Canada's – often have a paper-thin commitment to the rights of even their own citizens? Are we also reminded of the penchant of ordinarily democratic states to use international law as a reason for doing that which their domestic laws prohibit? These are the broader questions about the struggle for domestic observance of human rights in Canada that are raised by the RCMP's use of this particular international standard to justify its actions at the APEC protests.

Before discussing these broader issues, I would like to examine the persuasiveness of the major and subsidiary legal arguments put forward by the

RCMP in defense of their alleged misconduct. I will do so by considering the following questions:

1   Were the persons whose security ostensibly necessitated the alleged misconduct really entitled in law to special protection?
2   Was it the RCMP's duty to protect them from harm? If so, what was the nature of this duty, and what did it entail?
3   Did the RCMP act within its authority in adopting the specific measures that it did during the APEC summit?

Who Are Internationally Protected Persons?

In evaluating whether the RCMP was justified in behaving the way it did, we need to examine its stated justification for such behaviour. In the main, this justification is that the RCMP's duty to secure the persons, freedoms, and dignity of IPPs necessitated the specific measures that it took immediately before and during the APEC summit. Central to this argument is the premise that the principal participants at the summit were entitled to special protection as IPPs. On this point there is no debate. Indeed, Canada is obligated, under its own laws and under international law, to take special measures to protect those individuals who fall under the definition of internationally protected persons.

IPPs are defined in substantially similar terms by both Section 2 of the Criminal Code of Canada and Article 1 of the 1973 Convention on the Prevention and Punishment of Crimes Against Internationally Protected Persons, Including Diplomatic Agents (the Convention), which is legally binding on Canada. Both legal instruments include the following under the definition of internationally protected persons:

(a) heads of states, including any member of a collegial body performing the functions of a head of state under the constitution of the state concerned, and their foreign ministers, whenever such a person is in a foreign state and whether or not s/he is on official business
(b) any member of the family of a head of state or foreign minister accompanying him or her
(c) any diplomat or representative of a state who is carrying on his or her official duties in that country and who is entitled to special protection under international law in the state where the attack is expected to occur or has occurred
(d) any member of the family of such a diplomat or representative of a state who is part of his or her household

(e) an official or agent of an international organization of an intergovernmental character who is at the time and in the relevant place entitled to special protection under international law

(f) any member of the family of such an official or agent of an international organization who is part of the official's or agent's household.

This definition clearly includes the heads of state who attended the 1997 APEC summit, as well as all the family members who accompanied them. It also includes the diplomats, envoys, assistants, and officials who accompanied the heads of state, and all *their* family members. Furthermore, it includes the officials and agents of APEC itself – as a corporate, if loosely institutionalized, international organization – and all the members of their families.

The Canadian State Immunity Act, Section 7(10) of the Criminal Code, and the norms of customary international law vest a large measure of discretion in the executive branch of government regarding the entitlement of any person to claim special protection in Canada as an IPP. Thus, a certificate issued by the Secretary of State for External Affairs to the effect that any person is an IPP makes that person an IPP in the absence of evidence to the contrary. Such is the breadth of discretion afforded the executive branch of the Canadian government in matters relating to foreign relations that we can assume, for the purposes of this chapter, that the persons whose security the RCMP was concerned about were indeed entitled to special protective measures under both Canadian and international law.

What Is the Nature of the RCMP's Duty to Protect IPPs?

The RCMP, as agents of the Canadian government, had a special duty to ensure the security of the IPPs who attended the 1997 APEC summit. This duty is clearly stated in both Canadian and international legal instruments. Both the Convention and the Criminal Code (Sections 424 and 431) make it a serious crime to commit certain offences against an IPP. In particular, the Convention makes it an offence of a "grave nature" to intentionally commit the crimes of "murder, kidnapping, or other attack upon the person or liberty of an internationally protected person" or to intentionally commit a violent attack against the means of transport, official premises, or private accommodation "of any IPP that is likely to endanger his [or her] person or liberty." It is also a serious offence to threaten or attempt to commit any such attack, or to act as an accomplice in the commission of the attack. Moreover, the Convention mandates Canada and other states to take all practicable measures to *prevent* the commission of such attacks on the persons or liberties of IPPs.

It is instructive that the Convention does not explicitly state that an attack on the "dignity" of an IPP is a *criminal* offence. The Convention carefully delimits the nature of the criminal offences against IPPs that it establishes, and restricts them to offences that involve attacks on, or are likely to endanger, an IPP's person or liberty. The same applies to the Criminal Code: nowhere does it say that a mere attack on the dignity of an IPP constitutes a criminal offence.

To say, however, that attacks on the dignity (as opposed to the person and liberty) of an IPP are not within the purview of both Canadian and international criminal law is not to say that such attacks are not prohibited in other ways by both Canadian and international law; far from it. The point is that such attacks are simply not prohibited by the *criminal* law. Civil law is thought to be the appropriate remedy in cases of attacks on the dignity of IPPs, whereas criminal law is thought to be appropriate in the case of attacks on their persons or liberty. International law clearly prohibits attacks on the dignity of IPPs. Article 29 of the Vienna Convention on Diplomatic Relations (adopted as the domestic law of Canada by virtue of Section 3(1) of the Foreign Missions and International Organizations Act, 1991) states: "The person of a diplomat shall be inviolable ... The receiving [host] state shall treat him [or her] with due respect and shall take all appropriate steps to prevent any attack on his [or her] person, freedom, or *dignity*" (emphasis added). A similar provision is contained in the Vienna Convention on Consular Relations.

Moreover, the Canadian law on defamation also protects the dignity of IPPs. For instance, despite their immunity from Canadian judicial or penal processes, diplomats are entitled to sue in Canadian courts for compensation from persons who are found to have defamed them. Foreign heads of state can likewise choose to sue in Canadian courts to satisfy their claims for defamation or for any other kind of attack on or injury to their dignity.

Which brings us to the nature of the RCMP's duty with respect to internationally protected persons. First, it is important to recognize that because the RCMP is a crime prevention and law enforcement organization, its duty to afford special protection to IPPs does not extend to protecting IPPs from non-criminal attacks on their dignity. This is because such protection of dignity does not fall within the purview of the criminal law applicable in Canada (whether domestic or international in nature). Section 18 of the Royal Canadian Mounted Police Act is quite clear as to the nature of the duties that may be assigned to the RCMP by the government of the day. So are the relevant sections of the Security Offences Act, Section 6 of which empowers the RCMP to take steps to prevent the commission of offences referred to in Section 2. Section 2 implicitly includes offences against the person or liberty of an IPP (as defined in the Criminal Code). Clearly these sections do not authorize the RCMP to take any steps to prevent an attack on the dignity of an IPP. In addition, the RCMP's powers do not generally derive from the Canadian Security Intelligence Service Act (CSIS Act). The CSIS Act does not transform the RCMP into an enforcer of civil law. Nowhere does it give the RCMP jurisdiction over prevention of non-criminal attacks on the dignity of internationally protected persons.

It could of course be argued that even a non-criminal attack on the dignity of an IPP might, in certain instances, qualify as a threat to the national security of Canada, for example, if such an attack might cause an offended IPP to take steps to harm Canadian interests abroad or to refuse to cooperate with Canada on crucial military or economic matters. The implication of this argument would be that, pursuant to the powers conferred on it by Sections 2(1) and 6(1) of the Security Offences Act, the RCMP would be justified in taking steps to prevent a non-criminal attack on the dignity of such an IPP. This type of argument might be ingenious but it is unconvincing. It is unconvincing for the simple reason that the definition of threats to the security of Canada that applies to the Security Offences Act is the very same one contained in the CSIS Act. The definition contained in the CSIS Act clearly excludes from its purview such things as "lawful advocacy, protest or dissent" unless carried on in conjunction with activities clearly aimed at espionage, the overthrow of Canadian democracy, or other such aims. It is extremely difficult to conceive of any non-criminal attack on the dignity of an IPP (otherwise called an insult) that could qualify as a national security threat under that definition.

What, then, is the nature of the special duty of the RCMP in this context? In order to fully answer this question, it is important to appreciate the historical and legal bases for the establishment of such a duty. Attacks on the persons and liberties of heads of state and other government officials and diplomats have played an important role in world politics. From the 1934 assassination of King Alexander of Yugoslavia while on a visit to France, to the abduction of the senior British trade commissioner in Montreal by the Front de Libération du Québec (FLQ) in 1970, the international community has all too often been shocked by attacks on visiting foreign officials in the territories of their host states. This has led to sustained efforts to ensure that host states provide such officials with special protection from attacks on their persons, liberty, and dignity.

By agreeing to receive internationally protected persons, a state assumes international diplomatic obligations binding it to give them special protection from attacks on their persons, liberty, and dignity. The rationale is that because IPPs are personally inviolable under the existing norms of international law, host states are concomitantly bound to ensure that their inviolability is respected not only by its own officials or agents but also by every person within its territory. The performance of this duty, it is thought, necessitates extra effort on the part of the host state if the protection it offers internationally protected persons is to be seen as sufficient.

The measure of protection that is deemed sufficient under international law is termed "special protection." According to public international law scholars, this implies a higher level of protection than that usually accorded to either the private citizens of the host state or other aliens within its territory. Others prefer the term "increased protection." In both cases, it is clear that what is meant is the adoption of enhanced and special measures that would not ordinarily be adopted by the authorities in the host state if the objects of protection were private individuals and not IPPs. The specific nature of such measures would of course vary with time, place, and context. This context-dependent nature of the form that special protective measures would take ensures that the relevant authorities, in our case the RCMP, have some discretion as to how best to ensure the security of IPPs within their territorial domain. This is not surprising, given the vagueness of much criminal law and criminal procedure legislation and the broad discretion enjoyed on a day-to-day basis by police officers the world over. As we shall see, however, the fact that the RCMP have "special" powers with regard to protecting IPPs does not mean that such powers are draconian, untrammelled, or absolute. In fact, such special powers are still very much circumscribed in democratic states.

The discussion thus far has shown that the RCMP, as a Canadian law enforcement agency, had a duty to take enhanced measures to prevent attacks on the persons or liberty of the IPPs who attended the 1997 APEC summit. It has also shown that the RCMP had some discretion in determining what exactly it had to do in order to fulfil this duty. What remains to be analyzed is the measure of such discretion, as well as how RCMP officers used their discretion during the anti-APEC protests.

Did the RCMP Act within Its Authority during the APEC Protests?

Since the passage into law of the Canadian Charter of Rights and Freedoms in 1982, the discretion exercised by police officers in applying the criminal law of Canada has been substantially restricted by human rights law, both domestic and international, directly and indirectly. This implies that even while performing its special duty to provide enhanced protection to visiting IPPs, the RCMP is obliged to abide by the normal standards of behaviour mandated by both domestic and international human rights law, particularly the requirements of "due process." Thus, its preventive, investigative, and enforcement measures must conform to the normal standards by which it is required to operate. In other words, the human rights of Canadians or any other people are not required to leave town when IPPs ride in.

With this in mind, we can assess specific aspects of the alleged behaviour of the RCMP towards the anti-APEC protesters. Would it have been lawful for the police to assault, forcibly disperse, and pepper-spray the protesters in the name of preventing attacks upon the persons and liberty of IPPs? Would the RCMP have been entitled to take down or seize posters or flags displayed by the protesters in order to protect the dignity of visiting IPPs? It must be emphasized that the determination of the veracity of the allegations made against the RCMP by protesters is the province of the RCMP Public Complaints Commission panel established for that purpose. Important as such questions are, I am neither equipped nor inclined to delve into it in this brief and focused chapter. What I am more interested in is the question of whether such actions, if it were established that they had actually occurred, can be justified under international law.

Many of the alleged actions are not easily supportable under either domestic or international human rights law. For example, the RCMP and/or the Canadian government have been accused of:

- arresting British Columbia Civil Liberties Association director Craig Jones on 25 November for holding, well behind a security perimeter, a sign saying "Free Speech"
- cancelling Musqueam Nation Chief Gail Sparrow's scheduled address to APEC leaders at the last minute because it had a reference to human rights
- threatening UBC law graduate Karen Pearlston with arrest for displaying signs about APEC
- prohibiting protest signs within view of the APEC leaders
- unlawfully assaulting bystanders and protesters complying with police orders

- forcibly removing a protest banner made out of a student's bedsheet as he tried to hang it on private property
- detaining a well-known protest organizer a day before the APEC summit just to remove him from the summit venue
- stopping Kevin Dwyer, the president of the Graduate Student Society, from hoisting a Tibetan flag atop the GSS building.

In normal circumstances, such actions would clearly be serious violations of the Canadian Charter of Rights and Freedoms as well as the relevant international human rights laws.

For example, the RCMP's power to use force is subject to the requirements that such force be necessary and that the police act on reasonable grounds. The powers of arrest without warrant and of search and seizure without warrant that are conferred on RCMP officers by law are subject to the major restriction that they may be exercised only if an officer has reasonable and probable grounds to do so. Even though the constitutional rights of Canadians to such due process is not absolute, these rights may be derogated from only to the extent that is "demonstrably justifiable in a free and democratic society." Under international human rights law, the same limitation is imposed on the powers of the police to arrest a person, search a person or premises, and seize property.

The cancellation of speeches and the suppression of anti-APEC posters on arbitrary grounds would constitute a violation of the right to freedom of expression. This right cannot be derogated from either, except as is justifiable in a free and democratic society. Moreover, the concept that police officers *unauthorized by law* may not arrest or hinder Canadian citizens doing what they are lawfully entitled to do is an uncontroversial Canadian legal and constitutional principle. The mere fact that the alleged actions of RCMP officers occurred in extraordinary circumstances does not in itself justify a departure from this basic principle of Canadian, and even international, law.

It is difficult to imagine how any of the incidents listed earlier can be justified in a free and democratic society, and the attempts of the RCMP to do so on the basis of a perceived threat to the security of internationally protected persons has so far been unconvincing. For example, the RCMP has tried to explain its seizure of the bedsheet banner from a protester who was standing on private property behind a high-security fence by saying that he could have strung the banner several feet across a road that would be used by IPPs, thereby disabling one or more police motorcycle escorts!

The problem is that the RCMP's ultimate excuse for its behaviour during the summit is that its conduct was required by public international law. This necessitates a close reading of the two ostensibly conflicting strands of international and Canadian law. On the one hand, the RCMP is required to take all appropriate measures, including imposing some restrictions on the liberties of the Canadian public, in order to prevent attacks on the persons, liberty, and dignity of IPPs. On the other hand, it is also required to respect the requirements of due process in order to safeguard the persons, liberty, and dignity of the Canadian public. Performing one of these duties without violating the other requires a delicate balancing of competing rights, a balance that is all too often upset by the interjection of other social, political, and economic pressures.

Before examining these broader questions, however, it is important to emphasize that the special powers accorded the RCMP to protect an IPP from attacks on her or his person or dignity are not absolute or beyond challenge merely because such powers are characterized as "special." Such powers, as I have shown, are clearly circumscribed. They are delimited by the nature of the RCMP's functions as a crime prevention and criminal law enforcement agency. They are clearly limited by the provisions of Canadian and international human rights laws. And since derogations from both Canadian and international human rights laws *must* be "demonstrably justifiable in a free and democratic society," all the activities of the RCMP must also be reasonably justifiable. This includes all steps and actions taken by the RCMP under its special powers to prevent attacks on the persons and liberties of IPPs. Such special measures must still conform to the requirements of both Canadian and international law. While the events surrounding the 1997 APEC conference were hardly ordinary, under the law the extraordinary nature of those events is not in and of itself a justification for actions that violate Canadian and international law.

Broader Issues Raised by an Analysis of the "IPP Excuse"

At the beginning of this chapter, I indicated a number of broader issues raised by the RCMP's use of the "IPP excuse" to counter accusations that it abused its authority in its conduct towards Canadian citizens at the APEC protests. The seriousness of the alleged misconduct cannot be fully appreciated without an analysis of these issues. Such an analysis might yield a few lessons for Canadian and international human rights activism that go well beyond, but also include, the narrow context of the Canadian experience.

One such issue is the penchant of many presumably democratic states to do at the international level what they would ordinarily not do at the domestic level. Consider the alleged ease with which the Canadian government was able to barter away the human rights of its citizens in return for the participation of a foreign head of state at the APEC summit. Yet the same government would have considered it scandalous to have been asked by any domestic personage to beat, pepper-spray, and suppress local protesters in order to facilitate that person's attendance at the APEC meeting. It is as though the international plane were a zone without rights, without limits, without restraint – a zone where governments can behave in ways that are not ordinarily open to them.

The APEC protests also exposed as myth the notion that some states are somehow incapable of the crass police misconduct that the RCMP has been accused of. One of the lessons that the crackdown on anti-APEC protesters should teach Canadians and the rest of the world is that human rights violations are not the exclusive preserve of other lands, that human rights is not *here* and violations *there*. Instead, there may be lurking within Canada's institutional structure a tendency to do violence to the constitutional fabric upon which this country is supposed to be organized. Less powerful members of society, such as minorities and Aboriginals, who more often than not bear the brunt of police misconduct, are not always just crying wolf when they call for the RCMP and other police forces to be reined in. Rather, they speak with a voice that has been so enriched by their unique set of sad experiences that, in the interests of all of our rights, they ought to be listened to more often.

Yet another issue is the relationship between perceived economic benefit, through enhanced international economic activity, and a greater tendency of governments to violate the human rights of their own citizens. Did Canada exchange some of the basic rights of its citizens for Suharto's visit? And was this a metaphor for the continued inflow to Canada of trade and economic prosperity at the cost of basic human rights?

All over the world, enhancement of the bottom line through greater international trade is used by governments as an excuse for violating the fundamental human rights of their citizens. To be sure, many governments do need to shore up the bottom lines of their countries and alleviate the misery of their peoples. It is difficult to accept, however, that seizing flags and posters and roughing up non-violent protesters is necessary to achieve that objective. This is even more difficult to accept from a government that regularly lectures other states about the virtues of behaving otherwise.

Canada's corporate moral legitimacy is severely damaged by ethical inconsistencies – one more reason for discerning Canadians to be disturbed by the allegations of politically influenced RCMP misconduct at the APEC summit.

It is clear from this discussion that the root causes of the alleged ill-treatment of anti-APEC protesters by the RCMP have less to do with some autonomous capacity to do evil within that organization, and much more to do with the social, economic, and political pressures that underlay the entire APEC summit meeting. It is also clear that the "IPP excuse" is just that – an excuse for actions motivated not by the requirements of international law as such but by underlying social, economic, and political pressures.

That is what the "Suharto" metaphor represents. That is why a discerning observer who hears the "IPP excuse" may be wont to ask those around: *did someone say "Suharto"?*

13

A Whole Theatre of Others:
A Personal Account of APEC 1997

ARNAB GUHA

Now this overdone, or come tardy off, though it make the unskilful laugh, cannot but make the judicious grieve; the censure of the which one must in your allowance o'erweigh a whole theatre of others.
– Hamlet

Do you think anybody given the choice to change their birthright you think they wouldn't? You think if anybody could change bodies, you think Errol Flynn he didn't want to be Cary Grant? This is courage, it couldn't come at a worse time!
– Prologue to "Courage" by Gordon Downie of the Tragically Hip

I am an Indian. From India. I realize that in these parts that makes me East Indian. But I feel rather uneasy about that term. As I cannot trace my roots back to Java, Sumatra, or any of the beautiful and varied islands once lumped together as the "East Indies," and as I aspire to no renewed affiliation with either the British or the Dutch East India Company, I see no reason why, especially five decades after India's constitution as the world's most diverse democratic republic, I should have to borrow from an outdated colonial vocabulary to describe what is essential to me.

I say all this because it is fundamentally important to my appreciation of APEC 1997; because I have never felt my response to a public event so mitigated by my Indianness as I did in the period between April and November of Canada's Year of the Asia Pacific, when an unprecedented flood of the self-righteous and the pragmatic, the visionary and the indifferent, the profiteering, the prophesying, the opportunistic, and the well-meaning struck quiet Vancouver, surfing a slow Pacific, dazzling in designer dreams. Of all that I may bring to Canada, my Indianness, for all its small worth, must remain my most cherished contribution to this country's continued and proven commitment to maintaining a diverse and democratic house upon a foundation of liberal values.

I was born and raised in Jadavpur, a crowded Calcutta suburb that had its origins in a refugee colony set up hastily to accommodate those thrown up by a cruelly divided Bengal. I spent the first seventeen years of my life in a matrix of displacement that, though economically faltering, remained a bastion of civic discourse nourished by a hundred roadside tea stalls, bookstores, and a central bazaar where the old and the young met in huddled and earnest debate; where a publicly funded university throbbed with ideals of impartiality and excellence. Jadavpur engulfed us in the pungent and comforting smell of lamp oil and newsprint mingling to promote a tireless assessment of the state of the nation, and, in spite of a chronic lack of material resources, refused to indiscriminately vilify any colonizing power as the sole source of its current woes, but could and did welcome the English Shelley and the Bengali Tagore as equally powerful speakers for the disenfranchised of this world.

Given the trials and triumphs of a childhood in Jadavpur, where I never once wanted for food or education, but where hours without electricity made sweating over kerosene lamps a regular ritual in homework, and where my grandmother's repeated attempts at raising poultry on the terrace were a constant reminder of the millions who had been permanently evicted from their homes, I could never call myself a direct victim of any social calamity; but neither could I, especially upon coming to Canada, see my childhood as having been paved with the multitude of opportunities and choices that only a very strong economy can provide its resident members. As such, APEC in Vancouver put me in a rather difficult spot with its iconically simplistic politics that seemed to divide the world into easy lines separating villain from victim and democracy from dictatorship, while at the same time confusing dissident views with valid security concerns and seeking a voice for legitimate civil outrage in systemic racist vocabulary.

In the end such simplicity led to the dogmatic arrogance of self-righteousness, which was met with an equally ludicrous mechanism of censure, either premeditated by bureaucracy or simply executed in indecisive spontaneity by law enforcement agents. The price was and continues to be a whole theatre of others, pointing quick fingers in a harrowing circuit of accusation. This has, through a series of public complaints, hearings, resignations, adjournments, and renewals, prolonged the tedium of a witless morality play whose farcical slapstick makes the unskilful laugh and whose inconclusiveness must make the judicious grieve; for what we have missed, through all of this, is our ability to see the difference between holding a liberal democracy accountable to its citizens and going to the populist extreme of accusing one of the most open countries in the world of being a repressive police state.

A Public Complaints Commission that has bartered and bought, misled and mangled, traded and tripped, has now accrued a bill of some one million dollars and is still nowhere near uncovering a single dark corner of the intricate bureaucratic gothic of APEC 1997. On the one hand, no one has yet established the protesters' alleged provocation of the police to a point where the RCMP were justified in arresting and silencing anti-APEC activists well in advance of the implementation of the security blanket at the University of British Columbia; on the other hand, speculation on the involvement of the government in any perversion of the Canadian Charter of Rights and Freedoms has vacillated ludicrously between extremes, for example, from suggestions that the initials "PM" in police notebooks denote the Prime Minister and his high office to the occasional and somewhat tenuous suggestion that the letters stand for the first and second names of a senior RCMP official.

But what is most clear to anyone following even the barest of headlines is the regularity with which the federal government has now, over the course of a year, repeatedly had to swallow whole strings of proclamations, denials, and refusals, from former Solicitor General Andy Scott's resignation over a clumsy lie, to the belated granting of legal funding to the APEC Inquiry complainants. All these unnecessary delays and reversals have not only threatened to poison the relationship of trust between this democratic state and its concerned citizenry but have also come with a huge bill that is now being paid by the same "common person" in whose name the government has repeatedly entered into a string of dubious international partnerships, of almost every imaginable kind, in almost every imaginable part of the trading and tradable world.

No Place for a Centre

I can trace my involvement with APEC back to April 1997, when a comment of mine, supporting India's desire to be an APEC member, sparked words of anger from some participants in an e-mail discussion group at UBC. Most of my critics demanded that the university dissociate itself completely from the event. I chose to disagree. First, I believe that all universities, and especially publicly funded ones, play a vital role in hosting and promoting debates around decisions that affect the majority of the population who fund them. Second, knowing the history of APEC leaders' meetings, which in the past had been held in distant "resorts" strategically removed from any easily accessible public space, I could not but be impressed by Canada's decision to host the APEC leaders and bureaucrats at Canada Place, in the very heart of downtown Vancouver, and to allow one of the largest and most important universities of the country to serve as a venue for their final meeting and declaration.

It is true that APEC has traditionally failed to involve too many civic bodies in its core discussions and negotiations. In this, the decade-old Pacific Rim association simply emulates a host of such well-established and seldom challenged international alliances as the Organisation for Economic Co-operation and Development (OECD), which, as an elite club of First World economies based primarily in the North Atlantic bracket, does not quite rush to include the input of diverse non-governmental organizations, peace groups, or alternative peoples' forums in its fundamental decision-making process. If anything, Canada's Year of the Asia Pacific showed every promise of adding a civic component to APEC, be it through an affiliated conference focused solely on recognizing the economic contribution of women in our society, or through Canada's institution of a "Youth Commission" to enable young Canadians and foreigners like myself to take part in discussions on APEC through the Internet and videoconferences; not to mention the physical participation of a youth group, drawn from a nation-wide e-mail forum, at an actual APEC ministerial meeting in Montreal. Coupled with all this was Canada's repeated emphasis on the importance of education, sustainable environmental policies, and small and medium enterprises, or SMEs, to the well-being of all APEC member states. The working group on Food, Energy, Environment, Education, and Population, or FEEEP, is testimony to Canada's efforts.

While the core decision-making process of APEC would still involve closed-door meetings between bureaucrats and politicians, I could not help seeing the hosting of the centrepiece summit at a leading, publicly funded institution as being anything but beneficial to the process of generating popular debate about APEC. And I still believe I was correct in my assumption. Had the meeting been held in a specially commissioned leaders' retreat in some faraway scenic corner of northern British Columbia, in keeping with the tradition established by previous hosts of APEC, I doubt that subsequent debates would have gained as much momentum as they did across UBC, Vancouver, or Canada.

Moreover, whatever my thoughts on India's participation in the only major international economic alliance not dominated by OECD states, I have never fundamentally disagreed with the human rights concerns raised by the opponents of APEC. As an Indian, I know all too well the frustration resulting from a lack of any meaningful international acknowledgment of the heavy strategic and diplomatic costs incurred by a newly independent India, which, led by the liberal ideals of former Prime Minister Nehru, welcomed the Dalai Lama and his exiled Tibetan government into its borders at a time when the rest of the world chose to look the other way.

Nor do I doubt that unhindered free trade, fostered by the vested interests of a handful of multinational corporations, cannot be a panacea for the world's problems. Indeed, my position is, and has always been, that in a liberal democracy everyone has the right to be informed, and that true dialogue cannot arise from either promoting adversarial activism at the expense of other avenues of communication or resorting to institutional censorship in response to dissident political views, however expressed. Honest dialogue can be generated only by bringing diverse groups together, formally and informally, to challenge each other's opinions without ridicule, assault, or censure.

Unfortunately, what some of us saw at UBC, as early as May 1997, was an agenda for opposition that had already drawn strong conclusions about APEC, free trade, "Asian dictators," foreign investment, and developing economies, and that had, even before most Canadians had had a fair chance to learn the first thing about APEC, declared its unequivocal and rather dramatic intent to halt the leaders' meeting, to silence and disrupt events organized by any student group who may have felt otherwise about interregional trade, and to convince the campus community that the only valid starting point towards understanding APEC was to vehemently oppose and denounce it. Much as I remained concerned by many of the operational and philosophical aspects of APEC, I could not help feeling much more directly threatened by the dogmatic zeal of some of my UBC colleagues, who repeatedly claimed liberal democratic values as their justification for inflicting their own intractable views upon all those who chanced to cross their path. It was in reaction to such an environment on campus that a group of us started the APEC-University Forum in May 1997, with major logistical support from UBC's Green College.

The aim of the forum was to bring together people of different cultural, political, and educational backgrounds to ask each other questions, share information, and generally debate the merits and demerits of APEC as an organization; the role of Canada and UBC in APEC 1997; the universality of human rights in principle and in application; a studied consideration of international trade; and the growth and influence of multinationals as a historical continuum, from the armed East India companies of a previous era to the manipulation of national military forces by commercial corporations in our day, as in the ongoing struggle of the Ogoni people of Nigeria against oil producers in their land. Thus, between May and November 1997, the APEC-University Forum organized a series of informal events, speaker meetings, panel discussions, and information sessions at Green College. The events were attended by members of the UBC administrative community, officials from the Canadian Department of Foreign Affairs and other government branches involved in organizing APEC, students, academics, members of the APEC consular corps in Vancouver, and activists from the No-to-APEC coalition.

Such an attempt was doomed from the start, however. This became quite apparent at our inaugural event in the summer of 1997, an informal afternoon reception attended by UBC and Green College members; the American consul general and his colleagues from some of the APEC members' missions in Vancouver; former UBC president David Strangway, who was then at the vortex of the controversy surrounding the university's involvement in APEC; the president and the director of student affairs of the UBC Graduate Student Society, who, a few weeks later, passed a resolution in council formally opposing UBC's participation in the centrepiece event; representatives from the UBC Pacific Rim Club; and several members of APEC Alert, a group strongly opposed to APEC in general. The idea behind this event was to bring together those who, given their divergent opinions and approaches to politics, would seldom have had the opportunity to meet in a social setting and to hold personal conversations with each other, unhindered by the pressures of a publicly executed political agenda. And so it would have been, but for a couple of incidents that illustrate the sort of unnecessary tension generated from the earliest stages of any public discourse on APEC; tension that, in the months leading up to the meeting, helped build two political fortresses along such sharply divided lines that the media images that are now part of popular Canadian memory became inevitable.

On the morning of the reception, I received a telephone call from a liaison officer at the Indonesian diplomatic mission in Vancouver. This person, a young Canadian who had travelled throughout Indonesia, was now working, as I understood it, in a public relations capacity for the Indonesian diplomats here. He called to inform me that the head and deputy of their mission would not be able to attend, and to ask whether he could come to the reception in their place. I said we would be all too glad to have him at our party.

Almost as soon as he arrived, however, he began taking pictures of guests, including members of APEC Alert and the East Timor Alert Network, who had strongly denounced Indonesia's occupation of East Timor. He walked around as though documenting the event, without warning the guests or seeking their permission. Not only was this uncivil but it led to a ludicrous situation that threatened to undermine the very purpose of the gathering. Before we knew it, several anti-APEC activists were chasing this person around the College Hall, between clusters of amused onlookers who had by then traded politics for a gleeful recreation of a Punch and Judy fairground routine. Moreover, once the brief inaugural speeches had been made and the APEC-University Forum's objectives outlined, several of those who had been targeted by the intrusive camera took it upon themselves to stonewall the event by shouting about Canada's being a repressive police state that maintained itself on a policy of constant surveillance and that actually threatened the safety of all dissidents, whose lives it had documented in detail. Any chance there might have been of, say, an anti-APEC activist trading quiet questions with an APEC Canada organizer was eroded, first by the callous and unwarranted gesture on the part of the person from the Indonesian mission, and second by the subsequent refusal of some campus activists to respect their hosts' objectives in organizing such an event.

This, of course, was only the beginning. As the forum's various meetings got under way, I was approached by the young Canadian from the Indonesian mission on several occasions, either in person or by telephone, questioning the forum's inclusion of members of APEC Alert as featured speakers on our panels. At the same time, members of APEC Alert continued to make explicit public statements promising to do anything in their power, as "peaceful activists," to halt the leaders' meeting at the Museum of Anthropology at UBC. At one of the meetings, a prominent member of the group went on to announce to a full house his intention of executing a citizen's arrest on then Indonesian leader Suharto. While it is simple to understand why peaceful demonstrators have traditionally courted their own arrest as a fundamental part of civil disobedience, it was not so easy to see the passive or "peaceful" element in a group of protesters' attempting to physically capture an internationally recognized head of state at a summit meeting attended by more than a dozen other premiers and presidents in a country that is obliged, under international law, to accord the utmost security guarantees to all of them. However despicable General Suharto's policies may have been, and there is little doubt that he ranks among some of the worst despots of our time, it does not take much to appreciate that, as the head of his state, he was entitled to the same level of protection here as Canadians would expect their own leader to have when visiting other lands. Idle threats to arrest the visiting leader would only serve to justify, in an absurd inversion of moral ideal and political activism, the host country's concern for the safety of its dubious guest.

The RCMP may have read such a statement as a "threat," but some of us may see this as an exaggerated concern, based on our personal and social acquaintance with this particular member of the anti-APEC coalition. Indeed, some of us may have even seen the rhetorical escalation of APEC Alert as street theatre, elaborately designed to obtain the lawful arrest of Suharto under certain provisions of Canadian law concerning crimes against humanity, which would have made perfect sense given that the once sacrosanct principle of diplomatic immunity has now been turned several times on its head in the ongoing drama surrounding the extradition of former Chilean leader Augusto Pinochet from Britain to Spain on charges of human rights violations during his time in office. However, the Canadian government and law enforcement agencies had no personal acquaintance with and understanding of the anti-APEC protesters, especially when tension and hostility between activists and the police diminished the possibility of much non-adversarial interaction between them. This left them to rely on each other's slogans and platitudes, which were at their best insufferably banal and at their worst threatening or dismissive. Neither did the Canadian government show any inclination to acknowledge the fantastic duplicity of the current keepers of global order, who have sought to make Pinochet and Yugoslavia's Slobodan Milosevic the symbols of their Hollywoodesque sense of historical justice even as they have continued to provide practical support for the Indonesian massacres in East Timor and for the Turkish use of brute force to coerce Kurdish villages into submission.

Given the sorry absence of any sincere dialogue between the government and the protesters, the fierce rhetoric of some members of the anti-APEC camp may well have directed Canadian law enforcement agents towards the Canadian Security Intelligence Service Act, which allows "lawful advocacy, protest or dissent" but considers "activities within or relating to Canada directed towards or in support of the threat or use of acts of serious violence against persons or property for the purpose of achieving a political objective within Canada or a foreign state" to be a "threat to the security of Canada," which, once established, is then prosecutable under the Security Offences Act.

What is particularly unfortunate about the overblown rhetoric of APEC Alert is that the activists had, in fact, no intention of exceeding the limits of peaceful protest. Although I disagreed with them on many matters, my circle of friends included anti-APEC demonstrators. I know that the organizers did not intend any physical harm to any foreign guest or law enforcement agent, but only sought to voice their concerns over the fly-by-night crony capitalism that is fast becoming a global disease. Few Canadians would dispute the importance of the fundamental questions raised by those opposed to APEC. Quick-fix free trade agreements need the highest public scrutiny and, in chairing APEC 1997, Canada and UBC were indeed playing host to several dubious personalities. Given, however, that the world's problems cannot be reduced to a clear debit and credit ledger of historical accountability, and that there is more to foreign investment in developing economies than footwear and sweatshops, it was the intractability of much of the anti-APEC rhetoric that made any meaningful discussion impossible.

An Indian Perspective on APEC and Trade

The Indian question was fundamental to my response to the events surrounding APEC 1997 for several reasons. First, it was my support for India's membership in APEC that had gotten me involved in the debate in its earliest stages. Second, as popular discussions of Canada's liberal democratic role in the world gained momentum – both in official statements claiming "constructive engagement" as a way to cope with a desperate export situation and in their critics' questions about the validity of such an argument – I could not help pondering the remarkable similarities between the second largest and the second most populous countries in the world.

Both have a strong and common colonial heritage that they have overcome in their own ways, but without either a populist demonization of their former rulers or any compromise in the quality of their self-determination. Both nations struggle daily to maintain a pluralistic liberal democracy, and in both cases, each day's struggle seems to reinforce a fundamental commitment to democratic values. Both strive to play an unglamorous but important mediatory role in this world, and both nations are equally deluded in this regard: just as India's participation in the

Nonaligned Movement is seen as little more than symbolic, and the Nonaligned Movement seen as little more than a joke, so Canada's defiance of international sanctions against Cuba has been severely undermined by its ready support for the US missile attacks on Afghanistan and Sudan in 1998. Both countries, however, with their own internal separatist movements, their continual quest to seek better ways of including and incorporating minorities, and their perennial lack of easy answers, remain committed to a philosophy of equality. In Canada's case, this has resulted in higher taxes and lower high-end salaries but a much stronger welfare state than its mighty southern neighbour. In India, the ideal of egalitarianism has seen the absorption of members of several traditionally disenfranchised groups into an expanding middle class that is committed, above all, to education and democracy.

Indeed, it was my faith in democratic India that led me to defend its wanting to join APEC. India, unlike many developing economies, does not aspire to instant First World status. Ever since independence, India's focus has been on nation building and on the creation and expansion of a middle class. Thus, instead of spending valuable foreign exchange to send its best and brightest to be trained abroad, India concentrated on academic partnerships that resulted in such world-class academies as the Indian Institute of Technology and the Indian Institute of Management. This is why Nehruvian India closed its doors to a mass influx of foreign goods and went on an internal drive to sponsor the growth of Indian industry. It is not as though, in the absence of Coke, Indians went without cola; on the contrary, Indians developed their own vibrant soft-drink industry, to a point where, even after the re-entry of Coke into the country some ten years ago, Indian cola sales showed consumers' open support for the indigenously developed Thums Up over the Atlanta-based bubbly legend so vigorously advertised by Santa. While Malaysia was raising the world's tallest buildings in Kuala Lumpur, and Mexico City was being used by film production units to stand in for glitzy Los Angeles, New Delhi and Bombay were nowhere close to resembling the quintessential metropolis of the First World. At the same time, while Asia's tigers burned and Latin America wobbled on feeble economic feet, India continued to thrive, albeit unspectacularly, without any calamitous setback or fallout. While other developing countries created First World pockets inhabited by the super-rich, India, in spite of major economic inequalities, managed to create and expand its middle class into some four hundred million people who, though possibly without cars and CD players, have access to education and a free press. All of this, whether good or bad, is a direct result of India's commitment to democracy.

And yet, in spite of all the triumphs of building a democratic Indian nation, four decades of protectionist trade policies had created a colossal public sector that not only failed to guarantee the creation of new jobs but actually drove the nation to the verge of bankruptcy, until former Finance Minister Manmohan Singh decided to gamble on a more liberalized economic paradigm that opened India to foreign investors some ten years ago. Liberalization of the Indian economy had a twofold effect: on the one hand, it pushed Indian companies to re-evaluate their own quality control standards; on the other hand, it gave a small but distinct window of opportunity to those who had been left stranded between the noble ideals of a welfare state and a crippled economy that was in no position to meet some of the most basic needs of its common subscribers. When the Marxist chief minister of the Indian state of West Bengal now travels around the world seeking foreign investment, the most important bait that he can dangle is the lower cost of labour in his state and his country. The choice before him, and before millions of his constituency, is between unmanageable poverty on the one hand and a redeeming compromise on the other.

Moreover, it is important to note that the low cost of Indian labour relates not just to unskilled work. If a farmer in the state of West Bengal earns Cdn $2-3 a day, or Cdn $50-75 a month, then a space scientist developing satellite-launching technology for India's space program earns about Cdn $300 a month. The disparity between the two average salaries is akin to that between the salaries of a Canadian dish washer and a high-tech worker in Ottawa's silicon belt. Lower costs of production, together with a high level of education, constitute India's competitive advantage in the world. And any jeering at India's attempt to use this advantage to salvage its condition is analogous to the West's scoffing at cheap goods produced by postwar Japan, even though Japan's subsequent economic growth on the back of its early profits has made the Japanese tourist a much-courted icon of consumer spending in the Mazda- and Toyota-driving countries of the West. Indeed, one may well argue that, with India's firm commitment to democratic principles and deep understanding of regional societal concerns, some degree of foreign investment through such forums as APEC not only would be beneficial but is also desperately needed by the fifty-year-old nation attempting to reinvent itself. And once the immediate economic conditions have improved, as they did in Japan, India may well move on to the next phase, with its citizens negotiating with the rest of the world for such currently unimaginable luxuries as "backpacking" around a Lonely Planet, on a "shoestring" budget, in search of one's soul.

"Asian Dictators" and "Democratic Canada"

One of the most important reasons why India could not be left out of my response to APEC 1997 was the easy and all-too-frequent coupling of the words *Asian* and *Third World* with *dictators* and *authoritarian regimes,* both in the protesters' rhetoric and in the popular Canadian press. The most common examples of this were found in debates challenging the Canadian government's standard line on "constructive engagement." On these occasions, whether in newspaper columns or at open public forums, the pinnacle of self-righteousness was reached by much jeering at how, instead of "teaching" Asian countries the true principles of democracy, Canada was "learning" the mechanism of dictatorship from sundry Third World regimes. Indeed, all the talk about "teaching" and "learning," about "Asian dictators" and "Western democracies," could not but bring to mind an older vocabulary of colonial missionary zeal: it was as though Canada, as the bearer of the One True Faith into the hearts of darkness in the uncivilized world, had now corrupted its missionary self and "gone native" – oh, the horror! And what bandying about of words, hardly defined, explained, or understood – from *Fascist* and *Communist* to *genocide* and *Holocaust* – in an ironic echo of the hyperbolic jargon used by propagandists to justify the selective interventionist bombings of sundry dark patches of this world – oh, shame!

It was as though we had collectively bought into an easy assumption of the inherent racial propensity of Asians for totalitarianism and tyranny. It was as though we had forgotten that the world's largest democracy is both Asian and, to use that abhorrent term, Third World – a nation of one billion people, and some six hundred million voters, that remains one of the most remarkable examples of multiculturalism; that, in spite of economic hardship, has seen its democratic populace and independent judiciary declare a former prime minister of the stature of Indira Gandhi guilty of abusing the power of her office, both in court and in popular elections; that has supported, maintained, and expanded a free and unmonopolized press, and aborted the much-hyped Narmada Dam Project, which had already secured major international funding, because it was determined to be hazardous to the people and the land; and that, having learned the price of institutional censorship during the brief period of the Emergency some two and a half decades ago, would *never* seek to remove an able journalist from his or her position for doing a thorough job of reporting and fact finding, for presenting to the people what a democratic citizenry ought to know, and for doing what, in fact, remains the most important and sacred task of a free press in a free country. Ironically, while the Canadian government was actively seeking to bar the Canadian Broadcasting Corporation's Terry Milewski from reporting on APEC 1997, the Indian press was engaged in a healthy and vigorous debate on the country's revised nuclear policies; while the Canadian government was attempting to gag the voice of its Fourth Estate, the state-owned channels of the Indian television networks were broadcasting live parliamentary sessions in which the ruling political party had to explain its hawkish nuclear stand, clearly and completely, to a strong opposition bench and to the Indian people.

While the coverings and uncoverings of the RCMP Public Complaints Commission enabled the Canadian media to gloat over letters from Indonesian security officials asking whether they might be allowed to shoot Canadians, it took a book by a former American diplomat to clearly document how it was a visit from the president of the world's richest democracy, and Canada's largest trading partner, that resulted in an RCMP policy that now makes it legally possible for foreign agents to bring arms into this country. While the Indonesians, with their terrible record in East Timor, may have been callous and blunt in their query, Ambassador James Blanchard's account of his time in Ottawa suggests that American agents were simply unresponsive and forceful when it came to negotiating security for their leader on his Canadian visit in 1995. Indeed, while the RCMP did set clear restrictions on the Indonesians during APEC 1997, and even deported a couple of their guards, Blanchard's *Behind the Embassy Door: Canada, Clinton, and Quebec* describes how, in 1995, "the whole of Ottawa felt like it was being invaded by US Forces." The irony of the popular coupling of "Asian" and "dictators" was further heightened by the American firing of cruise missiles into Sudan and Afghanistan, albeit with characteristic free-world rhetoric, around the same time that the Canadian press was tut-tutting the Indonesians. This act of unilateral military aggression was made even more distasteful, this side of the 49th parallel, by Ottawa's instant support for its neighbour's unmitigated bullying of the world.

Courage

I am not a lawyer. Indeed, in my lack of any detailed knowledge of the fine print of the law, I belong to the popular median of this or any other free country. I consider myself *aware* of the law, and I like to think that I am alert to my basic rights. I am made to understand my place within society through my general education, by activists, by the media, and at times by some additional reading. But most of it is a marriage of common sense and an implicit guarantee of my rights that I have found in living and studying in three democratic countries – India, England, and Canada – and in visiting several others, including the United States.

It was on the basis of such an understanding that my friends and I initiated the APEC-University Forum. It was because of an assumption of an implicit guarantee of my rights that I was glad to participate as a youth delegate and volunteer at APEC 1997, and to speak at the panel on human rights organized by Amnesty International as part of the concurrent "Peoples' Summit" in Vancouver. It was my popular understanding of democracy and liberal values that led to my helping my friend Craig Jones set up his signs reading "Free Speech," "Human Rights," and "Democracy" outside Green College the night before the APEC leaders' meeting at the UBC Museum of Anthropology, and that caused me to be angered by his arrest the next day for displaying the very signs that I, in spite of my pro-APEC stance, had helped him set up. I heard about Craig's arrest as I worked at my volunteer's station at Canada Place, supporting the work of APEC 1997 and of the Canadian government in finding a much-needed market for exporting the produce of Canadian labour.

However, it is that same, though potentially flawed, ideal of fairness that asks me to withhold judgment on the RCMP's use of pepper spray on protesters whose ambiguous actions on the morning of the leaders' meeting resulted in the undoing of a security barricade; this, even as I remain firmly disappointed in the RCMP's use of force to disperse anti-APEC protesters and their audience at the UBC flagpole on another evening, some two hours before the area was to come under a security blanket. While I found it particularly hard to stomach the repeated denigration of Canada as a repressive police state, and even harder to swallow the simultaneous allegations of Canada's being infected by the totalitarian norms of sundry "Asian dictatorships," I found it equally difficult to accept the pre-emptive arrest of an anti-APEC protester, a few days before the centrepiece event, for allegedly compromising the hearing ability of a UBC security officer through the use of a handheld megaphone: clearly a censorial act based on a charge so ridiculous that the RCMP did themselves the biggest favour by dropping it. As one who spent a lot of time between May and November 1997 speaking at high schools and various public forums in Vancouver, dismissing several of his anti-APEC friends' prophecies of a violent suppression of free speech and democracy in Canada, and going out of his way on these occasions to cite numerous instances to assure his audience that Canada would never use unnecessary force to silence the voice of its citizens, I felt personally let down by such events as the arrest of Craig Jones and the clearly excessive and unnecessary use of pepper spray by the police in at least one instance during APEC 1997.

When I went out of my way to support UBC's role in APEC, it was because I believed that the role of the university was to actively foster debate on issues that had hitherto been muffled. And while UBC's hosting of the leaders' meeting did lead to a lot of discussion on issues surrounding APEC, I was most disappointed to see that the government did not view UBC or the Museum of Anthropology as more than physical loci, as being anything more than pretty buildings upon a prettier cliff. The university was thus reduced to a bare physical dimension, divorced from its intellectual, moral, and demographic contexts. Just as Canada is more than its spectacular mountains and its forests, even though both play a very important part in shaping Canadian consciousness, so UBC or any other university is far greater than a bland inventory of its buildings, gardens, and ponds. A university, by its very name, is about people and about universality; it is an institutional framework that seeks to educate through dialogue. And it is in this, if in nothing else, that Canadians have a right to feel cheated out of their contract of trust with their government.

It was in the absence of any public lecture delivered by a single visiting leader, or even by the Prime Minister of Canada, at a UBC venue during APEC that we demonstrated a distinct lack of understanding of the fundamental values and ideals of a liberal university education. And yet public lectures by visiting dignitaries have long been a tradition in many, many universities around the world. When President Clinton visited China last year, he addressed university students in Beijing and answered their sometimes harrowing questions about Sino-American relations. As a supporter of Canada, of trade, of APEC, and of democratic ideals, I was most upset by the lack of respect for the university.

As a pro-APEC organizer and as an Indian, I remain deeply disappointed by the suppression of free speech, by the improper arrests and detentions, and most of all by the institutional bullying of an award-winning national journalist, an act that cannot but hack deep into the very roots of any democracy. I support global trade because it is necessary, but also because I assume a democratic safety net against possible malpractice, if not outright injustice. I want India and other Asian nations to find a market in Canada for their intellect, their labour, and their products. I want small and medium Canadian enterprises, from Vancouver to St. John's, to be able to export their wares to sundry lands across the seas. This is not a twentieth-century dream, or an idea that is peculiar to me. The whole story of human civilization is one of trading and transmigration, of Silk Routes and sea voyages, of discovery and commingling. And while this has led to imperialism and slavery, the end result has not been all tragic. I, for one, can now sit and write in Canada after having been born, raised, and educated in Calcutta and after the benefit of a university education in England, and my friends and I are all the better for it. But whether any giant mechanism involving a demographic collective will do good or ill depends on the power vested in the conscience of every individual member of that group or nation. This is the ideal of democracy and it cannot be fulfilled without a continuous, open, and honest debate between its various subscribers. This is what we lacked at APEC 1997 and even afterwards, through the government's repeated attempts to stall the democratic process by at first refusing to providing funding for the legal fees of the complainants to the RCMP Public Complaints Commission and then by lies and counter-lies, omissions, and revisions.

It takes courage to stand in the line of fire and to defy the police, even in a proven democracy, when the sound of the rain creates an ominous alchemy with the persistent barking of guard dogs straining at the last leash of civility. It takes courage to stand against a mighty neighbour, not a hundred miles from our door, and to demonstrate the sovereignty of our values in however symbolic a manner. It takes courage to protest at a security barricade in the full view of snipers. There was no lack of courage at APEC, and all parties who risked their necks for their values are to be lauded. Through all the moves and countermoves, however, one vital democratic component was missing: the willingness of the different parties to talk to one another. In the absence of an open dialogue between people with divergent views, one cannot but adopt a reductive parameter for action. And it is such reduction that leads, in Marxian terms, not to revolution but to futile, catastrophic action.

Today, all the earnest debate around free trade, democracy, interregional alliances, and the role of foreign investment has been reduced to a banal quibbling between egos, and the government has done little to redeem itself of its part in the ongoing drudgery. In all that was done and said, there was courage. But one wonders if it did not come at a particularly bad time.

14

Whither APEC?

JANE KELSEY

A Decade of Turmoil

APEC – Asia-Pacific Economic Cooperation – has been aptly described as "four adjectives in search of a noun." Since 1994 its main formal commitment has been to free trade and investment across richer countries of the Asia-Pacific region by 2010 and poorer ones by 2020. APEC's mission is to serve the needs of the market. A senior US official explained in 1995: "APEC is not for Governments. It is for business. Through APEC, we aim to get governments out of the way, opening the way for business to do business." The official slogan for 1996 was "APEC means business." Canadian Christopher Butler, chair of APEC's Committee on Trade and Investment in 1997, called it "a product of the new era of globalization, an era in which business does business in an increasingly borderless world."

The APEC vision – deregulated markets, unrestrained foreign investment, and unrestricted trade – potentially affects every aspect of people's daily lives. Initially the APEC region embraced Japan, South Korea, members of the Association of Southeast Asian Nations, or ASEAN (Brunei, Indonesia, Malaysia, the Philippines, Singapore, and Thailand), the United States, Canada, Australia, and New Zealand. By 1993 it had expanded to include Chile, China, Chinese Taipei (Taiwan), Hong Kong, Mexico, and Papua New Guinea. Russia, Peru, and Vietnam became active members in

1998. Yet APEC claims to be a community of these *economies,* not of countries or their governments. This conveniently excludes from consideration the "non-economic" consequences for poverty, indigenous and human rights, employment, or environment, unless they are redefined in market-friendly terms. In APEC there is no perceived need, and no opportunity, to debate the deficiencies of the global free market model, let alone any alternatives.

The agenda is not APEC's alone. Free trade and investment, structural adjustment, and neoliberalism are variants within the global economic policies endorsed by the World Trade Organization (WTO), International Monetary Fund (IMF), World Bank, and Organisation for Economic Co-operation and Development (OECD), as well as misguided domestic governments. These policies deliver a bounty to international capital and domestic elites. They also mean deepening levels of poverty and inequality for hundreds of millions of people, who are denied any say in the decisions that will devastate their lives. APEC means big business; APEC does not mean people. It sees no downsides in the destruction of subsistence and family farms, small local industry, and government-provided social services that deregulation, tariff cuts, and privatization cause. It will never acknowledge the cultural genocide of indigenous peoples who are forcibly relocated and whose sacred sites are destroyed, or the plight of economic refugees who are forced to migrate from rural areas to cities and overseas. It will never concede that workers have rights to decent pay, safe conditions, and a secure livelihood. Nor will it recognize the feminization of poverty when women are denied the basis to sustain their families and when their burden of paid and unpaid work is increased. The environment is expected to somehow sustain the limitless pursuit of profit and growth.

The APEC agenda is therefore potent, but in a decade it has not progressed very far. Its visionaries tend to forget that processes of deregulation and governance are not self-executing. APEC might be called a community of economies, but the key players are governments, which have different and sometimes conflicting political, economic, and social agendas. The economies of APEC members remain rooted in diverse cultural, legal, and social forms. These realities are reflected in founding commitments to "flexibility," "voluntarism," and consensus as APEC's modus operandi. As APEC has tried to agree on concrete commitments, this pragmatic accommodation has given way to openly divergent positions. Most Asian members have insisted on voluntary economic cooperation within diversity. This has clashed with a universal, rules-based approach to trade and investment liberalization from the US, supported by Australia, Canada, and New

Zealand. On top of its inability to take effective action on the Asian economic crisis, these disagreements have left APEC virtually paralyzed. This was exemplified by the decision of the ministerial meeting in Kuala Lumpur in 1998 to pass the unresolved issue of sectoral liberalization on to the WTO.

This internal instability has been accompanied by external challenges, as knowledge about APEC has spread to those it affects but excludes. Some, mainly Western unions and environmental NGOs (non-governmental organizations), have asked for a seat at the table to represent their sectoral concerns. A broader-based network of workers' organizations, indigenous peoples, and human rights groups and NGOs, especially from Asia, have condemned APEC's operations as exclusive, secretive, and anti-democratic, and have also condemned its economic model for serving the interests of international capital and local elites while deepening injustice and inequality.

Mainstream media have joined the sceptics, openly questioning APEC's continued existence. An editorial in the *Weekend Australian* warned immediately before the Kuala Lumpur leaders' meeting: "If the forum cannot make progress on issues that promote recovery from the East Asian economic crisis, it must show cause why it should not be wound up – that is, if it is not punctured first by its own bloated structure." It did not.

Back in 1997, APEC leaders recognized that they faced a problem of legitimacy. Neither their governments nor supporters in business and academia were prepared to ask why, however. They assumed that the growing opposition to APEC could be solved with a public relations exercise. The 1997 leaders' statement said:

> To underpin our efforts, support among the people of the region for continuing trade and investment liberalization is essential. We welcome the decision by Ministers to develop an APEC-wide work program to assess the full impacts of trade liberalization, including its positive effects on growth and employment, and to assist members managing associated adjustments.

In May 1998 the APEC secretariat called for proposals from consultants to carry out the project. There was no pretence of objectivity: "By raising understanding and support for liberalisation, this project directly contributes to APEC's core trade and investment liberalisation objectives." The first phase would use case studies to illustrate APEC's benefits; the second would develop communications strategies for use by member governments. With the more sceptical Malaysian government in the chair, the

June 1998 APEC trade ministers' communiqué broadened this to talk of the need to promote "a broad-based and balanced understanding of the impact of liberalisation, taking into account *both benefits and the associated costs of adjustment*" (emphasis added). The results have not been made public, but a proposal for the third phase of the project was to be put before the Committee on Trade and Investment at its May 1999 meeting. This would be followed by a seminar in June 1999 in Auckland, New Zealand, on the "Impact of Liberalisation," with speakers who had practical expertise in selling ideas, such as "ministers, political pollsters, policy makers, academics, business people and the specialist media."

APEC remains a prisoner of its mission and its rhetoric. Because it has done nothing concrete to address or defuse mounting criticism of APEC process and goals, opposition has continued to grow. This opposition has become more visible at the time of the annual APEC meetings, wherever they are held. In Seattle in 1993 there was some limited NGO activity. From 1994 a regionwide counternetwork of NGOs, unions, and human rights and environmental groups began to emerge. A meeting of the People's Project for the 21st Century working group on APEC in Bangkok issued a statement that urged discussion and debate over APEC's role. They proposed an alternative people-centred approach to economic and social self-determination through a regional social charter "that will ensure that urban and rural workers, subsistence consumers, small scale and informal sector producers are effectively protected against the onslaught of economic globalization."

A Human Rights Watch Asia report in 1994 examined the impact of trade and investment liberalization on the region. The report agreed that rapid economic growth had benefited some; for millions of others, however, it meant low wages, erosion of health and safety standards, and restrictions on workers' right to organize. Indigenous peoples were dispossessed in brutal acts of cultural genocide. The traditional livelihoods of farmers were being destroyed without alternative jobs and incomes being provided. Trafficking in people, especially women and children, had increased. The natural-resource base was being depleted and environmental degradation in some places was life threatening. Human rights abuses accompanied free trade and investment regimes in many countries, as governments that promoted favourable investment conditions silenced those who were exploited, political opponents, and public critics.

From the Jakarta meetings in 1994 onward, the APEC meetings themselves began to symbolize this repression, as hosts sought to shield themselves and their guests from discomfort and embarrassment. In 1994 the Suharto government banned meetings and the press conference called by representatives of ten NGOs from various Asian and Pacific countries who had gathered to speak out against APEC. The streets were cleansed of itinerants and the poor. The military cracked down on dissident journalists, although they dealt more delicately with the East Timorese students who occupied the US embassy compound. Meanwhile, APEC leaders stood, smiling and waving, beside Suharto, in their batik shirts.

One year later, representatives of over a hundred NGOs and unions concerned with human rights, labour issues, the environment, and economic and social justice met before the APEC summit in Osaka. Their Kyoto Declaration supported cooperation among the countries and peoples of the region but condemned APEC's free market and trade liberalization paradigm for negating the developmental and democratic aspirations of the people:

> Economic growth and promotion of trade are not ends in themselves. Genuine development must be centred on the needs of people and nature, and deliver real social and economic justice. The form of indiscriminate, unregulated economic growth and trade which APEC advocates delivers the opposite of this.

The Japanese government did its own street cleaning. The homeless who lived in the square outside the conference venue were forcibly relocated to the other side of town; local journalists report that at least one person died in the ensuing intergroup conflict.

In 1996 APEC came under particularly heavy attack at meetings, rallies, and demonstrations across the Philippines. At least three different counter-APEC forums were held, several with a strong international presence. Two weeks before the APEC meeting began, the Philippine government announced that it had a blacklist of at least 100 people, from eighteen countries, who would be refused entry to attend the counter-APEC meetings. These included East Timor independence leader and 1997 Nobel Peace Prize co-winner Jose Ramos-Horta, Bishop Desmond Tutu, and Danielle Mitterand, wife of the former French president. Defending the decision, President Fidel Ramos said, "It is not so much the threat to national security that we are banning foreigners from this announced fora relating to APEC. It is that it is inimical to our national interest." The Indonesian government was already a major investor in the Philippines. One radio reporter portrayed Ramos as building a wall around APEC to keep his own people out. A column in the *Philippine Daily Inquirer* asked, "If you can allow goods to flow freely into countries, why can't you do the same thing for ideas?"

As part of a $1 million APEC "beautification" program, the government allegedly demolished the shanties of more than 33,000 families to create an "eyesore-free zone" for foreign dignitaries. Farmland in the Clark Special Economic Zone was cleared for runway extensions, despite farmers' protests that they were not allowed to harvest their crops first. A state of virtual martial law was declared in Central Luzon, with massive troop mobilization and reactivation of paramilitary groups, curfews, and checkpoints. Limousines of dignitaries sped up and down the APEC "friendship lanes," fatally injuring two pedestrians; workers stuck in traffic jams had their pay docked for being late. Locals who knew nothing about trade and economic liberalization became instantly anti-APEC. The notion that removing national protections and extending the hold of transnational enterprises over the Philippine economy would solve their problems of endemic poverty, inequality, and powerlessness seemed absurd. One senior columnist in the *Philippine Daily Inquirer* concluded that, in the eyes of APEC and Ramos, concepts of development

> are not about justice, they are not about dissent, they are not about people being free to say what kind of development they want. Freedom has no place in economic progress. Human rights have no place in economic progress. At the end of the day, principle must give way to expedience. Growth must take precedence over the moral imperative to right wrongs.

When the NGOs gathered in Vancouver in 1997, there was yet another "summit" of unions, human rights groups, and NGOs. The gathering had become even larger and more fragmented, and was largely unproductive; one New Zealand veteran of several summits referred to it as "the NGO Olympics." The people's assembly was also compromised by domestic politics, being partly funded by the federal Liberal and provincial New Democratic Party governments. This event posed no threat to APEC, but others apparently did. Security documents identified "long-standing native issues in British Columbia such as gaming, self-government, land claims, fishing rights and resource control over claimed lands, along with a collection of ad-hoc groups opposed to APEC" as "a potential security risk." Thus, when students protested at the site of the leaders' meeting at the University of British Columbia, their non-violent demonstration was broken up by Canadian Mounties who sprayed disabling pepper over protesting students and working media. This and other alleged excesses became the subject of a formal inquiry and civil suits. Official documents disclosed that the Prime Minister's Office had assured Suharto that he would be shielded from politically embarrassing protests.

During the Vancouver APEC meeting, the voice of indigenous peoples was heard for the first time. While an indigenous business conference, drawing on participants from several APEC countries, convened on the outskirts of the city, the Union of British Columbia Indian Chiefs, who were marginalized from the people's summit as well as the official event, issued their own challenge to the APEC process and agenda:

> The avoidance of dealing with our Peoples, on our terms, must cease. Treaty and non-treaty Indigenous Nations shall not surrender, cede our Aboriginal Title for an economic development agreement which deprives our future generations benefits from their sacred homelands. We give notice to the APEC state leaders and their corporate elite that investment, especially in British Columbia, remains very uncertain.

In Malaysia a year later, the formal NGO summit was partly funded by the Canadian government and predictably did little to further action against APEC. The gathering was more important as an opportunity for local unionists, women, and other activists who were seeking democratic and social reforms in Malaysia to be heard in some safety. Ironically, the United States' (self-interested) endorsement of the *reformasi* gave Prime Minister Mahathir ammunition to allege that the dissidents were part of a US-backed conspiracy. Several leaders, including a labour organizer of the APEC people's summit, were arrested within days.

To Engage or Oppose?

Most APEC governments remained hostile to, or dismissive of, the NGOs and their annual meetings. Their concerns and activities, however, were picked up by an often bored and increasingly sceptical international media. Some in APEC, especially host governments, felt that they needed to respond. In an attempt to defuse the potential for embarrassment, the Philippine official in charge of the APEC meeting in 1996 suggested that

> the networks of civil society deserve attention in a participatory framework of markets corrected for failures due to externalities and non-provision of public goods. Viewed this way, *truly representative non-government organizations* must therefore be given chances to present their

own agenda *for eventual incorporation* by the intergovernmental network of APEC in the implementation of action plans. [emphasis added]

This begged more questions than it answered. What would be considered a truly representative NGO, by whom, and according to what criteria? Could NGOs, by their very nature, ever be "truly representative"? To whom would they be accountable? On what terms might they be incorporated? Would only the well-resourced, well-connected NGOs, approved by their governments or funded by major US or European foundations, be allowed in? How would such NGOs need to perform to maintain their credibility and credentials with APEC? Given that the Pacific Economic Cooperation Council defines itself as an NGO, could employers' organizations or neoliberal think tanks seek inclusion too? With which parts of APEC's network would these APEC-mandated NGOs engage? The working groups? Ad hoc expert groups? Standing committees? Senior officials' meetings? Ministerial meetings? Leaders' meetings? The higher up the decision-making chain, the less likely access would be. In a nutshell, how could the democratic, social, cultural, and environmental deficits attributed to APEC be remedied by NGOs taking part on the periphery and on APEC's terms?

The Philippine government's solution was to offer the mildest critics a marginal role. In a highly publicized dialogue with a selected group of environmental NGOs, the government promised an APEC driven by sustainable development and with a human face. The senior official in charge claimed that the costs of structural adjustment would be a "hot issue" in official discussions. New Zealand's Foreign Affairs Minister Don McKinnon later said it was never discussed – nor, given APEC's economic parameters, would it have been appropriate or acceptable. Civil society and social costs were matters for each country to address domestically in its own way. Australia's Prime Minister John Howard likewise distanced himself from such moves.

Attempts to repackage APEC with a social face continued when Canada took the chair in 1997. The Canadian government's *Results Report* prominently recorded NGO participation in several "high level" APEC meetings, mainly on environment and "human resource development" issues. Alongside the formal summit, the Canadian government hosted an assembly of youth leaders, which included a walk-by of the "economic leaders" on their way "from their agenda meeting to the family photo." The second Women Leaders' Network meeting again addressed the concerns of the elite, with no attempt to explain how their proposals would alleviate the powerlessness and endemic poverty of hundreds of millions of women in the region. In Kuala Lumpur, Canada again proposed to broaden APEC's agenda to include social, human rights, and environmental issues, and to provide a role for NGOs; the suggestion fell on very deaf ears. The proposal was presumably brought forward for Canadian consumption since there was no remote chance that the proposal would be accepted by a consensus of APEC "economies."

As in APEC itself, fault lines emerged among its critics. Many, but not all, Western NGOs and unions sought to engage with APEC to gain some recognition of their concerns, mainly on labour standards and the environment, and convince APEC to moderate its free trade and investment paradigm. The chances of this seemed remote. APEC's interest in environmental issues was peripheral and defined in market-friendly terms. The first environment ministers' meeting, in March 1994 in Vancouver, was a Canadian initiative. There was no consensus in support of either the host's proposal for a new body to promote environmental cooperation or moves by New Zealand minister Simon Upton to promote economic environmental instruments, such as tradable pollution permits. A minimalist position emerged: a framework of principles on sustainable development would be "fully integrated" into the program of each working group and policy committee, which the senior officials would follow up on. The ministerial meeting on sustainable development in June 1997 was again hosted by Canada as APEC's chair. It had a narrow focus, responding to the leaders' call for a work program relating to sustainability of the marine environment, cleaner production, and sustainable cities. This complemented ongoing work on a Japanese-initiated project to reconcile economic growth, energy requirements, and environmental sustainability. APEC's Economic Committee also began to prepare a database of environmental measures that impacted on trade liberalization and facilitation. APEC had framed its environmental agenda to fit its free trade and investment goal.

Labour issues came under the rubric of human resource development. The main pressure for action came from the Asia Pacific Labour Network (APLN), the regional body of trade unions affiliated with the International Confederation of Free Trade Unions (ICFTU). Their position largely mirrored that taken by the parent body at the WTO. They met shortly before the Manila meeting in 1996 and prepared a "Trade Union Vision for APEC." This asked President Ramos to seek support for a Labour Advisory Forum within the APEC structure to parallel the APEC Business Advisory Council, and for acceptance of their network on the human resource development working group. The stated aim of the APLN was to harness the APEC objective of the internationalization of markets to the improvement of the conditions of work and life of the citizens of our populous region. The reality of economic globalization requires a strategic response reaffirming the human-centred purpose of all growth and development.

Ramos apparently agreed. The New Zealand Council of Trade Unions (NZCTU) report from Manila describes it as "surprising and refreshing to hear a Head of Government clearly articulate the view that Labour Standards were central to ensuring that the results of economic globalisation had to as a first priority alleviate poverty, improve living standards, and to enhance workers' well-being." This was consistent with official NZCTU policy, adopted in 1998, to seek a "social dimension in APEC," recognition of an APEC Labour Forum, and participation in APEC committees, working groups, and ministerial meetings. The New Zealand Trade Union Federation (NZTUF) likened the APLN's request to "urging a tiger to become a vegetarian."

Various APLN unions were subsequently included in national-level delegations to the Human Resource Development Working Group. This is a bottom-tier grouping that reports to the senior officials and to periodic ministerial meetings. The first ministerial meeting, in January 1996 in Manila, set up an action program focused on the needs for education and training to develop a flexible and adaptable workforce. When ministers met again in September 1997, education and training remained the priorities. The working group was directed

> to develop a project in which representatives of labor, management, and government from member economies can exchange views on best practices on training, skills development, the use of technology, and human resources development related issues in the workplace, avoiding duplication of work undertaken in other forums.

Union participation in the working group might improve some of its outcomes, but wider labour concerns, such as the rights of workers and unions, would not be addressed. The APEC Labour Monitor (ALARM), established in Hong Kong to coordinate action against worker repression in the region, condemned the APLN for legitimizing APEC's anti-worker agenda and delegitimizing the voices of workers and unions who wanted not to be co-opted but to resist. For the NZTUF, whose members included the clothing, textile, and footwear trade, it also showed the shallowness of the labour standards approach. During the New Zealand government's review of tariffs in 1998, for example, ministers had repeatedly justified zero tariffs by claiming that "the APEC agreement on tariff removal requires the removal of all tariffs between signatory countries by 2010 at the latest. New Zealand is a signatory to that agreement." The ministers never mentioned that APEC was non-binding and voluntary. The NZTUF, along with the sector's manufacturers and local communities, successfully challenged the proposal to eliminate tariffs by 2000 on textiles, clothing, and footwear – tariff cuts that the NZCTU's position on APEC would, logically, require it to support.

Most, although again not all, Asian NGOs and workers' organizations opposed "engagement," believing that it helped legitimize and stabilize APEC and that it redefined basic rights on APEC's terms. They preferred to challenge APEC's lack of political and popular legitimacy from outside. While they often shared a cultural sympathy for their governments' opposition to free trade and investment liberalization, their target was not simply non-Asian governments. They challenged the basic APEC paradigm that claimed that the unrestrained expansion of capital would improve the quality of life for the mass of the region's people. The joint campaign against APEC over the years had helped to build alternative networks at national and regional levels. The people's summits had been useful early on. By the late 1990s they lacked the focus and continuity for effective long-term opposition not just to APEC but also to the common agenda being pursued simultaneously through the WTO, MAI (Multilateral Agreement on Investment), and Enterprise for the Americas.

APEC 1999: New Zealand's Poisoned Chalice

The New Zealand government had eagerly awaited the chance to make its mark on APEC. In 1999 it took over the chair. The major ministerial and leaders' meetings were moved from November to September, one month before New Zealand's scheduled general election. This, however, was not shaping up to be the showcase the governing National Party had hoped for. New Zealand's APEC was hemorrhaging internally, its declarations and commitments were vacuous, and its credibility was under heavy external attack. The "great New Zealand success story" was also in trouble. Despite attempts to talk up the prospects of recovery, the economy was stagnant, unemployment was rising, and recent reports highlighted the growth of poverty and inequality since the free marketeers took control in 1984. The country's external current account deficit was more than 6 percent and foreign debt exceeded 100 percent of GDP – figures comparable with those of

Indonesia and Thailand before they collapsed in 1997. Even if fellow APEC economies turned a blind eye, it was not clear why New Zealanders would want to celebrate APEC's version of the New Zealand experiment.

Some traditional APEC supporters, including opposition leader Helen Clark, called on the government and officials to shift the focus away from free trade and investment and take a less doctrinaire approach to regional economic issues. Prime Minister Jenny Shipley remained committed to a hard-line liberalization approach. As former Prime Minister Jim Bolger told the APEC trade ministers when he opened their meeting in Christchurch in July 1996, the answer was more and better "p.r.": "There is no downside to opening up world trade. All you have to do is overcome political barriers, in other words, attitudinal barriers." Selling this message to New Zealanders became a matter of urgency. That was the responsibility of the Ministry of Foreign Affairs and Trade, whose officials were dedicated free traders. They faced an uphill task in convincing the public that spending $45 million on lavish banquets and security was more important than health, education, and pensions (all of which faced per capita cuts), or the people of Auckland that APEC was worth the disruption to their businesses and lives. The media needed convincing too. A scathing editorial in the main Sunday paper ridiculed "the proliferation of pointless conferencing on a global scale," called APEC a "monster out of control" and approved former Prime Minister David Lange's description of it as "a farcical waste of time." The editorial went on to observe:

> At a time when pensions are being cut and patients on hospital waiting lists are dying, it is also a scandalous waste of money ... A few photo opportunities and some bland communiques which will do nothing to improve the economic conditions of the citizens of the countries involved is hardly worth the expense of this conference. Or most of its kind.

The official strategy to co-opt NGOs, unions, and Maori was widely publicized and secured very little support. The APEC Monitoring Group (which brought together activists and academics working on fair trade, social justice, and human rights, and the NZTUF unions) decided against hosting another people's summit. The group announced that they would focus instead on educational campaigns that linked the APEC agenda to the government's neoliberal policies, as a platform on which to build debate on economic alternatives. Maori nationalists were set to highlight their opposition to the neocolonialism that APEC symbolized, and their struggle for economic and political sovereignty.

In mid-1998, the security issues around APEC attracted further unwelcome publicity for the government. The Court of Appeal found that the Security Intelligence Service (SIS) had acted unlawfully in breaking into and entering the house of Aziz Choudry in July 1996, when he was organizing an anti-APEC conference during the APEC trade ministers' meeting in Christchurch. In a double affront to the rule of law, an amendment to the legislation retrospectively legalized such break-ins. The furor that erupted forced the government to revisit a definition of security (introduced in 1996) that allowed the SIS to monitor those who were a risk to New Zealand's "international or economic well-being." The proposed changes would still mean that a number of New Zealand critics of free trade and investment policy, including active opponents of APEC in 1999, could be spied on legally. A further amendment to the Arms Act allowed the security personnel accompanying foreign leaders to New Zealand to carry firearms; the government conceded that it was simply regularizing another currently unlawful practice. Linkages to events in previous years left APEC looking far from benign. Other stories emerged of visits by APEC's security team to students, Chilean exiles, and other human rights activists. All these events were linked publicly to the suppression of dissent at previous APEC meetings.

Predictably, the formal APEC meeting achieved little beyond clearing some ground for the WTO negotiations in Seattle three months later. The government fortuitously gained some pre-election kudos from an agreement to intervene in East Timor that was negotiated outside the official meeting, and from a tour by US President Clinton. APEC seemed destined to limp on in Brunei in 2000 and China the following year.

The Future

At the cusp of the millennium, APEC's future is on the line. It appears increasingly impotent and discredited. Commitments to its goals of free trade and investment are few, voluntary, and retractable. The Asian miracle – APEC's much-heralded economic platform for the new millennium – lies in ruins. The setback is far from temporary. Popular opposition to the free market agenda is mounting as poor people in poor countries rebel against local conditions and a wind shift in richer countries suggests that a new global economic orthodoxy is emerging.

APEC faces a conundrum. Attempting to force commitments to a free trade and investment regime from its increasingly fractious members could cause it to self-destruct. Not forcing the issue, however, would discredit the goal of free trade and investment, which has virtually become its raison d'être. The grouping seems likely to limp on as an ineffectual shell. Meanwhile, the interests of capital in the region will find or create new vehicles to pursue their goal.

For long-term critics of APEC, whether APEC survives is therefore not the issue. Their focus is on the corporate interests, power brokers, and ideology that APEC represents. Their ability to contest any new developments will depend on the effectiveness of their local and sectoral organization, their regional linkages, and their insistence on not being co-opted into a fruitless and counterproductive collaboration with APEC itself.

BIBLIOGRAPHY

Bakan, Joel. *Just Words: Constitutional Rights and Social Wrongs*. Toronto: University of Toronto Press, 1997.

Berger, Thomas R. *Fragile Freedoms: Human Rights and Dissent in Canada*. Toronto: Clarke, Irwin, 1981.

Bloomfield, Louis M., and Gerald F. Fitzgerald. *Crimes against Internationally Protected Persons: Prevention and Punishment: An Analysis of the UN Convention*. New York: Praeger, 1975.

Borovoy, A. Alan. *The New Anti-Liberals*. Toronto: Canadian Scholars' Press, 1998.

–. *When Freedoms Collide: The Case for Our Civil Liberties*. Toronto: Lester and Orpen Dennys, 1988.

British Columbia. Commission of Inquiry into Policing in British Columbia (Oppal Commission). *Closing the Gap: Policing and the Community*. Victoria, 1994.

Bryden, Philip, Steven Davis, and John Russell, eds. *Protecting Rights and Freedoms: Essays on the Charter's Place in Canada's Political, Legal, and Intellectual Life*. Toronto: University of Toronto Press, 1994.

Canada. Commission of Inquiry Concerning Certain Activities of the Royal Canadian Mounted Police (McDonald Inquiry). *Second Report: Freedom and Security under the Law*. Ottawa: Supply and Services Canada, 1981.

Canada. Commission of Inquiry into the Deployment of Canadian Forces to Somalia (Somalia Inquiry). *Dishonoured Legacy: The Lessons of the Somalian Affair: Report of the Commission of Inquiry into the Deployment of Canadian Forces to Somalia*. Ottawa: Minister of Public Works and Government Services Canada, 1997.

Canada. Commission of Inquiry Relating to Public Complaints, Internal Discipline and Grievance Procedure within the Royal Canadian Mounted Police (Marin Inquiry). Ottawa, 1976.

Canada. Prime Minister's Office. Letter to CBC Ombudsman: <http://pm.gc.ca/cgi-win/pmo_view.dll/ENGLISH?846+0+NORMAL>

Canada. *Royal Canadian Mounted Police Act*. R.S.C. 1985, c. R-10.

Canadian Broadcasting Corporation. APEC Files: <http://www.tv.cbc.ca/national/pgminfo/apec/index.htm>

–. CBC Ombudsman's Report on Terry Milewski: <http://www.tv.cbc.ca/national/pgminfo/apec/report.html>

–. *The National*. News story of 8 September 1998: <http://www.tv.cbc.ca/national/real_video/apec980908.ram>

–. *The National*. Transcripts: <http://tv.cbc.ca/national/transcripts.html>

–. *The National Magazine*. Documentary of 9 September 1998: <http://www.tv.cbc.ca/national/real_video/apec980909.ram>

Convention on the Prevention and Punishment of Crimes Against Internationally Protected Persons, Including Diplomatic Agents, 1973.

Corbin, Charles B., and Ruth Lindsay. *Concepts of Physical Fitness.* Dubuque, IA: Brown and Benchmark, 1994.

Denza, Eileen. *Diplomatic Law: Commentary on the Vienna Convention on Diplomatic Relations.* Dobbs Ferry, NY: Oceana Publications, 1976.

Desbarats, Peter. *Somalia Cover-Up: A Commissioner's Journal.* Toronto: McClelland and Stewart, 1997.

Edwards, J. "Ministerial Responsibility for National Security." A study paper prepared for the Commission of Inquiry Concerning Certain Activities of the Royal Canadian Mounted Police. Ottawa: Minister of Supply and Services Canada, 1980.

Ericson, Richard, and Aaron Doyle. "Globalization and the Policing of Protest: The Case of APEC 1997." *British Journal of Sociology* 50 (1999): 587-606.

Farenholtz, D.W., and E.C. Rhodes. "Police Officer's Physical Abilities Test Compared to Measures of Physical Fitness." *Canadian Journal of Sports Sciences* 17, 3 (1992): 228-33.

Francis, Daniel. *National Dreams: Myth, Memory and Canadian History.* Vancouver: Arsenal Pulp Press, 1997.

Friedenberg, Edgar Z. *Deference to Authority: The Case of Canada.* White Plains, NY: M.E. Sharpe, 1980.

Graves, Franklin R., and Gregory Connor. "The FLETC Use of Force Model." *The Police Chief* (February 1992): 56-8.

Griffiths, Curt T., and Simon N. Verdun-Jones. *Canadian Criminal Justice.* Toronto: Harcourt Brace, 1994.

Hogg, Peter W. *Constitutional Law of Canada.* 4th ed. Toronto: Carswell, 1997.

Horowitz, Gad. "Conservatism, Liberalism, and Socialism in Canada: An Interpretation." *Canadian Journal of Economics and Political Science* 32, 2 (1966): 147-71.

Irvine, A.D. "Let Truth and Falsehood Grapple." *University of Toronto Quarterly* 67 (Spring 1998): 549-66.

Jessop, Bob. *State Theory: Putting the Capitalist State in Its Place.* Cambridge, UK: Polity Press, 1990.

Jones, David Phillip, and Anne S. de Villars. *Principles of Administrative Law.* Toronto: Carswell, 1994.

Lustgarten, Laurence. *The Governance of Police.* London: Sweet and Maxwell, 1986.

Macleod, R.C. "The RCMP and the Evolution of Provincial Policing." In *Police Powers in Canada: The Evolution and Practice of Authority,* edited by R.C. Macleod and David Schneiderman, 44-56. Toronto: University of Toronto Press, 1994.

Mann, Edward, and John Alan Lee. *RCMP vs the People: Inside Canada's Security Service.* Don Mills, ON: General Publishing, 1979.

Marshall, Geoffrey. *Police and Government: The Status and Accountability of the English Constable.* London: Methuen, 1965.

McClanahan, Grant V. *Diplomatic Immunity: Principles, Practices, Problems.* London: C. Hurst, 1976.

Mewitt, A.W. *An Introduction to Criminal Process in Canada.* Toronto: Carswell, 1996.

Milewski, Terry. Letter to CBC Ombudsman: <http://www.tv.cbc.ca/national/pgminfo/apec/milletter.html>

Mollard, Murray. *The Citizenship Handbook: A Guide to Democratic Rights and Responsibilities for New Canadians.* Vancouver: BC Civil Liberties Association, 1997.

Nevitte, Neil. *The Decline of Deference: Canadian Value Change in Cross-National Perspective.* Peterborough, ON: Broadview Press, 1996.

Nova Scotia. Royal Commission on the Donald Marshall, Jr., Prosecution (Marshall Inquiry). *Commissioners' Report: Findings and Recommendations.* Vol. 1. Halifax: Nova Scotia Government Printer, 1989.

Palango, Paul. *Above the Law: The Crooks, the Politicians, the Mounties and Rod Stamler.* Toronto: McClelland and Stewart, 1994.

–. *The Last Guardians: The Crisis in the RCMP – and in Canada.* Toronto: McClelland and Stewart, 1998.

Phillips, Ruth B. "APEC at the Museum of Anthropology: The Politics of Site and the Poetics of Sight Bite." *Ethnos* (forthcoming).

Pross, A. Paul, Innis Christie, and John A. Yogis, eds. *Commissions of Inquiry.* Toronto: Carswell, 1990.

Przetacznik, Franciszek. *Protection of Officials of Foreign States According to International Law.* The Hague: Martinus Nijhoff, 1983.

Puder, G. "Re-thinking Use of Force Theory: A Comprehensive Approach." *RCMP Gazette* 55, 10 (1993): 7-10.

Pue, W. Wesley. "Letter from Mr. Wesley Pue to Mr. Peter Donolo": <http://www.cbc.radio-canada.ca/htmen/2_1_8.htm>

Reith, Charles. *The Blind Eye of History: A Study of the Origins of the Present Police Era.* London: Faber and Faber, 1952.

Robb, J. "The Police and Politics: The Politics of Independence." In *Police Powers in Canada: The Evolution and Practice of Authority,* edited by R.C. Macleod and David Schneiderman, 167-83. Toronto: University of Toronto Press, 1994.

Rodrigues, Gary P., ed. *Pocket Criminal Code.* Toronto: Carswell, 1994.

Roman, Andrew J. *Effective Advocacy before Administrative Tribunals.* Toronto: Carswell, 1989.

Savoie, Donald J. *Governing from the Centre: The Concentration of Power in Canadian Politics.* Toronto: University of Toronto Press, 1999.

Sawatsky, John. *Men in the Shadows: The RCMP Security Service.* Toronto: Doubleday, 1980.

Schmidt, Richard A. *Motor Learning and Performance: From Principles to Practice.* Champaign, IL: Human Kinetics Books, 1991.

Sen, B. *A Diplomat's Handbook of International Law and Practice.* Dordrecht, Netherlands: Martinus Nijhoff, 1988.

Simmonds, R. *Internal Review of the Royal Canadian Mounted Police Investigation of the Hatfield Case.* Ottawa: RCMP, 1985.

Smallwood, Joseph Roberts. *I Chose Canada: The Memoirs of the Honourable Joseph R. "Joey" Smallwood.* Toronto: Macmillan, 1973.

Smith, David E. *The Invisible Crown: The First Principle of Canadian Government.* Toronto: University of Toronto Press, 1995.

Stenning, Philip Cherrill. "Police and Politics: There and Back and There Again?" In *Police Powers in Canada: The Evolution and Practice of Authority,* edited by R.C. Macleod and David Schneiderman, 209-40. Toronto: University of Toronto Press, 1994.

–. "Trusting the Chief: Legal Aspects of the Status and Political Accountability of the Police in Canada." S.J.D. Thesis, Faculty of Law, University of Toronto, 1983.

United Nations General Assembly. *Report of the Secretary-General on Consideration of Effective Measures to Enhance the Protection, Security and Safety of Diplomatic and Consular Missions and Representatives,* A/39/456; A/39/456 Add. 1-4; A/40/453, 1984.

Yergin, Daniel, and Joseph Stanislow. *The Commanding Heights: The Battle between Government and the Marketplace that is Remaking the Modern World.* New York: Simon and Schuster, 1998.

Cases

Alberta (A.G.) v. *Putnam* (1981), 62 C.C.C. (2d) 51 (S.C.C.).

Bisaillon v. *Keable and Attorney General of Quebec* (1980), 62 C.C.C. (2d) 340 (C.A. Qué).

British Columbia (Public Service Employee Relations Commission) v. *BCGSEU* (1979), 96 D.L.R. (3d) 86 (B.C.S.C.).

Campbell v. *Ontario (Attorney General)* (1987), 31 C.C.C. (3d) 289 (Ont. H.C.).

Canada (A.G.) v. *Canada (Commission of Inquiry on the Blood System in Canada - Krever Commission),* [1997] S.C.J. 83.

Canada (Royal Canadian Mounted Police) v. *Malmo-Levine,* [1998] F.C.J. 1912 (F.C.(T.D.)).

Dixon v. *Canada (Commission of Inquiry into the Deployment of Canadian Forces to Somalia - Letourneau Commission),* [1997] F.C.J. 986 (F.C.A.).

Entick v. *Carrington* (1756) 19 St. Tr. 1030, 95 E.R. 807.

Hunter v. *Southam Inc.,* [1984] 2 S.C.R. 145.

Jones v. *Canada (Royal Canadian Mounted Police Public Complaints Commission),* [1998] F.C.J. 1051 (F.C.(T.D.)).

Libman v. *Québec,* [1997] 3 S.C.R. 569.

Muttray v. *Canada (Royal Canadian Mounted Police Public Complaints Commission),* [1998] F.C.J. 1289 (F.C.(T.D.)).

R. v. *Campbell and Shirose* (1999), 133 C.C.C. (3d) 257 (S.C.C.).

R. v. *Metropolitan Police Commissioner, Ex parte Blackburn* [1968] 2 Q.B. 118. [1968] 1 All E.R. 763 (Eng C.A.).

Reference Re Manitoba Language Rights [1985] 1 S.C.R. 721.

Reference Re Remuneration of Judges of the Provincial Court, [1997] 3 S.C.R. 3.

Reference Re Resolution to Amend the Constitution (Patriation Reference), [1981] 1 S.C.R. 753.

Reference Re Secession of Quebec, [1998] 2 S.C.R. 217.

Roncarelli v. *Duplessis,* [1959] S.C.R. 121.

CONTRIBUTORS

Joel Bakan of the Faculty of Law at the University of British Columbia is one of Canada's leading constitutional law scholars. He is currently working on issues relating to corporate regulation and human rights and is a frequent media commentator on constitutional issues, including those related to APEC 1997. Educated at Simon Fraser University, Oxford, Dalhousie, and Harvard, he has taught at Osgoode Hall Law School of York University and at the University of British Columbia. A former Rhodes Scholar and law clerk to former Supreme Court of Canada Chief Justice Brian Dickson, he teaches constitutional law, contracts, and sociology of law. He has won the Faculty of Law's Teaching Excellence Award twice, in addition to a UBC Killam Research Prize.

Karen Busby, Associate Professor in the Faculty of Law at the University of Manitoba, teaches courses on civil procedure, administrative law, and gender inequality. After articling and practising in the area of administrative law in the early 1980s, she worked for the Federal Court of Appeal as a clerk and research assistant for three years. She is the editor of *Manitoba Queen's Bench Rules, Annotated.* In addition to research on public interest litigation, she has participated in numerous interventions by the Women's Legal Education and Action Fund (LEAF) before the Supreme Court of Canada and other courts and tribunals on equality issues.

Arnab Guha was president of the APEC-University Forum in Vancouver from June 1997 to January 1998. A graduate of Cambridge University, where he was a Nehru (Chevening) Scholar from India, he participated in an international study session on the Universal Declaration of Human Rights at the Institut International de Droits de l'Homme in Strasbourg, France, in July 1998, and has since worked as a research associate at the Center for Democracy and Technology in Washington, DC, and served on the Executive Committee of the UBC Graduate Student Society as director of student affairs. A freelance journalist and published poet, he is currently a member of Green College, UBC, working on a doctoral thesis on hypertextual communication. He was elected Fellow of the Cambridge Commonwealth Society in 1994.

Andrew D. Irvine is Associate Professor of Philosophy at the University of British Columbia. As a past president of the BC Civil Liberties Association, he has long been involved in the promotion and protection of basic democratic rights and freedoms in British Columbia and across the country. Founded as a non-profit, non-partisan organization in 1962, the BCCLA is the oldest continuously active civil liberties association in Canada. A graduate of the University of Saskatchewan, the University of Western Ontario, and Sydney University, Australia, Professor Irvine is also an occasional contributor to the *Vancouver Sun* and other Canadian newspapers. He has either held academic posts or been a visiting scholar at the University of Toronto, Simon Fraser University, the University of Pittsburgh, and Stanford University.

Jane Kelsey is a Professor of Law at the University of Auckland and one of the foremost experts on APEC. Educated at Victoria University (Wellington), Oxford, Cambridge, and Auckland, she has written three books on the restructuring of New Zealand's economic and social life, including *The New Zealand Experiment: A World Model for Structural Adjustment?* (1995). Her newest book, *Reclaiming the Future: New Zealand and the Global Economy* (1999), examines the impact of globalization on New Zealand life and future options. Dr. Kelsey was a speaker at the peoples' summit held in conjunction with the 1997 APEC conference in Vancouver.

Terry Milewski has filed reports from thirty countries during twenty-one years as a Canadian Broadcasting Corporation correspondent based in Toronto, Ottawa, Jerusalem, Washington, and Vancouver. In December 1997, the CBC broadcast his documentary revealing the role of the Prime Minister's Office in the security arrangements at the APEC summit. In September 1998, he reported further details, and in October the Prime Minister's Office filed a public complaint against him. The CBC then announced that Mr. Milewski would be removed from covering the APEC affair "permanently." In March 1999, however, the CBC's Ombudsman rejected the PMO's complaint, ruling that Mr. Milewski's work "cannot be faulted, from the point of view of accuracy and fairness."

Gerald M. Morin, QC, is a barrister and solicitor in practice in Prince Albert, Saskatchewan. Appointed to the RCMP Public Complaints Commission, he chaired the first RCMP PCC tribunal inquiring into the APEC affair.

Obiora Chinedu Okafor is an expert in international law. He was educated at the University of Nigeria and the University of British Columbia (where he was a Killam Doctoral Fellow). Currently an assistant professor in the Department of Law at Carleton University in Ottawa, he is a Social Sciences Research Council MacArthur Foundation Fellow on Peace and Security in a Changing World. Between April and August 1999, he was a Visiting Fellow at the Harvard Law School's Human Rights Program. He has worked widely in the fields of public international law, international human rights law, international institutions, legitimate governance, comparative constitutional law, and legal theory. He has just published *Legitimate Governance in Africa: International and Domestic Legal Perspectives* (edited with Edward Kofi Quashigah) (The Hague: Kluwer Law International, 1999). His newest book is *Re-defining Legitimate Statehood: International Law and State Fragmentation in Africa* (2000).

Constable Gil Puder was a decorated eighteen-year veteran of the Vancouver Police Department and an expert in the use of force. An active martial artist, he taught at both the Justice Institute of British Columbia's Police Academy and the Langara College Criminal Justice Department. He also performed research for the Honourable Mr. Justice W.T. Oppal's Commission of Inquiry into Policing in British Columbia (1994). Gil regularly published in police journals and the popular media, and was an outspoken advocate of criminal justice reform. He was a featured speaker at several conferences, including the Drug Policy Foundation's international conference and the Hoover Institution's Law Enforcement Summit at Stanford University (both in 1999). His forthcoming book, *Crossfire: A Street Cop's Stand against Violence, Corruption and the War on Drugs,* is scheduled for publication in spring 2000 by Douglas and McIntyre.

W. Wesley Pue is Nemetz Chair in Legal History and Professor of Law at the University of British Columbia. He has taught at York University, Oklahoma City University, Carleton University, and the University of Manitoba, and has served as Distinguished Visiting Professor at both the University of Adelaide (1999) and La Trobe University (1996) in Australia.

Donald J. Sorochan, QC, was called to the Bar of British Columbia in 1972. He joined the Vancouver law firm Swinton & Company, where he is presently Managing Partner, as an articled student the previous year. Mr. Sorochan's advocacy work has resulted in several landmark decisions in Canadian law in the areas of criminal, constitutional, and construction law. He has acted as lead counsel in several provincial and federal inquiries and royal commissions, and was General Counsel to the former British Columbia Police Commission. Mr. Sorochan is a director and executive board member of the International Society for the Reform of Criminal Law. He was a founding director of the Justice Institute of British Columbia and has served on various boards and committees, including the Western Correctional Association, the National Parole Board of Canada, the Canadian Bar Association Criminal Justice Review Committee, and the Law Reform Commission of Canada Consultation Committee. Mr. Sorochan has acted as Commission Counsel at hearings of the RCMP Public Complaints Commission, and is currently member of the board of directors of the Canadian Association for Civilian Oversight of Law Enforcement.

Philip C. Stenning is an Associate Professor at the Centre of Criminology, University of Toronto, which he joined in 1968. His research has focused primarily on public and private policing, the prosecution process, criminal law and procedure, accountability in the criminal justice system, firearms abuse and gun control, and Aboriginal policing and justice. He has acted as a consultant to several federal and provincial governments and commissions of inquiry, including the federal McDonald Inquiry into the RCMP in the late 1970s and the Marshall Inquiry in Nova Scotia in the late 1980s. Most recently he was a consultant to the review of the public prosecution service in Nova Scotia by the Honourable Fred Kaufman, QC.

Nelson Wiseman teaches political science at the University of Toronto. A frequent media commentator and a specialist in Canadian politics, he has written extensively on provincial political cultures, party politics, and constitutional politics.

Margot E. Young is Associate Professor of Law in the Faculty of Law at the University of Victoria, where she was appointed in 1992. Professor Young holds degrees in political science, law, and jurisprudence and social policy. She teaches and writes in the fields of constitutional law, social welfare law, civil liberties and the law, and feminist legal theory. Currently she sits on the National Steering Committee of the National Association of Women and the Law. She is a research associate with the Canadian Centre for Policy Alternatives – British Columbia, and is a member of the national executive of the Canadian Law and Society Association.

INDEX

Campbell v. *Ontario (Attorney General)*
(1987), 109
Canada: similarities with India, 205-6
Canada Act 1982, 43
Canadian Bill of Rights (1972), 58
Canadian Broadcasting Corporation
(CBC). *See* CBC
Canadian Security Intelligence Service
(CSIS), 35-6, 91
Canadian State Immunity Act and IPPs, 188
Carle, Jean, xiv, xvi, xxii
CBC (Canadian Broadcasting Corporation):
Milewski taken off APEC story, ix, 21,
141, 156; Ombudsman exonerated
Milewski, ix, xix, xxi, 21, 156-8, 173
Censorship laws, 37-8, 38-9
Charter of Rights and Freedoms: growth
of liberal democratic ideas, 119-20;
impact on political culture, 122; part of
Constitution Act, 1982, 44; and rule of
law principle, 46, 57, 58
"Charter-free zone" (CBC documentary),
6, 146-8
Choudry, Aziz, 225
Chrétien, Jean: attitude re APEC affair, 41,
144; compared APEC with Clinton
impeachment process, 13-14; impact of
APEC on reputation, 13
"Citizen police," 61-2. *See also* Police
Clark, Helen, 224
Clinton, Bill: impeachment process coinci-
dent with APEC affair, 13-14
Common law peace officer ("citizen
police"), 61-2. *See also* Police
Conference on Security and Cooperation
in Europe (CSCE), 59-60
Considine, Chris, xviii, 150, 163-4
Constitution: amendment procedures, 44;
articulation of rights, 42-3; composed of
numerous documents, 43-4; democracy
a fundamental principle, 42, 45, 48-9;
entrenched, 44; foundation of liberal
democracies, 42-3; importance of vigilant citizenry, 3-4, 29, 37-40, 56, 195; key
principles, 42, 45; lawful use of state
powers, 42-3, 63-4; other constitutional
elements, 44-5; subtlety of APEC affair,

12-15, 15-17, 25; "unwritten constitution,"
19. *See also* Rights; Rule of law
Constitution Act, 1867 (*formerly* BNA Act),
43, 46, 57, 58
Constitution Act, 1982, 43-4
Contingency fee arrangements, 175
Convention on the Prevention and
Punishment of Crimes Against
Internationally Protected Persons,
Including Diplomatic Agents, 187-8, 189
Cory, Peter, 36-7
Court Challenges Program, 175
Courts: accountability mechanism, 20, 22-3,
64-5; international criminal court, 61; lit-
igants' access to resources, 22-4; protection
vs. unlawful police power, 9. *See also*
Legal system; Supreme Court of Canada
Criminal Code of Canada, and IPPs, 187-8
Crosbie, John: on Airbus Affair, 110-11
CSCE (Conference on Security and
Cooperation in Europe), 59-60
CSIS (Canadian Security Intelligence
Service), 35-6, 91
CSIS Act (Canadian Security Intelligence
Service Act), and IPPs, 190, 204-5

Democracy: freedom of speech essential,
36-7; fundamental principle in constitution, 42, 45, 48-9; fundamental rights,
29; interconnection with rule of law, 49;
need for vigilant citizenry, 3-4, 29, 37-40,
56, 195; selective questioning of police
abuses, 52-6; trade-off, economic benefits vs. human rights, 195
Denning, Lord: on police independence,
92-3
Dicey, A.V.: on rule of law, 47
Dictatorship, line of authority, 17-18
Dingwall, Bill (RCMP Inspector), xv, xvi,
32, 144
Dohm Commission of Inquiry (BC, 1971),
66
Donolo, Peter: actions vs. Milewski, xviii-
xix, 143, 154-5, 156; civil rights vs.
security, 144; concern re Suharto's
embarrassment, xiii; on PMO involvement in security, 145, 146

Douglas, Robb, 144
Dwyer, Kevin, 193

Elections Canada, and anti-APEC organizers, xvii, xxi
Entick v. Carrington (1756), 58

Federal Court rulings: on funding issue, 168-70, 172-3; on superiority of different interests, 180; on withholding of documents, xxi-xxii
Federal Police Ombudsman, 68-9
Federalism, and the constitution, 119
FLQ Crisis (1970), 98-9
"Forces of darkness" remark (Milewski), 155-6, 157
Fraser, Keith, 152
Freedom of association: alleged restrictions by RCMP, 6, 29-31, 33, 35, 78-9
Freedom of movement: alleged restrictions by RCMP, 6, 33
Freedom of speech: alleged restrictions by RCMP, 6, 29-31, 78, 193; mark of democracy, 36-7; restricted through "undertakings," 33-4; separate from security issue, 32
Fulton, E. Davie: on police independence, 87-92, 93-5, 97
Funding for APEC complainants. See APEC affair

Gastown Riot inquiry (Dohm Commission, 1971), 66
Government: accountability mechanisms re rule of law, 20, 24-5; authority re complaints vs. RCMP, 67; checks and balances lacking, 25, 27; internalization of constitution/rule of law, 19-20; and police power (see Police; Rule of law); relationship with police (see Police independence). See also Parliament; PMO; Prime Minister
Gray, Herb: and Airbus Affair, 109-10
Gustafsen Lake dispute, 53

Harber, Anton, 38
Hatfield, Richard, 104-6

Hatfield case (1985), 104-6
Heafey, Shirley: alleged interference with Morin Commission, xx, 160-1, 163-5, 166-7; appointment of Morin Commission, xvii
Hitler, and rule of law, 61
Hughes, E.N. (Ted). See Hughes Commission under PCC and APEC
Human Resource Development Working Group (of APEC), 222
Human Rights Watch Asia report (1994), 216

ICFTU (International Confederation of Free Trade Unions), 221
IMF (International Monetary Fund), 214
India: commitment to democracy, 208-9; economic development and trade, 206-7; possible benefits of APEC membership, 206-8; similarities with Canada, 205-6
International law and APEC affair, 186, 192-4, 195. See also IPPs (internationally protected persons)
International Monetary Fund (IMF), 214
Internationally protected persons. See IPPs
Intervener funding, 176
Ipperwash Provincial Park affair, 52
IPPs (internationally protected persons): with armed agents, 209; definition, 187-8; nature of RCMP's duty to protect, 185-6, 188-90, 191, 194; protection of dignity, 189-90, 194

Jakarta APEC meeting (1994), 216
Jones, Craig: arrest because of signage, xv, 8, 145, 192; e-mail messages to Milewski, 148, 150-2; lawsuit vs. authorities, xvi, 145; statements in Milewski documentary, 147
Judiciary. See Courts; Legal system

Kaplan, Robert: on police/government relationship, 104-5
Keable Inquiry (1981), 102-3
Key Point Act (South Africa), 38
Klein, Naomi, 155, 183

24-6. *See also* Government; PMO; Prime Minister

Parwoto, Benjamin, 150

PCC (RCMP Public Complaints Commission): adversarial nature of, 178-9; and APEC affair (*see* PCC and APEC); appointment of members, 74; establishment, 67-9; functioning and role, 161-2, 171-2; jurisdiction limited by RCMP lobbying, 70, 76; powers, 70-1; role of commission chair, 161-2; under Royal Canadian Mounted Police Act, 69-70, 161

PCC and APEC: complainants' duties and rights, 180-1; complaints re inappropriate police conduct, 6, 8, 71; complaints re political interference, 9, 71-2 (*see also under* RCMP and APEC); complex legal issues, 177-8; cross-examination of Jones re e-mail messages, 150-1; Federal Court rulings, xxi-xxii, 168-70, 172-3, 180; funding, possible sources, 174-7; funding refused for complainants (Morin Commission), xvii, xviii, 74-5, 163, 164, 172-3, 177-80; funding approved for complainants (Hughes Commission), xxi, 23, 75, 174; funding imbalance, government vs. complainants, 22-4, 74-5, 172; Hughes appointed sole commissioner, ix, 72-3, 174; Hughes Commission, mandate, 141; judicial inquiry undesirable, 73; Milewski-Jones e-mail messages tabled, 150-2; Morin, allegations of bias, ix, xix, 160, 165-6, 167-8, 174; Morin Commission, alleged interference by commission chair, xx, 160-1, 163-5, 166-7; Morin Commission, and proposed statement regarding legal assistance for complainants, 164-5, 168-70; Morin Commission, mandate, xvii, 159-60; Morin Commission resigns, xx, 160-1, 174; role of commission counsel, 74, 163-4

Pearlston, Karen, xiii, 145, 192

Peel, Robert: on policing, 62

Pépin, Marcel (CBC Ombudsman): exonerated Milewski, ix, xix, xxi, 21, 156-8, 173

Pepper spray, 136, 144, 159, 210

Perceptual narrowing (in crises), 139

Piper, Martha (UBC president), 32-3, 146

Plante, Lloyd (RCMP Staff Sergeant), 146

Pluralist ideology, 80-1, 84

PMO (Prime Minister's Office): alleged use of RCMP for political ends, 6, 8, 9, 15-16, 30, 31, 34, 71-2; civil liberties vs. security risks, 82-3, 144; complaint to CBC re Milewski, ix, 21, 141, 154-5, 156-8, 173; control of parliament, 24-6, 27; denied orders re protest signs, 145; Milewski's facts not challenged, 150, 154; request to move protest area, 32-3, 145, 146, 147; seriousness of charges, 8, 18-19, 34, 36-7, 39-40, 49-50, 51-2, 78-9, 82-3. *See also* Government; Parliament; Prime Minister

Police: autonomy and power, growth of, 127; Canadians' expectations of, 11, 128-32; Canadians' respect for, 124; "citizen police," development, 61-2; civilian oversight crucial, 36, 50-2, 60; core elements of policing, 62-3; distance from politicians growing, 121; and government bidding, 10, 25; "Nine Principles of Policing," 63-4; redress against, through courts, 9; restrictions on actions, 129-30; and rule of law, 9-11, 12, 61-2; social acceptance of actions necessary, 54-6, 130; subject to the law, 64-5. *See also* Police accountability; Police independence; Police use of force; RCMP

Police accountability: under Charter, 122; courts, 20, 22-3, 64-5; and democracy, 50-2, 63; internal proceedings, 65-6; mechanisms for, 20-6, 50-1, 64-7, 129; to Parliament, 20, 25-6, 50, 51; the press, 20-1; public inquiries, 20, 22-3, 66-7

Police independence: in Airbus affair (1993-97), 109-12; during anti-separatist policing (early 1970s), 99-101; classic notion, 89, 92; consensus lacking re scope, 92-4, 95, 96-8, 112, 113-14; during FLQ Crisis (1970), 98-9; "grey zone" of politics/policing, 126; in Hatfield case (1985), 104-7; illegal activities and government knowledge, 99-101; insulating ministers from conduct of investigations, 109-12; in investigating and laying charges, 64, 93, 107-8, 109; Keable Inquiry (1981) view, 102-3; "law enforcement," definitions, 95-6; Lord Denning's view, 92-3, 95, 97, 105; Marshall Inquiry Report (1989) on improper interference, 108-9; McDonald Inquiry (1981) view, 50, 51, 101-2, 111; ministerial direction of police, 93-4, 107-8; need for, 9-10, 18-19, 50-2, 60, 63, 64; in Nicholson affair (1959), 87-92, 93-5, 97, 106-7; in Olson case (1982), payments to Olson wife, 103-4; political control vs. accountability, 96-8, 115; public attitude, 125; reporting relationship with Solicitor General, 91; Small case (1989), 107-8; suggestions to define police/government relations, 114-16; Supreme Court discussion, 112-13

Police state, defined, 11, 12, 106, 125-6

Police use of force: abuse, complacency re, 52-3; as armed political force, 125-6; attitudes of Canadians, 128-32, 139-40; control tactics, in general, 131-2; factors to be assessed by police, 132-4; physical fitness of police and level of response, 133-4, 137-9; physiological arousal in crises, 139; reasonable response, factors, 132-4, 137; response options, 135-7; restrictions on, 129-30; socioeconomic class of target, 52-6; "tunnel vision" in crises, 139; underlying question of APEC affair, vii. *See also* RCMP and APEC

Political culture, Canadian: APEC affair as "business as usual," 123-4; authority, shift from political to legal, 121; British origins, 117-18; civil liberties consciousness, 122; deference to authority gone, 120-2; democratization/popularization of, 120; federalist principles, 119; pillars of constitution, 118-20; public outrage short-lived, 123; responsible government, 118

Political culture, US, 118

Politicians, and accountability, 121-2

"Politicians' Indigestion Protection Act," 15-17

Porter, Dennis, 33

Press. *See* Media

Prime Minister: consequences of wrongdoing, if provable, 25, 26; constitutionality of police deployment, 25; control of parliament, 24-6, 27; decline of media deference, 122; relationship with RCMP, 18. *See also* Government; Parliament; PMO

Proctor, Dick, xviii

Protesters (at APEC): behaviour, 132-3; description, 5, 7-8, 80; motives/concerns, 5, 57, 80, 82; "radicals"/students dismissed by Canadians, 14-15; status affects response of Canadians, 53-6

Province: article on Milewski, 152-3, 157

Public Complaints Commission, RCMP. *See* PCC

R. v. *Campbell* (1999), 65

R. v. *Metropolitan Police Commissioner, Ex parte Blackburn* (1968), 92-3

R. v. *Shirose* (1999), 112

Ramos, Fidel, 217-18

Ramos-Horta, Jose, 217

Ratushny, Ed: proposed PCC statement, 164, 168-70

RCMP (Royal Canadian Mounted Police): APEC affair (*see* RCMP and APEC); armed foreign agents permitted in Canada, 209; complaint mechanisms, under federal government, 67; contract policing, provincial, 119; "Mountie myth," 125; national security intelligence gathering to CSIS, 35-6; PCC (*see* PCC); relationship with Prime Minister, 18; and unlawful orders, 28. *See also* Police; Police independence

RCMP and APEC: alleged civil rights violations, 5-6, 29-31, 33-4, 78-9, 193; alleged illegal surveillance, 30, 31, 35-6; alleged pre-emptive arrests, xiv, 79, 134, 146, 149, 193; alleged use of excessive force, 30, 31, 136, 192; allegedly used for political ends, 6, 8, 9, 15-16, 30, 31, 34, 51-2, 71-2; and APEC Alert group, 204-5; factors to be assessed, 132-4; international law as justification, 192-4; IPPs, nature of RCMP's duty to protect, 188-91; "law enforce-

Set in Minion, Univers, and Flightcase
Printed and bound in Canada by Friesens
Copy editor: Francis J. Chow
Designer: George Vaitkunas
Proofreader: Karen Mason
Indexer: Patricia Buchanan